Crossword Dictionary

B.J. Holmes

Titles in this *Bradford's* series:

Crossword Solver's Dictionary	1-901659-67-4
Crossword Key Dictionary	1-901659-40-2
Pocket Crossword Dictionary	1-901659-91-7
How to Solve Crosswords	1-901659-95-X

you might also find some of our range of specialist dictionaries useful:

Dictionary of Shakespeare	1-901659-39-9
Dictionary of British Military History	1-901659-80-1

for details of our complete range of English and bilingual dictionaries, visit our website: www.petercollin.com

Bradford's

Pocket Crossword Dictionary

B.J. Holmes

PETER COLLIN PUBLISHING

First published in Great Britain, October 2001

Published by Peter Collin Publishing Ltd
32-34 Great Peter Street, London, SW1P 2DB

British Library Cataloguing-in-Publication Data

A catalogue record for this book is available from the British Library

ISBN 1-901659-91-7

Text computer typeset by PCP
Printed and bound in Finland by WS Bookwell
Cover artwork by Gary Weston

Crossword Clues and Extracts

Throughout this book we have used parts of clues and clues to illustrate a particular style of puzzle and how to solve the clue. It would have been difficult and confusing to include the source of each clue in the main layout of the book. Instead, we have credited the sources below. The clues we have used have come from a range of newspapers and magazines - we are indebted to the crossword setters for making the puzzles interesting, challenging and enjoyable to solve!

The publications used as sources include:

The Daily Express, The Daily Mail, The Daily Mirror, The Daily Record, The Daily Telegraph, The Financial Times, The Guardian, The Independent, Independent on Sunday, The Observer, The Radio Times, The Sun, The Sunday Telegraph, The Sunday Times, The Times

INTRODUCTION

Crosswords are a waste of time. There's always something more useful to do. Like pursuing a career, raising kids, wallpapering, walking the dog, writing a novel. At least, that's the way I saw it for many years.

That is until I found myself flat on my back with a chronic illness. In that situation even the delights of TV, radio and records began to pall and, in frustration, I turned my attention to the cryptic puzzle in my daily paper. Up till then I had never given the wretched, impenetrable thing more than a glance. At first I had little success, managing maybe a couple of answers if I was lucky before throwing it aside in frustration. However, in time and using assorted reference books, I eventually completed my first grid – to my surprise and immense satisfaction. From then I was hooked, and was soon sampling all the broadsheet and tabloid papers - buying, begging, borrowing or stealing.

And, in time, I was picking up prizes from national newspapers such as *The Financial Times* and *The Independent.*

Looking back, I can see that my interest in cryptics was kick-started when it dawned on me that there was some regularity in the tricks that compilers got up to. As I couldn't keep all their little dodges in my head I began writing them down, solely for my own reference. In time the notes became a thick file by the side of my bed.

Although I use assorted dictionaries, thesauruses, reference books and so on - it was when I realised my own file had become not only my **first** means of attack when facing a virgin grid, but also my **most-used** source, it occurred to me there was a book in it that could be useful to others. And you hold the results in your hand.

BACKGROUND

The story goes that the first crossword appeared in an American newspaper (the Sunday edition of the *New York World*) at the beginning of the last century. Since then crossword puzzles have spread to most cultures and have taken a variety of forms – from the original straightforward definitional type requiring factual answers to the more abstruse cryptic kind characterised by the use of convoluted clues, using puns and the playing of language games *(see next page)*. Today's grids can be square, rectangular or odd-shaped and can have either black squares or thick lines to separate the answers.

WHAT'S THE POINT?

For a start cryptic crosswords must be enjoyed by a large number of the population because virtually every British newspaper, national and local, carries one. And there have been many famous addicts, notably film star Richard Burton, who we are told, had to have daily access to British cryptics no matter to what part of the world his job or wealth had taken him.

Moreover, there is mounting medical opinion that they are downright healthy! Regular mental exercise is just as important as daily physical exercise and several prominent doctors have extolled the virtues of the crossword habit in staving off the ravages of age on the brain.

THE NATURE OF CRYPTICS

Crosswords can be classified broadly into two groups. Firstly there is what is called the definitional type. They are easily recognized because their clues are usually short and their solution calls for knowledge rather than language manipulation. They appear under various titles such as Quickie, Coffee-break and Concise. They have two main sub-categories: the general knowledge type and the specialised, the latter appearing in magazines and drawing on the specialist knowledge of their particular readership from pop music and golf to train-spotting.

Then there is the cryptic which has less the nature of a knowledge test and more the character of a game – a naked battle of wits between the compiler and the punter. And, like a game, it has its rules and conventions. An understanding of these is necessary and that is one of the purposes of this book.

CRYPTICS - CRACKING THE CODE

In order to solve cryptics it is useful to look at the exercise from the point of view of the compiler. The setter of a crossword is actually on a par with a conjuror. In both activities the name of the game is deception. Deception has two forms. Firstly, **disguise**. A conjuror will disguise the trappings of his trade: what seems like a solid box, can be hollow. Similarly, through the clever use of words a crossword compiler will draw a veil over his actual intent. For example,

`'Serve held by the Italian superstar' (4)`

embodies a couple of disguises. 'Serve' is dressed up in the clue as a **noun**, whereas the underlying intention is that it should be equated with the **verb** 'to DO' (ie. as a charlady). On the other hand, 'Italian' is disguised as an adjective relating to 'superstar', yet its role lies in the **two** words 'the Italian' (ie. Italian for 'the') which is IL. Finally, DO 'held by' IL yields the solution IDOL, a term which can be applied to a superstar.

Conversely a noun can be dressed up as a verb to throw you off the scent. Take

'Hide article held by Goneril's father' (7)

Sitting at the front 'Hide' looks for all the world like a verb and you probably wouldn't realise it isn't until you start putting the thing together from the clue's other parts. Goneril's father is LEAR - don't worry if you didn't know this, it's the kind of thing we have in our glossary. Then, LEAR goes around THE (article) to produce the answer LEATHER, a noun synonymous with hide.

The second form of deception is **misdirection**. The astute observer knows that whenever a conjuror says 'Look, nothing in my hand', the real business is likely to be taking place somewhere else, like the magician's other hand. And so too, with the crossword. One must fight the temptation to look where the compiler is directing our attention.

Example:

'Set meal' (2,6)

This is a familiar phrase describing restaurant fare. Once we are on our guard that we might be being misdirected, the **last** thing we should think of is a restaurant! So, what else can the word 'set' imply? A radio set? A television set? Bells might ring at that point, leading to the notion that, in that context, a 'set meal' is in fact a TV DINNER.

Remember, the crossword clue has to be synonymous with the solution (or at least be strongly suggestive of the answer) so the compiler will be very wily in using the only tools available to the craft: **disguise** or **misdirection**, usually both at the same time.

EQUIPMENT FOR THE JOB

The beginner really needs to have a handful of reference books handy. Now, there is a feeling amongst many solvers that the use of books, etc. is in some way cheating. I have no such qualms. Of course, there will be expert solvers who will pride themselves on finishing a broadsheet cryptic with no use of aids, but these lucky people must be a minority, an enviable elite. My attitude has always been that the compiler has many books and aids at his disposal so why should the common-or-garden solver (like me and most of the readers of this book) be at a disadvantage?

So you need:

1 a standard **dictionary**, the bigger and the more up to date the better. Obviously you can only use a dictionary if you already know what you are looking for, so the main function of your dictionary will be for confirming spelling. However it can also be used for checking the existence of a word you've never heard of.

As an example, the word 'barathea' may mean nothing to you - as it meant nothing to me when I tackled the following clue:

`'Arab returns holding two articles made from a fine woollen cloth' (7)`

However, 'Arab returns' gives you BARA, while THE and A are 'two articles'. Putting the articles into BARA leads you to BAR-A-THE-A. Never heard of it, we say. But you look it up in your regular dictionary and discover (again, as I did) that BARATHEA is some kind of fabric.

Another valuable use for dictionaries is to search for some combination or phrase, provided you know the first word. Say you are faced with

`'Tossed aside?' (9,6)`

and the letters you already have suggest that the first word might be 'throwaway' but you have a mental block over 'aside' (mental blocks do happen). Looking through a dictionary can reveal the expression THROWAWAY REMARK — and you're there.

2 a **thesaurus**, which will provide synonyms. The original thesaurus (Roget) now has several versions on the market.

3 an **atlas**. One of the side benefits of crossword puzzles for me is that I am pushed into brushing up my geography.

4 a **UK Gazetteer** (for example, an AA book) as almost any town and village in the UK is fair game. Also be warned: a knowledge of London landmarks and suburbs, not to mention Underground stations and lines, is assumed. If you live out in the sticks like me you will need some kind of map of the capital.

In addition you will find useful

5 **Brewer's Dictionary of Phrase and Fable**. I had never heard of this wonderful tome until someone bought me one as a present. It is invaluable as a reference work on Classical Mythology and a whole range of literary and linguistic material.

6 a **book of quotations**. Not essential but you will get the occasional quotation thrown at you. But don't be too worried because the quotes will be well-known ones.

7 anything with **elementary** French, German, Spanish, etc. (say, a tourist phrase book) as compilers are prone to include basic words from the major languages when they have a mind to. However, the most common borrowings from foreign tongues that are used in solution construction will be found in our glossary.

8 a **book of lists**, usually with Crossword in the title. Such a book not only gives all kinds of lists (flowers, mountains, etc.) but does so very helpfully in order of word-length. For example, the *Bradford's Crossword Key Dictionary,* Peter Collin Publishing. (In the present book we do incorporate lists but we restrict ourselves to the short words amenable to being used as components.)

Also, some of these books (and some dictionaries) list **abbreviations**, which figure constantly in cryptics. The present book does not aim for comprehensiveness in the provision of abbreviations, but most common ones have been included in the glossary along the way.

9 finally, the kind of books that you might find on the family bookshelf - **the Bible, history books, general knowledge books, the works of Shakespeare** and so on - will not come amiss. The characters created by Messrs Shakespeare and Dickens are regular cast members on the crossword stage. See the *Dictionary of Shakespeare*, Peter Collin Publishing.

Incidentally, don't be put off by the length of the above list. One or two books you probably have already and you can pick up the others piecemeal. I found that once people close to me knew of my new pastime, I began receiving appropriate books as presents.

A daily dose of cryptic puzzle solving not only keeps the mind active – and you'll be surprised how many people you meet (strangers included) who share your pastime once you get into the swing of it - it is also an ongoing educational experience. That is why it is no sin to use the back-up of reference books - indeed, even a pocket crossword machine. I received one of the latter as a present and am not ashamed to include it in my armoury.

My technique is to tackle a puzzle in three stages:

1 I go through and see what I can do unaided;

2 then use books (starting with this one), and finally

3 take recourse to my little battery-operated friend, when there are any obstinate holes left in the grid, as there usually are. Again, this isn't 'cheating'. Professional compilers use them, so why shouldn't we?

Interestingly, it is one of the constant pleasures of crossword solving that, after hitting a brick wall with a particular grid and putting the thing aside for a while, a critical answer can come easily when one returns to it. As in other areas of activity, the value to the mind of a break is a mysterious but real phenomenon. (Hey, phenomenon – that's a word I can now spell, thanks to crosswords.) Still a mystery to psychologists as to its exact workings, the phenomenon seems to come about either because a break allows the brain to come at a problem from a different angle, or during the break the subconscious still works on the problem in some mysterious way.

Finally, there is a clear pecking order in terms of difficulty with regard to the different national newspapers. Generally, the more popular the paper, the easier is the paper's cryptic. So, the beginner may choose to start with a tabloid. However, test runs have shown that using this book, the novice can actually start with one of the broadsheets – the 'Ivy League' of crosswords – if so choosing.

Before we go any further let's get some technical words out of the way.

CROSSWORD TERMS

Definition: It is one of the basic rules of the game that the compiler includes a word or phrase which defines the answer in some way. It will be in the form of a definition or an example. If the answer is MARSUPIAL the clue will include either a definition of marsupial or an example (for instance 'kangaroo' or 'jumper'), the latter usually prefixed by 'say' indicating it is an example.

Synonym: A word or phrase that has the same meaning as another (dog, cur, canine and so on). Because compilers will not usually give precise dictionary definitions of what they are after, the term 'definition' and 'synonym' themselves have the same meaning for our purposes.

Component: The most common form of cryptic clue is the compound type where one is required to build up the solution from given bits. These bits are letters, groups of letters or complete words, and throughout this book we call them components or elements. They can be used as they stand or require adaptation (shortening, reversing etc) as signalled by indicators.

Indicator: We use the term indicator to describe a coded instruction about handling components. For instance, anagrams (mixing up letters) are one of the commonest devices and are signalled by indicators such as 'mixed up', 'changed', etc.

GUIDELINES AND CROSSWORD TRICKS

A SIMPLE STARTING POINT

About 80% of cryptic clues will contain the vital synonym either at the beginning or the end of the clue. Effectively this reduces the cryptic, at least in part, to an easier 'concise' puzzle. So one can make a start by limiting one's attention to the beginning of a clue, and if this doesn't throw up anything useful, concentrate for an equal amount of time on the end. Consider the following clue:

'Move quickly to squeeze Conservative out' (4)

In this example the synonym lies at the **beginning**. Hence we need a synonym for 'Move quickly'. Well, we take CRUSH (ie. squeeze) from which we omit or 'out' C for Conservative, leaving us with the answer – RUSH.

On the other hand, the synonym lies at the **end** of

'Beat veteran to the starting place' (9)

Some kind of 'starting place' is what we require and THRESH (beat) + OLD (veteran) leads to THRESHOLD.

So remember, about 40% of the time the definition of your answer is the first word or words of the clue, and about 40% it is the last word or words.

Which leads us to another tip: if you can't solve a clue straight away but notice the first and last words end in S, then there's a good chance the answer ends in S. But use a pencil when you put it in, just in case.

LITTLE WORDS MEAN A LOT

(AND MAY NOT BE AS INNOCENT AS THEY LOOK)

Often the definite and indefinite articles (a, an, the) and other parts of speech are openly used in the clue to build the answer itself. For example,

'The gilt-edged alternative' (5)

is deliberately written in a way that encourages you to overlook 'The'. Yet its very letters are the bulk of the answer! THE edged with OR (ie. gilt) is needed to construct O(THE)R which we run together to give the answer OTHER, the required synonym for 'alternative'.

The trick is a little more abstruse when we not only have to focus on a small word that our eye may skim over, but then be required to use only part of it. Consider the following cleverly constructed clue:

'Split half of capital' (5)

On the face of it, this looks like we are seeking a word synonymous with 'Split' which consists of half the letters of some capital city. If we think this then we have been successfully misdirected because, in fact, the 'half' applies to 'of'. Then, with QUIT for 'split' and adding the O from 'of', we get QUITO, the capital of Ecuador. So keep an eye on the little words!

WORDS PUT INTO THE 'WRONG' CONTEXT

The compiler will try to nudge your brain in the wrong direction by deliberately confusing parts of speech (using nouns as verbs, adjectives as nouns etc) as in the following.

`'Not the main sort of crustacean' (4-4)`

'Main' is made to look like an adjective in the sense of 'principal' or 'chief'. In fact it needs to be seen as a **noun** meaning 'sea'. Thus, a crustacean **not of the sea** leads to the answer LAND-CRAB. (Incidentally, the compiler's use of a noun as an adjective is not cheating in the sense of being grammatically illegal. Unlike many other languages which severely restrict parts of speech, English positively thrives on its looseness.)

SPOONERISMS

If you didn't already know it, The Rev. W.A.Spooner of Oxford is credited (or discredited) with the slip in speech where initial sounds of words are transposed so as to form some ludicrous combination, such as 'The Lord is a shoving leopard' (for 'loving shepherd'). As a result the so-called spoonerism makes an occasional appearance in crosswords. A convoluted example is demonstrated by

`'Not served by Hatter, one at tea-party put to sleep (as the eccentric Oxford don had it!)' (10)`

Ready? Then here we go: 'One at tea party' = HARE (remember the March Hare from 'Alice in Wonderland'?). 'Put to sleep' = BEDDED. This gives us HARE-BEDDED which is then **spoonerised** to provide the answer BARE-HEADED (ie. not served by hatter – or more plainly, without a hat). Phew!

WORDS DO NOT HAVE SACROSANCT BOUNDARIES

A component word can be used to cross from one word to another in the answer. For example:

`'City porter's to carry on to the end' (4,3)`

The 'City' is LA (ie. the American city) and the required synonym for porter (ie. the drink) is STOUT. This gives us LASTOUT – which we have then to split appropriately to give us LAST OUT ie. to carry on to the end,

MISDIRECTION

As we have said, misdirection is a standard ploy. For instance, the compiler can give a string of elements which automatically suggest a certain group or idea. In the following clever example one has difficulty avoiding the notion of publications when, in fact, the compiler has a completely different grouping in mind:

'Common feature of The Times and The Guardian - but not Punch' (7, 7)

The important classification is not 'publications' but 'parts of speech', thus what is common to the first two titles but not the last is 'The'. From this example, the answer: LEADING ARTICLE.

IGNORE PUNCTUATION!

Beware of punctuation. While used to make some kind of sense to the clue, punctuation will also be used to misdirect the solver. Consider:

'Improvise after trade gets into difficulty, in a way' (7,3)

'In a way' looks separate from the rest, being split off with a comma. However, we should ignore the comma and read the last four words as a whole - because we need to look for something synonymous with 'difficulty in a way'.

Thus, 'Improvise' (JAM from jazz) placed **after** 'trade' (TRAFFIC) gives a 'difficulty in a way': TRAFFIC JAM, the answer. Note how the compiler has naughtily thrown in the comma to break up the synonym and put the solver off the track - as 'difficulty in a way' should be read as a whole without a break.

THE SENTENCE ITSELF

One of the aspects of playing with words is to refer to the sentence itself while misdirecting attention or simply aiming to confuse.

Consider:

'This would define it where you have to get it' (6,6)

This could send your brain off in search of some form of shop. Following this train of thought you might come up with something like RETAIL OUTLET which has the requisite number of letters. But you should be uneasy with this, as it is only partially satisfactory. Further consideration might suggest that 'it' is actually the definition and we come up with the answer, DIRECT OBJECT, which is the grammatical function of 'it' in the sentence that makes up the clue.

THE DREADED PUN - WHERE BOOKS AREN' T USEFUL

A small number of clues are not based on synonyms and therefore are not amenable to book research. These are usually pun-based or otherwise tongue-in-cheek. With these cases there is nothing for it but to put on the old thinking cap. For instance:

```
'Might one be worn by a feller?' (6-6)
```

A question mark often indicates that some extra trickery is going on. Here, the compiler is playing with the word 'feller', suggesting it is a casual way of spelling 'fellow' where in fact a **feller of trees** is the base reference, which directs us to the answer: LUMBER-JACKET.

OLD WORKHORSES

These are the clichés of the game that are frequently used ('feller' in the above example is one of them), confounding beginners - and arousing an amused 'Oh not again' response from veterans. If you're a beginner you'll soon join the ranks of the groaners. For the record, amongst the commonest are 'flower' to denote a river and 'number' to denote some kind of painkiller. Another one, which we might call **The Hidden 'And'**, requires AND to be inserted, without a direct reference to it in the clue. An easy example is:

```
'Measurement of horse's extremities?' (5)
```

The extremities of the word 'horse's' are the letters H and S. Inserting the implied AND we get H AND S, giving HANDS. Do I hear a groan already?

PLAYING THE GAME

We have likened the crossword compiler to a conjuror. However, the analogy is not total because, unlike a conjuror, the compiler is not supposed to cheat. While a conjuror can tell us downright lies, a compiler is obliged to tell us the truth - albeit in a convoluted form. In this sense he is playing a game and like all games there are rules.

One of these is that all words must count. No words must be thrown in just to make the clue look better. The implication of this is that the solver should consider every word. If you're stuck, a useful tactic is to go through the clue again looking at each word **separately**. Having said that, there is some bending of this convention with little words. For instance, some setters do use definite and indefinite articles which are not strictly necessary for the definition.

Another rule is that each clue must contain at least one definition of, or synonym for, the answer. What you are looking for – either as a word or phrase – is in there somewhere! In addition, the definition is supposed to be a good match with the solution. Again a reservation, as opinions do differ on this one with regard to particular cases. For example, "The Times" team are not allowed to equate CAN and ABLE. But the entries in this book are geared to what appears in a wide spread of puzzles and as other setters regularly use this specific pair they are included. I have to say that quite a few times I have quibbled with an example that I have come across – maybe it was a little unfair, clumsy or even non-PC – but my rule in compiling the glossary is that if it has appeared in practice it merits inclusion.

FORMS OF CLUE

Usually the clues in a cryptic crossword fall into one of four categories: the compound, single definition, double definition and one that, for want of a better term, I call the whimsical clue.

The Compound Type

This is the most common form. Here the compiler provides components with instructions on how to put the solution together like a set of Lego bricks. The instructions are largely in the form of indicators (described later). This type has also been compared to Charades, being similar to the parlour game where hand signals are the coded instructions and mimes supply the components to make up the answer.

Compound clues can be short and straightforward as:

`'Stupid person departs with tear' (4)`

D (for departs) along with RIP (for tear) gives DRIP, a stupid person.

The following is much longer but still straightforward:

`'Not generating a profit, one French company has no managing leader in charge' (10)`

UNE (one French) + CO (company) + NO + M (managing leader) + IC (in charge) adds up to UNECONOMIC, not generating a profit.

Some help on the compound type comes later when we look at indicators.

Single definition

Masquerading as a clue from an 'easy' or 'quick' crossword this type gives what appears to be a straightforward definition, usually two words. However, for it to justify its position in a cryptic there must be a twist. Example:

`'English flower' (5)`

The uninitiated might immediately start trawling a book of lists for a flower (ie. a bloom) of five letters. However one should realise that the word 'English' is in there for a reason, denoting some kind of twist, The problem with these apparently simple ones is that even a seasoned solver cannot be sure of the answer until he has a few letters in. Say we have T-E-T and we are still having trouble finding a flower that fits. With experience we come to realise that 'flower' is an old standby for river (mentioned earlier), and we get TRENT.

Double Definition

This consists of two words (or phrases) that are synonymous with each other. Again, no indicators are used leaving the solver to rely entirely on his knowledge of words (or the books beside him). Example:

`'Medium number' (5)`

The 'medium' that was assumed in former days to permeate space is ETHER, and it is also a 'number' (with a silent 'b'), one of the old workhorses we have mentioned.

Whimsical Clues

The clues for these (and their answers) are usually longer than normal. A phrase or sentence is given very often with a question mark signalling that the answer is related to it in some quirky or humorous way. Of the four types of clue this is the one where reference books are of the least use because, with no indicators or other conventional help, the field is so open. Example:

`'Not the monarch at Bannockburn?' (6,3,5)`

You can look up monarch and get a whole list of kings and queens. You can look up Bannockburn, with little effect, apart from maybe suggesting a Scottish king, say Robert the Bruce – another red herring. Then it might occur to you to split up the last word and look up 'bannock' separately. That gives you 'Scottish bread or cake'. Still no sense. Eventually, hopefully, you might relate 'cake' to 'burn' and, bingo, you come up with ALFRED THE GREAT.

This type of clue can be quite a stumbling block in the completion of a grid and is thankfully restricted in use, although they do provide satisfaction and maybe a chuckle when cracked.

Now, back to the most common type of clue, the **compound**.

INDICATORS

The compiler will get up to all kinds of tricks to misguide the solver in building up the compound solution but the rules of the game require that he plays fair. Namely, he needs to specify what kind of legerdemain he is up to and he does this by using a set of codes that we have called indicators.

A large number of such indicators has been built up and the most common ones will be found in this book. However, such a list can never be complete because adventurous setters are continually designing new ones. For our purposes indicators consist of the following groups.

Anagram indicators

Examples: mixed up, replaced, gusty, fixing, clumsy

An anagram is a word of phrase formed from transposed letters of another word or set of words. eg. LAIR and RAIL. Where the answer requires the construction of an anagram, an appropriate indicator will be given. Anagram indicators are many and varied but they all have in common the notion of something being **wrong** (eg. broken, off) or **changed** (eg. altered, redistributed) or **worked on** (eg. hammered, sorted), that kind of thing.

In the simplest form, the letters to be reworked will be contained in a single word as in the following example:

```
'Exceptionally good purse distributed' (5)
```

Here the anagram indicator is 'distributed' telling us we have to shuffle some letters. The indicator is usually adjacent to the word (or words) to be operated on and in this case the target word is PURSE. The definition is 'exceptionally good' and, juggling the letters of PURSE leads us to the answer SUPER. A little more difficult is when we have several words or components to work on, as in:

```
'Draw entailed clashing with European' (9)
```

The word 'clashing' signals an anagram. However, there are not enough letters in 'entailed' and we have to throw E (signalled by European) into the mix. Our task then is to rearrange ENTAILED along with E to get a synonym for 'draw' – DELINEATE.

Omission indicators

Examples: drop, leave, quit

Here target letters, words or components have to be omitted in order to help construct the answer. This requirement is signalled by such words as 'out', 'not entirely' and so on.

Example:

```
'Out east, sell vehicle for writer' (4,5)
```

'Out east' suggests we should drop E (for east) from 'sell' or a word meaning the same. Thinking about it leads hopefully to MARKET which, with the E 'outed', becomes MARKT. 'Vehicle' clues WAIN while 'writer' is the definition, telling us a writer's name is required. Putting MARKT and WAIN together, then splitting them appropriately we get the answer, the novelist MARK TWAIN.

Reversal indicators

Examples: return, rising, northern

These make an appearance in the form of straightforward words like 'back', 'over', or more subtlely in words like 'retiring'.

Once we suspect a reversal we have to decide whether it requires us to reverse **letters** or **whole components**. In the following example, 'retiring' is the reversal indicator and it is the **letters** that have to be reversed:

'Papal diadem represented by retiring Italian painter' (5).

IT (for Italian) is reversed, followed by ARA (ie. an Associate of the Royal Academy) to give the Papal diadem: TI + ARA, that is TIARA.

On the other hand, letter-order is to remain the same but the order of **components** is to be reversed in:

'Cheerful mug? Just the reverse' (6).

'Mug' clues BEAT UP, then the two **words** are put in reverse order to give 'cheerful': UPBEAT.

In this second form, the reversal indicator can also be thought of as an ordering indicator - see later.

Nesting indicators

Examples: accepted, accomodation, nursing

Here one component is to be nested or embedded **within** another. The instruction can be in one of two forms. Firstly there is the notion of one component going **into** another (penned in, engaged in etc) as in:

'First (first of Romans) engaged in building empire' (7)

'First' gives us the synonym for the word we are looking for, while 'first of Romans' gives us 'R'. 'Building' is an anagram indicator signalling that 'empire' is an anagram. Fiddling around with the letters we get PEMIER. Into this we have to 'engage' or nest R to get PREMIER (ie. first).

Secondly, the indicator can focus on one component **going round** the other (examples: penning, restricting, absorbing, circling, choking etc) as in:

'Rank ivy choking short bough's vitality' (8)

'Rank' indicates that 'ivy' is an anagram (VIY). 'Short' indicates that a synonym for 'bough' (BRANCH) should be shortened, specifically BRANC. Then 'choking' signifies that VIY should encircle BRANC to give 'vitality', namely VIBRANCY.

Homophone indicators

Example: audition, spoken, we hear

A homophone is simply a component or word that sounds like another but has a different meaning eg., HEIR and AIR, and is a common device in crosswords. That such a target is sought is signalled by such words as 'soundly', 'sounding', 'broadcast', and phrases like 'on the radio' etc. as in:

'Facilitate the sounding of notes' (4)

Firstly, the word 'sounding' can be a homophone indicator, so we might be looking for sound-alikes. The notes required are EEs which is a homophone for EASE, the answer, ie. 'facilitate'.

Another way the homophone game is played is to misguide us by the use of capital letters which are **appropriate** for the sense of the clue but **inappropriate** for getting the answer. For example:

'Popular accommodation inside Hull, we hear' (7)

'We hear' is a popular homophone indicator and its role in this clue is to suggest to us that we go by the **sound** of 'Hull'. So we should read it, not as the town with a capital H, but as the common noun 'hull'. In other words we are looking for something indicative of the interior of a boat. 'Popular' clues IN, 'accommodation' clues BOARD and we have the answer: INBOARD.

Run indicators

Examples: run, piece of, outburst, occurring in

In this case the setter is signalling that the answer (or required component) is embedded in the clue itself as a run or series of consecutive letters, usually crossing from one word to another.

Common run indicators: 'part of', 'not all', 'sampled in', 'section'. The beauty of this type is that once we have identified it as a straight 'run' clue it is the easiest to solve because the answer is staring us in the face as in the following:

'Oriental city with a noisy section' (5)

'Section' is cluing that we should look for a run, which inspection reveals to be within the phrase 'with a noisy' - HANOI which is the Oriental city of the answer.

Strictly, 'Hanoi' requires a capital letter but another lesson that might be learned from the above example is that the normal rules about the use of capital letters are invariably ignored. So you may have to **imagine** the capital letter, as in the above. On the other hand, as in our Hull example, you might have to **discount** a capital letter to get to the answer. Here's another one:

`'Specific humidity as sampled in Cape' (5)`

'Sampled' suggests that the answer lies in a run, and it does, But we are misdirected by the capital letter to Cape which suggests the answer is geographic. However, the answer is FICHU, which appears as a clear run of letters within the clue. And a fichu, our dictionary shows us, is a cape, an item of women's clothing.

As this type is one of the easiest to solve, there is rarely more than one within a crossword. But to confuse the issue, such a run may be in reverse or consist of alternate letters, the sequence of which can be signalled by odd, even, etc. as in

`'Sway, creeping in at regular intervals' (5)`

'Sway' is the definition and the answer is REIGN, indicated by the even-numbered letters (ie. at regular intervals) in the sequence 'creeping in'.

Whimsy indicators

Examples: ?, " ", !

When the compiler takes a flight of fancy, pursues some caprice, uses poetic licence, stretches a point or otherwise breaks the rules, usually with humorous intent, there will be some indication by what we may call a whimsy indicator. The most common such indicator is the use of a question mark. Also beware of an exclamation mark or quotation marks.

Example:

`'A "silly" place for flowers' (6,3)`

The answer is WINDOW BOX – the logic being that a window box is on a sill and therefore may be described as "silly". Do I hear another groan?

The remaining indicators require little explanation.

Abbreviation indicators

Examples: short, little, small

Abbreviations are probably the most common device of all in cryptics and can be cued by words such as 'briefly'. However, that an abbreviation is required is not always signalled, presumably because they are seen as a part of everyday speech. They fall into two types.

Firstly, acronyms like RAF. Ideally the solver should have a separate abbreviations reference list but the present book includes most of the common examples and you'll soon get used to the popular ones anyway, such as 'artist' calling for RA or ARA; 'defence body' for NATO, 'accountant' for CA and so on. Of course, computer acronyms are becoming increasingly common – DOS, RAM, ROM etc.

The second kind are common shortenings and diminutives, and these are often signalled by 'little' for example. 'Boy' and 'little boy' call for a shortened first name (RON etc). The same applies to 'little girl' with DI coming near if not at the top of the list. She makes one of her many appearances in this one:

`'Absent-minded little girl with crazy artist' (8)`

which emerges as DISTRAIT (DI + an anagram of ARTIST)

Colloquialism indicators

Example: commonly, Cockney

Apart from a small number (such as AINT) these are not very frequent and call for slang or other informal speech. If regional dialect is called for it will usually be signalled eg. GANG requires 'Scottish' in the clue, NOUT and OUT (for nothing and something) requires 'Northern' or 'Yorkshire', and so on.

Probably the most widespread use of colloquialism is the dropping of initial H signified by an apostrophe (') as in

`'Courageous London coppers start to take over the French 'abitation' (10)`

where the last word clues OME (ie. 'ome). Result: MET + T + LES + OME = METTLESOME.

Repetition indicators

Examples: again, repeatedly

Just as it says, some letter or component (or its synonym) has to be repeated to complete the answer.

Initial letter indicator

Examples: leader of, hint of, pointer

The signal that you are to use only the first letter of a word usually comes in the form of straightforward words like 'front', 'beginning' or 'start', as 'start of hostilities' cues H.

However, the compiler may use a more abstruse word such as 'top' as where 'top-sail' clues S. Even more abstruse is the use of a synonym for 'top' that fits the character of the clue. Consider:

`'Old boat's load seen with hatch removed' (4)`

The initial letter indicator is 'hatch' (ie. top). Removing the initial letter from CARGO (load) we get ARGO, an 'old boat', the vessel of Jason and his Argonauts.

Other specific letter indicators

Examples: last, finally, middle

Apart from the initial letter indicator, indicators can call for the last or central letters of words to be used. Occasionally, a **numbered** letter may be stipulated. For example 'the fourth of July' identifies Y. With me being an avid classics fan, it took a long time to sink in that, in the context of cryptics, Beethoven's Fifth has got nothing to do with old Ludwig at all.

Ordering indicators

These specify the order in which components are to be set and are usually self-explanatory in the form of 'first', 'last', 'before' and so on. In the following, 'chases' is an ordering indicator:

`'Wild lady chases thousand in a crazy manner' (5)`

Its function is to tell you that 'wild lady' (an anagram of LADY) follows M (for thousand) – giving MADLY.

Palindrome indicators

A palindrome is a word which is spelled the same whichever way you read it eg. LEVEL, ANNA and their use is indicated by phrases such as 'in both directions'. In the following 'whichever way you look at it' plays the role of a palindrome indicator:

`'It's to be done whichever way you look at it' (4)`

which is satisfied by DEED. Such words do crop up but, just as they are rare in reality, they are rare in crosswords too.

Combinations

Most compound clues will contain a combination of indicators, usually two but three or more are possible. For example,

`'Singer pockets rearward ball, then another, in pool' (9)`

incorporates three:

'pockets' is a nesting indicator

'rearward' is a reversal indicator

'another' is a repetition indicator

Here we go. 'Ball' is **reversed** – LLAB, to be followed by **another** ball (ie. O) to give LLABO. This is then **nested** within the singer BING (the compiler assumes you remember him) yielding BI-LLABO-NG, ie. BILLABONG, an Australian word for pool!

SUMMARY

1 Remember that in the majority of cases the synonym for the answer is the **first** or **last** part of the clue.

2 Ignore the obvious. Remember that the setter is trying to trap you with the obvious, so look for a **less** obvious meaning.

3 Consider each word **separately**, especially when the words have been made to look as if they go together.

4 Be on the lookout for the code words and phrases that serve as indicators.

5 When you reach an impasse with a particular grid, don't lose your cool and give up. Just put it aside for a while, do something else and return to it at another convenient time. Remember, these things are supposed to be fun.

A LAST WORD

Finally, it has to be said that a book such as this can never be complete. New words are being coined everyday and old words are taking on new meanings, so even an imposing authoritative dictionary can never be up-to-date.

Bearing that in mind, the entries in this book can be seen as being of two kinds. Firstly there is the core of standard indicators and components that are a part of the compiler's armoury. While we hope that most of them are contained here, it must be borne in mind that compilers are an ingenious lot and are forever devising new tricks with which to challenge us.

The glossary's other entries may be seen as peripheral in the sense that they surround this core and are themselves at the edge of the vast lexicon that is the evolving and expanding English language. This is where your dictionaries and other reference books come in.

Therefore, if you are a beginner and are prepared to persevere, this book should certainly help you to make some inroads into a grid. And, if it does that for you, it's done its job.

As implied at the beginning, I now have a modicum of experience at puzzling, but the following glossary is still my main source of reference – so I'm sure even case-hardened veterans will find it of use.

OK, keep your wits about you, be alert to the continual flood of new words and, if this is your copy, don't be afraid to write your own discoveries in the margins - that's what they're there for.

Lastly, to beginners and veterans alike – happy puzzling!

HOW TO USE THIS DICTIONARY

Cross referencing: Only a minimum of cross-referencing between entries has been included where the connections may not be obvious. So if you do not see anything that fits the bill under one entry, look up other likely words in the list.

Abbreviations: rem: remember – this is to remind the user of some meaning of a word that may have been forgotten.

Few other abbreviations are used in the text and those that are, are standard eg., Gael. for Gaelic and so on.

Square Brackets: Although lists against entries are largely confined to those words and components that can be used in word-building a few words have been included in square brackets at the end of lists. These are longer words whose link may be a little obscure but might in themselves constitute a fully-fledged answer.

Aa

a, A ONE; PER; TOP; UPPER; be wary that 'a' is often used in the guise of being part of the grammar of the clue sentence when it is in fact a component to be used in constructing the answer

a follower B

a foreign EIN; UNE; UNE

A4 SHEET

a French UN; UNE

a German EIN

a head EACH; PER

a Parisian UN; UNE

AB RATING; TAR; can indicate something to do with sailors, boats, navy etc.

abandon CEDE; DITCH; DROP; DUMP; FREE; JILT; LEAVE; QUIT; SCRAP; SHED; SLOUGH; STRAND; YIELD

abandoned EX; FREE; LEFT; LOOSE; OFF; QUIT; SHED; anagram indicator; omission indicator

abandonment CESSION

abash SHAME

abase LOWER

abdominal pain COLIC

abide BEAR; DWELL; LIVE; STAND

Abigail MAID

ability ART; FLAIR; SENSE; SKILL; TALENT

able ACUTE; BRAINY; BRIGHT; CLEVER; DEFT; FIT; HANDY; QUICK; SHARP; SLICK

able, be, is CAN

aboard ON; nesting indicator which is usually disguised in a seafaring context as "Family aboard tanker" clues OILSKINS (ie. KIN is nested within OIL S.S.)

aboard ship can indicate for a component to be nested within SS

abode PAD; *see* DWELLING

abound TEEM

about A; AROUND; ASTIR; C (ie. circa); CA; ON; OVER; RE; UP; anagram indicator; reversal indicator; nesting indicator

about to go READY; SET; indicator for C to be omitted

above OVER
Abraham' s nephew LOT
abroad AWAY; GONE; OFF; OUT; anagram indicator
absence BLANK; LACK; NEED; WANT
abscond BOLT
absence of NO
absent AWAY; GONE; MISSING; OFF; omission indicator; *see* ABROAD
absent oneself GO
absolute UTTER
absorb EAT; nesting indicator
absorbing nesting indicator
abstainer TT
abstainers AA
abstentionist DRY
abstinence, period of, time of LENT
abstract painting OPART (ie. OP ART)
absurd DAFT; SILLY; WILD; anagram indicator
absurdly anagram indicator
abuse CHEEK; CURSE; ILL; MUD; RAIL; RAILING; anagram indicator
abused HURT; anagram indicator
abysmally anagram indicator
abyss DEEP; HELL; HOLE; PIT
academic BA; DON; FELLOW; LECTOR; MA; PROF; GRADUATE; *see* DEGREE, GRADUATE
academic achievement BA, MA; *see* DEGREE
academic establishment LSE; MIT; SCHOOL; U; UNI; *see* COLLEGE, UNIVERSITY
academic position CHAIR
academic stream CAM
academic terms SESSION
academician ARA; RA
accent ACUTE; BEAT; BROGUE; BURR; GRAVE; PITCH; SOUND; STRESS; TONE
accept PASS; TAKE; WEAR; nesting indicator
acceptable DONE; MEET; NICE; ON; OK; WORTHY
acceptable, socially DONE; IN; U
acceptance from France OUI
accepted IN; nesting indicator
access DOOR; ENTREE; ENTRY; GATE

access, gain HACK
accessory EXTRA
accident BUMP; CHANCE; CRASH; FLUKE; SMASH; anagram indicator
accidental FLAT (mus.)
accident, no MEANT
accidentally anagram indicator
accommodate nesting indicator
accommodation BB; BOARD; DIGS; FLAT; HOME; HOUSE; MANSE; MOTEL; NEST; ROOM; nesting indicator; *see* BUILDING
accommodation, temporary TENT
accommodating nesting indicator
accompanied by WITH
accompanied by Cockney WIV
accompany BACK
accompanying WITH
accomplished ABLE; DID; OVER; *see* ABLE
accomplishment SKILL
according to AFTER
accordingly SO
account AC; ACC; BILL; RELATION; REPORT; RESUME; STORY; TALE; VERSION; can indicate something to do with a novel
accountant AUDITOR; CA; CLERK
accurate EXACT; RIGHT
accusation CHARGE; SLUR
accusation, bring an LODGE
accuse BLAME; BOOK; BRAND; CHARGE; NAME; SMEAR; SUE; TAX
accustomed USED
ace A; BEST; CARD; CRACK; ONE; SERVE; STAR; STROKE; SUPER; TOP
ace, flying BADER
ache LONG; YEARN
achieve DO; GET; HIT; MEET; PASS
achieved DONE; GOT; HIT; MET
achievement FEAT
acknowledge ACK; ALLOW; KNOW; NOD; OWN; WAVE
acid PHENOL; TART
acidity, soil PH

acknowledged ACK
acknowledgement LETTER; NOD; ROGER; WAVE
acquire BAG; CATCH; EARN; FIND; GAIN; GET; LAND; NET; TAKE; WIN
acquire unfairly; *see* STEAL
acquired BOUGHT; FOUND; GOT
acquisition BUY
acquit BEAR; CLEAR; FREE; RELEASE
acrid BITTER
acrobat TUMBLER
acrobatic FLEET; anagram indicator
across AX; OVER
act BILL; BLUFF; DEED; DO; LAW; MOVE; PLAY; POSE; SHAM; TURN
act in exaggerated fashion HAM
acted DID
acting anagram indicator
action BATTLE; CASE; DEED; FIGHT; PLAY; SUIT; WAR; anagram indicator
activate BOOST; CHEER; HEAT; MOVE; ROUSE; STIR; WAKE
activated, activating anagram indicator
active SPRY; anagram indicator
actively anagram indicator
activity BUSTLE; FERMENT; FEVER; HUM; RUSH; anagram indicator
activity, corrupt VICE
activity, non-serious PLAY
actor EXTRA; GABLE; HAM; LOM; OLIVIER; PLAYER; TREE
actor, bad, poor HAM
actor, leading STAR
actor, old TREE
actors CAST; can indicate something to do with acting, role, part, stage
actual REAL; TRUE; VERY
acute KEEN; SHARP
ad see ADVERTISEMENT
adage SAW
Adam's ale HYDRO; WATER
adaptable, adapted, adapting, adaptation anagram indicator
add PUT; SUM; TOT; TOTAL
add secret ingredient LACE

added ON
adder SNAKE; SUMMER; can indicate something to do with an accountant, calculator etc
addict USER
addicted HOOKED
addition PS; SUM
additional EXTRA; OTHER; OVER
additional item PS
address FACE; HOME; PAD; PLACE; NUMBER; ORATION; SPEECH; TALK
adequate AMPLE; ENOUGH; OK
adhere CLEAVE; STICK
adherents CAMP
adhesive GLUE; GUM; PASTE; STICKY
adjacent BESIDE; CLOSE; NEAR; NEXT; ordering indicator
adjust ALIGN; ARRANGE; FIT; ORDER; TUNE
adjustable, adjusted anagram indicator
adjustment, needing anagram indicator
administered RAN; anagram indicator
administrative division PARISH; REGION
administrator HEAD; REGENT; *see* CHIEF
admirable person BRICK; HERO; ST; TRUMP
admiral ADM; DRAKE; HOOD; NELSON
admire REVERE
admired man HERO
admirer BEAU; FAN; LOVER; SUITOR
admission ENTRY; IM (ie. I'M)
admission office RECEPTION
admission, publicise OUT
admit ALLOW; GRANT; OWN; LET
admitted IN
adolescence YOUTH
adolescent TEEN; YOUTH
adore LOVE
adorn DECK
adornment see GEM, JEWELLERY, STONE
adornment, with little BALD; PLAIN
adrenalin, source of GLAND
adrift FREE; LOSE; OFF; OUT; anagram indicator
adult A; BLUE

advance COME; CLIMB; LEAD; LEND; LOAN; MOVE; RAISE; STEP; SUB
advance, amorous PASS
advance cautiously INCH; NOSE
advance payment ANTE; SUB
advance stealthily CRAWL; CREEP; EDGE; INCH
advanced FORWARD; LENT; NEW
advanced in years AGED; OLD
advances, made LENT
advancing one letter to be moved to beginning of word
advantage ASSET; BOON; EDGE; PLUS; START
advantage, take MILK
advert see ADVERTISEMENT
advertise PLUG; PROMOTE; PUSH
advertisement AD; HYPE; NOTICE; PLUG; POSTER; PUFF
advice CLUE; HELP; HINT; TIP
advisable WELL
advisable, more BETTER
advocates BAR
aeroplane BUS; CRATE
aesthetic ARTY
affair AMOUR; CONCERN; MATTER
affect, badly DENT
affect slightly TINGE
affectation POSE
affected ARCH; CAMP; anagram indicator
affectionate FOND; TENDER
affirm AVER; OK; STATE
affirmative AY; AYE; OK; YES
affirmative yore AY
affixed STUCK
afflicted LANE; anagram indicator
affluence EASE
affluent RICH
Afghan DOG
aforesaid DITTO
afraid DREADING; LEERY; SCARED
afresh RE
African MOOR; RIFF
African party ANC

African port ORAN
after PAST; POST; SEEKING; SINCE; ordering indicator
after hours LATE
after that time SINCE
afternoon PM
afterthought PS
afterwards LATER
again MORE; OVER; RE; can indicate an element to be repeated
again, perform REDO
against AGIN; ANTI; AVERSE; CON; CONTRA; V
age CYCLE; ERA; EON; TIME; PERIOD; YEAR
age, at a young EARLY
ageing GREY; OLD
agency BUREAU; CIA; HAND; MEANS
agency, intelligence CIA
agency, news TASS
agency worker TEMP
agent BOND; FACTOR; FED; REP; SPY
agents CIA; MI
ages YONKS; *see* AGE
aggravate IRK; NETTLE; PRY
aggregate, mineral ORE
aggressive HARD
aggrieved SORE; anagram indicator
agile SPRY
agitate FLUSTER; IRK; NEEDLE; SHAKE; STIR
agitated SHOOK; anagram indicator
agitation LATHER
agony PAIN
agony, cause RACK
agree CHIME; MATCH; NOD; OK; SETTLE; SQUARE; TALLY; UNITE
agree, don't DEMUR
agreeable FINE
agreeably WELL
agreed DONE; OK; OKED; ON
agreement AY; AYE; BOND; DEAL; NOD; OK; PACT; SAYSO; SYNC; TREATY; UNION; YEA; YES
agreement, old, traditional YEA
agricultural business FARM; HOLDING

ahead FORWARD; LEADING; ON
ahead, go LEAD
ahead, went LED
aid ABET; CRIB; HELP
ail TROUBLE
ailment, minor COLD
aim END; GOAL; PLAN; POINT
aim high LOB
air AURA; PORT (Gael.); SIDE; SONG; STRAIN; TED; TUNE; WARM; WIND
air, go by FLY
air, in the UP; anagram indicator
air-intake VENT
air-trip HOP
airborne soldier PARA
airborne, to get FLY
aircraft CRATE; JET; MIG; PLANE
aircraft component FIN; PROP; WING
aircraftman AC
aircraftsman ERK
airhole VENT
airman FLIER; PO
airmen RAF
airplane CRAFT; *see* AIRCRAFT
airport LUTON
alarm APPAL; BELL; PANIC; RATTLE; SIREN; WORRY
alarm, cry of O; OH
alarmingly anagram indicator
albeit THOUGH
albeit briefly THO
album DISC; LP
alcohol BEER; CIDER; GIN; *see* DRINK
alcohol, add extra LACE
alcohol-free DRY; TT
alcohol, not having DRY; TT
alcohol, not having much LITE
ale. long drink of YARD
Alfred ALF
alfresco OUT
alien ET; STRANGER

align ARRANGE; DRESS
all FULLY; LOT; QUITE; SUM; TOTAL; U; WHOLE
all over the place anagram indicator
all right APT; FINE; FIT; GOOD; OK
allegro FAST
alley MARBLE
alliance AXIS; BLOC; MATCH; NATO; UNION
allocated anagram indicator
allocation QUOTA; RATION; SHARE; anagram indicator
allot ASSIGN; GRANT
allotment GARDEN; GRANT; PART; SHARE; RATION
allow ENABLE; GRANT; LET; PASS
allow, don't BAN; BAR
allow, not BAN; BAR
allowance GRANT; RATION
allowed LET; LICIT; ON
allowed, is MAY
allowed, not BANNED; OUT
allowed, what's RATION
alloy BRASS
allure CHARM
ally PAL; *see* FRIEND
Almighty GOD
almost NEAR; NEARLY; NIGH; omission indicator, usually one letter from the end of a word
almost at once SOON
aloft HIGH; UP
alone SOLO
along with AND
aloof COLD
aloud homophone indicator
also AND; TOO
also known as AKA
alter CHANGE
alter eg.o HYDE
alteration anagram indicator
altered anagram indicator
alternate can indicate the use of alternate letters as "Theorize air's iamb as showing alternate rhyme scheme" gives TERZA RIMA
alternative OR; OTHER

alternatively OR; anagram indicator
alternatively named AKA
altitude HEIGHT
altogether NUDE
aluminium AL
always AY (Middle English); EER; EVER
amass GATHER; HOARD; SAVE
amateur LAY
amazement AWE; WONDER
amazing anagram indicator
Amazon can indicate something exclusive of men
ambassador HE (abbr. for His Excellency)
ambit RANGE; SCOPE
ambition DREAM; END; GOAL; GRAIL
ambitious type PUSHER
amble STROLL
amend FIX
amended anagram indicator
amending, needs anagram indicator
amendment CHANGE; FIFTH; anagram indicator
amends, make ATONE
amenities NT
America AM; STATES; US
America, in can indicate American spelling as "beauty in America" clues LUSTER
America, small profit in BUCK
American A; AM; GI; US; YANK
American associate BUD; PARD
American bill CHECK; TAB
American bonnet HOOD
American chap BO
American college *see* AMERICAN UNIVERSITY
American colony, founder of PENN
American flag COLOR
American fool SHMO
American hero REVERE
American Indian BRAVE; CREE; CREEK; CROW; HOPI; UTE
American kid BUB
American lawyer DA
American letter ZEE

American money BUCK; CENT; DIME; FOLD; QUARTER; ROLL
American people CREE; HOPI; UTE; *see* AMERICAN INDIAN
American prosecutor DA
American, serving GI
American ship *see* AMERICAN VESSEL
American side ENGLISH
American's mood COLOR
American state AL; ALA; ALAS; ARK; CAL; COL; COLO; CONN; DAK; DEL; GA; I; IA; ID; ILL; IND; KANS; KS; KY; LA; MA; MASS; ME; MICH; MINN; MISS; MONT; NEB; NEV; NH; NJ; NY; OK; OR; ORE; PENN; RI; SC; SD; TENN; TEX; TX; UT; VA; VT; WASH; WIS; WYO
American tone COLOR
American university MIT; YALE
American vessel US; USS
American volume LITER
American waistcoat VEST
American warrior *see* AMERICAN INDIAN
American wood LUMBER
American woman, vulgar BROAD; DAME
Americans GIS
Amerindian CREE; HOPI; UTE; *see* AMERICAN INDIAN
amid nesting indicator
ammo, old GRAPE
ammunition BULLET; ROUND; SHOT
amorous, be BILL; COO; SPOON
among MID; nesting indicator; run indicator
amount DROP; LOT; SOME; STAKE; SUM; TON
amount, large TON
amount, say can refer to a mountain (where 'say' is acting as a homophone indicator)
amount, small DAB; DOT; DRIB; SPOT; TOT
amount, unspecified SOME
amour BEAU; LOVER
amphetamine SPEED
amphibian CROC; EFT; FROG; NEWT; TOAD
amply WELL
amuse TICKLE
amusement FUN
amusing DROLL; FUN; FUNNY
an rem: AN itself can be part of the solution

anaesthetic ETHER; LOCAL; NUMBER
analyse PARSE
analyzing anagram indicator
ancestors LINE
anchor KEDGE
ancient AGED; OLD
Ancient Briton PICT
ancient city ILIUM; ROME; TROY; UR
ancient letter RUNE
ancient oath ODS
ancient vessel ARGO
and rem: AND itself can be part of the solution
and not NOR
and others ET AL
and so on ETC
anecdotes ANA
anew anagram indicator
anger BILE; FURY; GALL; HEAT; IRE; IRK; RAGE; RILE; WRATH
anger, showing CROSS; MAD
angle BEND; CAST; CORNER; FISH; LINE; SLANT; TURN; VIEW
angler's equipment CREEL; NET; REEL; ROD
Anglican CE
angrily anagram indicator
angry CROSS; HEATED; HET(UP); IRATE; RED; SORE; WILD; anagram indicator
angry, be FUME; RAGE; RANT
angry display PADDY
angry feeling IRE
angry, get FUME
angry-looking BLACK; RED
angry, visibly BLACK; RED
anguish WOE
animal APE; ASS; CAT; CONY; DOG; KID; LION; MOOSE; PET; RAT; SOW; STAG; YAK
animals FLOCK; HERD; MICE; PACK; STOCK; SWINE
animals, inferior CULL; CULLS
animals. lots of ZOO
animal specialist VET
animation shot CEL

animosity PIQUE
announce SAY; STATE
announced, announcing homophone indicator
announcement AD; BILLING
anon SOON
annoy BUG; GALL; GRATE; IRK; MIFF; MARK; NETTLE; PEEVE; RIDE; TEASE
annoyance, express TUT
annoyed ATE; CROSS; RODE; SORE; *see* ANGRY
annoyed, get RILE
anonymously usually a signal that N is to be omitted from indicated word
anorak NERD
another SECOND; anagram indicator; when used with a verb can indicate use of prefix RE-
another way, in anagram indicator
annulment, to effect an CANCEL
answer A; ANS
answer, near to WARM
answer, short A; ANS
antelope ELAND
anti-aircraft AA
anti-smoking group ASH
anticipation HOPE
anticyclone HIGH
antique OLD; PERIOD
anxiety ANGST; STRESS; WORRY
anxious KEEN; TENSE; anagram indicator
anxious, be FRET; WORRY
any SOME
anybody ONE
anyhow anagram indicator
anything AUGHT; OUT
anyway anagram indicator
apart ASUNDER; anagram indicator
apart from SAVE
apartment APT; FLAT; PAD; ROOM
ape COPY; GIBBON; MIMIC; ORANG
apex PEAK; TOP
Aphrodite, son of EROS

apostle PETER; SPOON

apostrophe (') when an apostrophe is placed before a word it usually signals the omission of the initial 'h' which in turn indicates that 'h' is to be dropped from the beginning of the target word to provide the solution; when an apostrophe appears at the end of a word it usually signals the omission of the 'g' in '-ing' which in turn indicates the omission of the final 'g' in the target word

appal SHOCK

appalling DIRE; anagram indicator

apparatus RIG

apparent CLEAR; PLAIN

apparently AP

appeal CRY; IT; O (i.e. as in 'O Jerusalem'); SA (ie. sex appeal); SUE; UMP

appear BE; EMERGE; LOOK; SEEM; SHOW

appearance AIR; CAST; ENTRY; FACE; FRONT; GUISE; LOOK; LOOKS; MIEN

appearance, deceptive FRONT

appended ON; something to be appended to a component

applaud CHEER; CLAP; PRAISE

applause CHEER; CHEERS

apple COX

appliance anagram indicator

application APP; COAT; USE

application for cut PLASTER

applied anagram indicator

apply USE

appoint ASSIGN

appointment POST; JOB

appraisal anagram indicator

appreciate DIG; GROW; KNOW; LIKE

apprehension DREAD; FEAR

apprentice LEARNER; TYRO

approach ANGLE; DRIVE; MODE; NEAR; TAKE; WAY

approaching ALMOST; NEAR; TO; one element to precede another

appropriate APT; DUE; FIT; FITTING; POCKET; RIGHT; STEAL; TAKE; PROPER; WHIP [ASSUME; PILFER]

appropriately WELL

approval AMEN; FAVOUR; NOD; OK; YES

approval, cry of BRAVO

approve ALLOW; GRANT; OK; PASS

approximate NEAR; ROUGH
apt ABLE; FIT; FITTING; MEET; RIGHT
apt, are TEND
apt, increasingly FITTER
aptitude TALENT
aquatic creature OTTER
Arab HORSE
Arab country OMAN
Arabian AR
arbiter REF
arc BEND; BOW
arch BOW; CHIEF; anagram indicator
Archbishop RUNCIE; TUTU
archdeacon VEN
archer HOOD; TELL
architect NASH; WREN
architects RIBA
architecture, type of IONIC
Arctic, in the, of the POLAR
ardent AVID; KEEN
are EXIST
are French ES
area A; ACRE; AREA; DEPT; FIELD; LAND; REGION; ROOM; TRACT; ZONE
area, copper's MANOR
area, in the immediate BY
area, military SECTOR; ZONE
area of land ACRE; ROOD
area, playing COURT; FIELD:
area, specialised DEPT
arena LISTS; RING
argue BICKER; PLEAD; REASON; SPAR
argument DO; ISSUE; PLEA; RIFT; ROW; SPAR; SPAT; TIFF; TODO (ie. todo); WORDS
argument against CON
arise EMERGE
aristocracy GENTRY
aristocrat EARL; LORD; NOBLE; PEER
aristocratic NOBLE
aristocratic young man BUCK

Arizona AZ
Arkansas AR
'arken EAR (ie. 'ear)
'arkened EARD (ie. 'eard)
arm BRANCH; GUN; LIMB; RIFLE
armed assailant GUNMAN
armed men POSSE
armed services FORCES
armour MAIL
army HOST; TA
army branch, corps, part of RA; RE; REME; RI; UNIT
army chief, supremo OC
army corps *see* ARMY BRANCH
army craftsmen REME
army doctors RAMC
army drill BULL
army, part, unit CORPS; *see* ARMY BRANCH
army vehicle JEEP; TANK
Arnold, Dr HEAD
aroma SCENT
aromatic ingredient SPICE
around C; CA; anagram indicator; nesting indicator; reversal indicator
arouse STIR
aroused, arousing anagram indicator
arrange ALIGN; DO; DRESS; EDIT; FIX; ORDER; RIG; SORT
arrange to meet DATE
arranged LAID; anagram indicator
arrangement ORDER; anagram indicator
arrayed anagram indicator
arrest BOOK; BUST; COLLAR; COP; GRAB; NAB; STEM; STOP; STUNT; nesting indicator
arresting nesting indicator
arrival ARR
arrival, expected time of ETA
arrive ARE; COME; REACH
arrived ARR; CAME
arrogance SIDE
arrogant COCKY
arrogant person SNOB
arrow DART

arsenic AS
art CRAFT; PIC; SKILL
art, classical ARS
art, French ES (ie. French verb)
art, work of BUST; MURAL
artfully anagram indicator
Arthur ART
article A; AN; DER; DIE; EL; IL; ITEM; LA; LE; LES; LOS; PAPER; THE; THING; UNE; UNE
article, old YE
articles articles (see articles above) in some kind of combination eg. ANTHER; ILDER
article, useless LEMON
articulate FLUENT
artillery RA
artist DALI; HUNT; MONET; MUNCH; RA; TITIAN; TURNER
artistic society RSA
as LIKE; QUA; SINCE
as before DO (abbr. of ditto)
as far as TO
as if anagram indicator
as it were QUASI
as new anagram indicator
as soon as ONCE
as well TOO
ascend CLIMB; MOUNT; RISE; SCALE
ascent CLIMB; RISE
ascetic FAKIR
ashen PALE; PALING
Asia EAST
Asian INDIAN; PATEL; THAI
Asian dish BALTI
ask BID; DEMAND; POSE; QUIZ; REQUEST
ask piteously BEG
asked BADE
aspect FACET; HUE; SIDE; TONE; VIEW
aspersion SLUR
asphyxiate SMOTHER
aspiration DREAM
aspire HOPE; LONG; YEARN

aspiring, one HOPER
ass FOOL
ass, sound like an BRAY
assassin BOOTH
assassinated, assassination anagram indicator
assault HIT; RAID
assault, serious RAPE
assemble BUILD; EDIT; GATHER; HOARD; MEET; MUSTER; SIT; anagram indicator
assembled SAT; anagram indicator
assembly DIET; MEET; MEETING; RALLY; SITTING; anagram indicator
assent OK; YES
assess GAUGE; GRADE; MARK; RATE
asset PLUS
assign PIN; POST
assignation DATE
assignment JOB; MISSION; TASK
assist ABET; AID; BACK; HELP
assistance AID; HAND; HELP
assistance, without ALONE
assistant ABETTER; ADC; AIDE; DRESSER; MATE
associate MATE; PAL
association CLUB; RING; UNION
Association member GUIDE
assorted anagram indicator
assuage ALLAY
assume DON; PUTON (ie. put on)
assurance NERVE
astern AFT
astonishing anagram indicator
astray anagram indicator
astray, go ERR; SIN; WANDER
astronomical unit EPACT
astute SHREWD
at all EVER
at first IST (ie. 1st); initial letter indicator as "Honour kept us doing our shoes at first" clues KUDOS
at heart insertion indicator; can indicate that middle letter(s) are to be used, as 'liberal at heart' clues E or BER
at home IN

at last last letter indicator
at sea ADRIFT; anagram indicator
at that time THEN
Athenian TIMON
Athenian character TIMON; can indicate a Greek letter needs to be used as a component (*see* GREEK CHARACTER)
Athens, in can indicate the use of a Greek letter (see Athenian character)
athlete BLUE; RUNNER
athletic type BLUE; RUNNER
atmosphere AIR; AURA; FUG
atrocious DIRE; anagram indicator
attached ON
attachment BOND; LINK; LOVE; TIE
attack ASSAIL; CHARGE; CHECK (i.e. in chess); FIT; GOAT (ie. go-at); PUSH; RAID; SORTIE; TILT; *see* UNDER ATTACK
attack with explosives SHELL
attacked BIT; HIT
attempt BID; CRACK; GO; SHOT; SHY; TACKLE; TRY
attempts TRIES
attend APPEAR; GRACE; HEED; SHOW
attendant BUTLER; CARER; GROOM; PAGE; USHER
attending AT; PRESENT
attention CARE; EAR; HEED; INTEREST
attention, pay HEED
attention, requiring TODO (ie.to-do)
attic GARRET; LOFT
attire DRESS; FROCK; GOWN; SHIRT; SKIRT
attitude AIR; LINE; MANNER; POSE; TONE
attract DRAW; ENGAGE; LURE; PULL; TEMPT
attraction DRAW; IT; LURE; PULL; RIDE
attractive CATCHY; CUTE; FETCHING; NICE; PRETTY; TAKING
attractive female, girl, woman DOLL; DISH; LOOKER
attribute of run indicator
auction SALE
auction item LOT
audacious BRAVE; COOL; FORWARD; LIPPY
audacity NERVE
audible disapproval BOO; HISS
audibly homophone indicator

audience HEARING; HOUSE
audience, appreciative CLAPPERS
audit CHECK
audition, auditioning homophone indicator
auditor EAR
auditor, to homophone indicator
augur SEER
August AUG
Aunt Sally BUTT
aura CHARM
aureole HALO
Aussie fellow SPORT
Aussie party DING
austere DOUR
Australia AUS; OZ
Australian AUS
Australian fool DILL
Australian lake EYRE
Australian sheep-shearer RINGER
Australian utility, fire UTE
Austria A
authentic REAL; TRUE; GEN
author BARRIE; ELIA; ELIOT; HOPE; LEWIS; ORWELL; PARENT; PEN; POTTER; SAND; URIS; WELLS; YEATS; *see* NOVELIST, WRITER
authorisation OK
authorisation, give *see* AUTHORISE
authorise OK; ORDER; SIGN
authority CLOUT; EXPERT; MIGHT; SAGE
Authority BOARD
authority, position of CHAIR
autobiography LIFE
automatic reaction TIC
autumn FALL
avail USE
available AROUND; ON; OPEN; OUT; TAP
available, not OFF; OUT
availing USING
avant-garde VAN
avarice GREED

avenue AVE; DRIVE; WAY
aver AFFIRM; STATE
average AV; AVE; MEAN; MEDIUM; NORM; PAR; SOSO (ie.so-so)
avoid FLEE; SHUN; WARE
await BIDE
award CUP; EMMY; GOLD; GRANT; MM; OSCAR; PALM; PRIZE; *see* HONOUR, MEDAL
aware HIP; ONTO
aware of trends HIP
away ABROAD; HENCE; OFF; OUT; anagram indicator; omission indicator, such as initial or final letter
away, put DINE; EAT
awe DREAD
awful BAD; CHRONIC; LOUSY; anagram indicator
awfully anagram indicator
awkward STICKY; anagram indicator
awkward position CORNER; SPOT
awkwardly anagram indicator
axe CUT; HATCHET; HEW; SACK

Bb

babble PRATE; PRATTLE
Babe RUTH
baby CHICK; CHILD; CUB; KID; KITTEN; PUP
baby food RUSK
babywear NAPPY
bachelor B; BA; SINGLE
back AFT; BET; END; HIND; REAR; SECOND; SPINE; STERN; reversal indicator; last letter indicator
back at sea AFT
back-numbers SON

back-room DRAW; MOOR
backbone SPINE
backchat LIP
backed reversal indicator
backed by joint run and reversal indicator as in "Statesman backed by Labour henchman" gives NEHRU; can indicate a component is to come last in the solution
backfired reversal indicator
background PAST; REAR; STORY
backing AID; reversal indicator; element to be placed at end of word
backslapping HEARTY
backstreet ALLEY; TS
backtracking reverse indicator
backward reversal indicator
backwards AFT; reversal indicator
bad DIRE; EVIL; HARD; HIGH; ILL; OFF; POOR; ROTTEN; anagram indicator
bad actor HAM
bad, become ROT
bad behaviour CRIME; SIN
bad feeling ODIUM
bad hat CAD; ROTTER
bad, is not as EASES
bad name MUD
bad service FAULT
bad smell BO; PONG
bad-tempered MEAN; TESTY
bad, very CHRONIC; EVIL
bad weather FOG
badger BROCK; HARRY; HOUND; NAG; PESTER
badly ILL; anagram indicator
badly, behave SIN
badly made TRASHY; anagram indicator
baffling anagram indicator
bag CARRIER; CASE; CATCH; GRIP; NET; POKE; PURSE; SAC; SACK; SACHET
bagel ROLL
baggage CASE; SLUT
baggage man PORTER
bagging nesting indicator
bags LOTS; OODLES

bait KID; LURE; RIB; TEASE
bake COOK; TAN
baked anagram indicator
baking HOT
balance POISE; WEIGH
bald BARE; PLAIN
ball BLACK (ie. colour in snooker); BLUE; BROWN; DANCE; DELIVERY; GREEN; LOB; MARBLE; O; ORB; PILL; PINK; RED; SLUG; YELLOW; YORKER
ball, high LOB; SKYER
ball of yarn SKEIN
ballad AIR; LAY; SONG
ballet leap JETE
balloon O; SWELL
ballot POLL; VOTE
balls OO; OVER
Baltic port RIGA
balustrade FENCE; RAILING
ban BAR; BLACK; DEBAR; STOP; VETO
banal FLAT; TRIPE; TRITE
bananas BATS; HAND; HANDS; NUTS; anagram indicator
band BAR; BELT; CIRCLE; FESS; GANG; GIRD; HOOP; LINE; O; RANGE; RING; SASH; SHOE; STRAP; STREAK; STRIP; STRIPE; TROOP; ZONE
band, metal SHOE
band performance GIG
bandage DRESS
bandit BRIGAND
bang BLOW; CLAP; KNOCK; REPORT; STRIKE
banger CRATE; HEAP
bank BAR; BLUFF; BRAE; CAMBER; CAY; HEAP; LEAN; MASS; REEF; RELY; ROW; SCARF; SHELF; SIDE; SHORE; SLOPE; TIER
bank employee TELLER
bank worker TELLER
banker CAMBER; a favourite with compilers, indicating a river (in the form of banked, between banks etc); *see* RIVER
banking CAMBER
banknote BILL; FIVER; TENNER
banknotes ROLL; WAD
bankrupt BROKE; BUST

banks indicates first and last letters to be used
banner FLAG [HEADLINE; PROHIBITIONIST]
bannock BREAD; CAKE; LOAF
banquet FEAST
banter CHAFF; JEST; RALLY
bar BAN; BAND; BANK; BILLET; BLACK; BUT; COUNTER; EXCEPT; FRET; GATE; INN; LATCH; LEVER; LINE; LOCAL; PUB; RAIL; RAY; ROD; SAVE; SHELF; SHOAL; STREAK; STRIP; STRIPE; TAVERN; often indicates something to do with the legal profession; in singular or plural can indicate something to do with music or composer; can indicate something to do with a pub
bar, seedy DIVE
bar, type of PUBLIC
barbaric person GOTH
barbarism TERROR
Barcelona NUT
bare BALD; NAKED; NUDE; PLAIN
bare teeth GRIN
barely JUST
barely sufficient SCANT
bargain DEAL; HAGGLE; SNIP; TRADE
barge BOAT; BUMP; LIGHTER
barge through tunnel, propel LEG
bark BAY; GRAZE; SCRAP; SNAP; TAN; YAP
barker DOG; can refer to a specific breed of dog; *see* DOG
barking anagram indicator
Barnaby RUDGE
barometer GLASS
baron B; LORD
baron, Scottish HOME
baronet BART; BT
baroque anagram indicator
barracks CAMP
barrel B; BIN; BL; DRUM; KEG; PIN; TUN
barrel-part STAVE
barren BLEAK; DRY; DULL; STARK
barricade FENCE ; WALL
Barrie's dog NANA
barrier BLOCK; DAM; FENCE; GATE; HEDGE; PALE; PLUG; RAIL; RAILING; WALL

barrister BRIEF; COUNSEL
barrow CART; GRAVE
barter TRADE; TRUCK
base BED; EVIL; FOOT; FOUND; HOME; LOW; MEAN; MOUNT; REST; VILE
base of final latter indicator
baseball game INNING
bash DO; RAM; *see* HIT
bashful COY; SHY
basic RUDE
basic instinct ID
basil HERB
basin BOWL; SINK
basis STAPLE
basket CREEL; HAMPER; TRUG
bass DEEP; FISH; SINGER
bastard SHAM
bat BLINK; CLUB; WILLOW
bath DIP; POOL; SALINA; TUB
Bath can refer to some aspect of the city
bathroom LAV
bathroom accessory TOWEL
baton ROD; STICK; can indicate something to do with relay race, conducting
batsman STRIKER
batsman's hit STROKE
batten down NAIL
battery, part of CELL
batting IN
battle CLASH; FIGHT; FRAY; SCRAP; WAR; can refer to a specific battle eg. ALMA; LOOS; MARNE; MONS; SOMME
battle, do FIGHT; WAR
battleship RAM
bawl CRY
bawdy BLUE
bay BARK; BELLOW; BIGHT; BROWN; COVE; HOWL; NICHE; ROAN; SPACE; can indicate something to do with a house
Bayeux can indicate something to do with sew, sewing
BBC AUNTIE
be EXIST
be able CAN

be angry RANT; *see* ANGRY
be first LEAD; WIN
be given GET
be paid EARN; GET
be, to (with some indication of France) ETRE
be told HEAR
be upset CRY
beach LIDO; SAND; SHORE; STRAND
beak BILL; HOOTER; NEB; NOSE; RAM
beam BAR; GLOW; LIGHT; RAFTER; RAY; SHAFT; SHORE; SMILE
bean HEAD; PULSE
bear ABIDE; ACQUIT; BALOO; BROOK; CARRY; POOH; SELLER; SHOW; STAND; TOTE; WINNIE
beard AWN
bearing AIR; E; EAST; MIEN; N; NE; NORTH; NW; S; SE; SOUTH; SW; W; WEST
bearings *see* BEARING
beast ASS; BRUTE; CAMEL; *see* ANIMAL
beast of burden ASS; MULE
beastly accommodation, place etc DEN; LAIR; STY
beasts STOCK
beat ALLIN (ie. all-in); CAP; CANE; CLOCK; CLUB; DRUB; FLOG; LAM; LASH; LICK; PASTE; PIP; PULSE; RAP; STRAP; STRIKE; THRASH; THRESH; THROB; TICK; TOP; TROUNCE; WHIP
beaten, be, get LOSE
beaten (up) anagram indicator
beating LASH
Beau NASH
beautiful creature PERI
beautiful girl PERI
beautiful lady, woman BELLE; VENUS
beauty DISH; GEM; GLAM; LOOKS; can indicate something to do with sleep
beauty competition, entrant in MISS
beauty in America LUSTER
beauty queen MISS
beauty spot EDEN
because FOR; SINCE
become FIT; GET; SUIT; TURN

become tired FLAG
becoming FIT
bed BUNK; COT; COUCH; CRIB; DIVAN; FORM; KIP; LITTER; PATCH; PLOT; REST
bed, French LIT
bed, in NOT UP (which reverses into PUT ON for instance)
bed, out of UP
bedding, Japanese FUTON
Bedouin ARAB
bedspread COVER
bee rem: apart from an insect, a bee is also a form of social gathering
beef BARON; BRAWN; BULLY; CARP; GRIPE; GROUSE; MIGHT; ROAST; STEER; can indicate a cut of beef eg. RUMP, TOPSIDE
beef producer COW
beer ALE; BITTER; BREW; DRAUGHT; KEG; LAGER; MILD; PILS; PINT; PORTER; SWIPE(S); WALLOP
Beethoven, like DEAF
before ANTE; ERE; PRE; preceding indicator
before, as DO
before long ANON
before noon AM
before now ALREADY
before time EARLY
befuddled anagram indicator
beg ASK; PLEAD
began AROSE
begin ARISE; OPEN; SETTO (ie. set-to); START; *see* START
begin again RENEW
beginner L; LEARNER; TYRO; initial letter indicator
beginning BIRTH; DAWN; SEED; START; initial letter indicator
beginning of life EGG
beginning of new era OAD (ie. zero AD)
behave badly SIN
behaviour ACTION; PLAY
behaviour, silly ANTIC; PRANK
beheaded first letter omission indicator
beheaded king CR
behind AFTER; BACK; LATE; REAR; RUMP; STERN; TAIL; can also indicate the last letter or letters of the answer
behind bars INSIDE

behind, show MOON
behind time LATE
behold ECCO; LO
being LIVER
being performed ON
being staged ON
Belgian FLEMING; [LEIGE]
Belgian province NAMUR
belief CREED; FAITH; ISM; TENET
belief in God DEISM
believe CREDIT; FEEL
believer DEIST
believer in God DEIST
belittle DECRY
bell-sound CLANG; DING; RING; TING
Bellini heroine NORMA
Bellini's work NORMA
bellow BAWL; BAY; ROAR
bellows-mender FLUTE (character from 'Midsummer Night's Dream')
bells PEAL
belly PAUNCH; POT; TUM; TUMMY
bellyache MOAN; GRIPE
belonging to run indicator
beloved DEAR
beloved Parisian CHER
below UNDER
bemused MAD
belt BAND; HIT; HURRY; KNOCK; ZONE
bench FORM; PEW; SEAT; SETTLE
bend ARC; ARCH; BIGHT; BOW; FOLD; HOOK; KNOT; PLY; S; STOOP; U
bender KNEE
beneath BELOW; LOW; UNDER
Benedictine DOM
beneficiary HEIR
benefit AID; ASSET; AVAIL; BOON; DOLE; GAIN; GOOD; HELP; PERK; RIGHT
bent ASKEW; CROOK; CROOKED; LEANING; anagram indicator
bent one CROOK; LIAR

berate SCOLD
berated anagram indicator
berth BUNK; DOCK
beserk anagram Indicator
beside ON; NEAR
besmirch SMEAR
besmirching STAIN
besom BROOM
besotted anagram indicator
best BEAT; CAP; CREAM; DEFEAT; ELITE; FLOWER; PASTE; PEAK; PICK; PLUM; TOP; TOPS
best China MING
best part CREAM
bestow AWARD; GRANT
bet ANTE; BACK; GAMBLE; LAY; NAP; PUNT; STAKE; TREBLE; WAGER
bet, good CERT; EVENS
betray SHOP; RATON (ie, rat on)
betrayal TREASON
better BACKER; FINER; FITTER; LAYER; MASTER; PUNTER; TOP; something to do with betting eg. TOTE; in conjunction with a verb can indicate the use of OUT, as "be a better pilot" clues OUTFLY for example
better, to get CAP; RALLY; RISE
better half MATE
betting record BOOK
betting system TOTE
between sides component to be nested between R and L, or L and R
beverage CUP; *see* DRINK
bewail KEEN; LAMENT
bewildered anagram indicator
bewitch ENCHANT
bias SKEW; anagram indicator
biased ASKEW; anagram indicator
bib POUT
Bible AV; RV
Bible, part of HEB; NT; NUM; OT; VERSE; *see* BOOK
Bible story PARABLE
Biblical character JOB; LOT; MARK
Biblical mountain SION
Biblical writer LUKE; MARK

bid CALL; CHARGE; INVITE; OFFER; ORDER; TENDER
biff BLOW
big HUGE; OS; TALL; VAST
Big Apple NY
big car LIMO
big hit SIX
big house GRANGE
big noise VIP
big one WHOPPER
bigger than average OS
bighead B
bight BAY; BEND; COVE; LOOP
bigwig CHEESE; NOB; VIP
bike CYCLE; MOPED
Bikini ATOLL
bill AC; ACT; AD; ADVERT; BEAK; INVOICE; NOSE; POSTER; TAB; can indicate something to do with a bird
Bill W
bill in U.S. CHECK; NOTE; TAB
billet BAR; JOB
billow SWELL
Billy BUDD; GOAT; KID
bind FASTEN; HOLD; HOLE; PEST; STRAP; TIE
binder FOLDER
binding CORD; TIE
bingo LOTTO
biography LIFE
bird CAPON; CHAT; CHOUGH; COCK; COOT; CROW; DIVER; DRAKE; DUCK; EMU; FINCH; FOWL; GANNET; GOOSE; HEN; JAY; KITE; KNOT; LARK; LIFE; LORY; MINA; MOA; PEN; PIE; RAIL; RAVEN; REE; ROOK; ROOSTER; RUFF; SAKER; SCOTER; SHRIKE; SNIPE; SPARROW; STINT; STORK; SWALLOW; SWAN; TEAL; TERN; TIME; TIT; WREN [ROOST; WING]
bird, fabulous, legendary, mythological ROC
bird disease GAPES; ROUP
bird, male DRAKE
bird no longer DODO; MOA
bird, old DODO; MOA
bird sanctuary NEST
bird song TRILL

Birmingham BRUM; rem: can refer to Alabama or the American South as well as the English Midlands city
Birmingham venue NEC
birth date AGE
birth, of NATAL
birthplace MANGER
biscuit NUT; SNAP; WAFER
bishop B; MAN; PIECE; RR
bishop's domain SEE
bishop's office SEE
bishopric ELY; SEE
bit CRUMB; GRAIN; JOT; LITTLE; LUMP; MORSEL; ORT; PART; PIECE; PINCH; SCRAP; SHRED; SNAFFLE; TASTE; TRACE; run indicator
bit of run indicator; can indicate the initial letter(s) of the following word
bit of fun LARK; LAUGH
bit-part CAMEO; EXTRA
bite GNAW; NIP; SNACK; TANG
biting RAW; nesting indicator
bitter ACRID; BEER; ICY; PARKY; SOUR
bizarre OUTRE; RUM; anagram indicator
black B; BAN; BAR; CARBON; EBONY; INKY; JET; SABLE
black eye MOUSE
Black Horse BESS
black magic BART (ie. black art)
black stuff JET; TAR
black, very BE
blackguard CAD
blackleg RAT
blade OAR; SHARE; SWORD; VANE
blame RAP
bland MILD
blast RAIL
blasted anagram indicator
blatant GLARING; LOUD
blaze MARK
blemish DEFACE; FLAW; MARK; SCAR; SMEAR; STAIN; TAINT
blending anagram indicator
blessed HOLY
blessing BOON

blight BANE; MAR; RUST
blighted anagram indicator
blimey COR
blind DAZZLE
blind man PEW
blink BAT
blinking BALLY; DANG
bliss HEAVEN; JOY
blob BLOT
block BAR; BARRIER; BRICK; CUBE; DAM; DIE; SET; SETT; STEM; STOP; VETO; WEDGE
block of paper PAD
block off road CONE
blocked run indicator
bloke CHAP; COVE; LAD; SID; *see* MAN
blokes MEN
blonde FAIR
blood GORE; RACE; RED; STOCK; STRAIN
blood group A; AB; O
bloodshed GORE
bloodthirsty GORY
bloody RARE; RED; GORY
bloom BLUSH; FLUSH; FLOWER; can refer to steel-making
bloomer BISH; BREAD; ERROR; LOAF; SLIP; rem: can refer to a flower eg. ASTER; *see* FLOWER
bloomimg OUT
blossom MAY
blot SPLODGE
blotchy anagram indicator
blow BIFF; CUFF; GUST; HIT; PUFF; SMACK; STRIKE; STRIPE; STROKE; TAP; THUMP; TOOT; WAFT; WIND
blow, light TAP
blow-out FEAST
blown up anagram indicator
blub CRY; SOB; WEEP
blue ADULT; AZURE; BLOW (slang for 'squander'); CAM (ie. university colour); DOWN; LOW; NAVY; RIBALD; RIGHT; ROYAL; SAD; SKY; TORY
blue, be MOPE
blue-eyed boy PET
Bluegrass state KY

blue material DENIM
bluebottle COP; FLY; *see* POLICEMAN
bluff KID
blunder BISH; BONER; ERR; ERROR; GAFFE; TRIP; *see* BLOOMER
blunt DULL; PLAIN
blurb PUFF
blush BLOOM; REDDEN
blushing PINK; RED
boa FUR; STOLE
board COUNTER; DEAL; DECK; DIRECTORS; EMBARK; PENSION; PLANK; TABLE; also can refer to material used in boards eg. DEAL; can indicate something to do with chessboard (commonly MAN, MATE); can indicate something to do with dartboard (commonly BULL, INNER, OCHE, OUTER)
board game GO
board, on can indicate that an element is to be inserted between the letters SS (ie. for Steamship)
boarding PENSION
boarding house PENSION
boast BRAG; CROW; VAUNT
boasting, idle BLUSTER
boat ARK; BARGE; CRAFT; DHOW; GIG; HOY; KETCH; PRAM; PUNT; REEFER; SHELL; SHIP; SMACK; STEAMER; SUB; TRAMP; TUB; TUG
boat-trip ROW
boatmen CREW; EIGHT
bob CUT; DIP; S (ie. shilling); can indicate something to do with haircut
bobbin SPOOL
Boche HUN
body MASS; MUMMY; SOMA; STIFF
body, as a ALL
body-builder STEROID
body of work CORPUS
body, part of ARM; CHEST; FOOT; HEAD; HIP; LEG; ORGAN; SHIN; SPINE
body-snatcher HARE
bodyguard HEAVY
bog MARSH; MIRE; SWAMP
boggy area FEN

Bohemian ARTY
Bohemian girl MIMI
boil HEAT; SIMMER
boiling anagram indicator
boisterous ROUGH; anagram indicator
bold BRASH; BRAVE
bolt ARROW; FLEE; LEVANT (old slang); LOCK; PIN; RUN; WOLF
Bolshevik LENIN
bomb A; ATOM; eg.G; FLOP; H; VI
bombard SHELL
bond KNOT; MANACLE; TIE
bone ILIUM; INCUS; RIB; SHIN; STEAL
bones TARSI
bonfire BLAZE
bonnet HOOD
bonnet, American HOOD
bonus EXTRA; PLUS
bony THIN
book ACTS; AMOS; AV (for authorised version); B; DAN (for Daniel); ENGAGE; EDITION; EPH; HEB; JER; JOB; JUDGES; KINGS; LIB; LOG; MARK; NT (for New Testament); NUM; NUMB; OT (for Old Testament); PRIMER; PSALMS; RESERVE; RUTH; TITLE; TOME; VOL
book, change EDIT
book-end FINIS; K
book, French ROMAN
book, good JUDGES; *see* BIBLE, BOOK
book, OT NUMB; *see* BIBLE, BOOK
booked can indicate novel or fictional character
bookmaker BINDER; WRITER
books AV; NT; OT ; *see* BOOK
boom BANG; SPAR
boomeranged reversal indicator
boor LOUT; YAHOO
boost KICK
boot KICK
booth STALL; TENT
booze BEER; *see* DRINK
boozer TOPER; *see* DRUNKARD
bop DANCE

Bordeaux CLARET; rem: can be a place as well as a wine therefore signifying something French
border ABUT; BOUND; EDGE; EDGING; FRINGE; HEM; LIMIT; LINE; MARCH; MARGE (old word); RIM; SIDE
borders can indicate first and last letters
bore BRED; DRAG; DRILL; DRIP; EAGRE; FAG; IRK; PAIN; PIERCE; REAM; WELL
boring DEAD; DRY; FLAT; can indicate some cognate of NUMB
boring type NERD
boring-bit BROACH
boring place WELL
boring, something AWL
born B; NEE
boss HEAD; STUD
bosses BOARD
Boston institute MIT
botch BUNGLE
both TWAIN
bother BANE; CARE; DO; EAT; FUSS; HECK; HINDER; NARK; PEST; RATS(!); ROW; TIFF; WORRY
both flanks (sides) RL; LR
bothered ATE; anagram indicator
bottle NERVE
bottle, with extra BRAVER
bottom BASE; BED; BUM; END; FOOT; LAST; PRAT; RUMP; SEAT; TERN; last letter indicator
bottomless omission indicator for last letter of associated word
bottom, river, sea BED
bottle FLAGON; MAGNUM; NERVE; PHIAL; VIAL
bough BRANCH
bought it something to do with having died
bounce BOB
bouncer BALL
bouncy anagram indicator
bound END; HEADED; HOP; JUMP; LEAP; LOPE; SPRING; TIED
boundary BORDER; EDGE; FENCE; FOUR; HEDGE; IV; METE (boundary stone); RIM; RUNS; SIX; VI
bounder CAD; FENCE; HEEL; ROD
bouquet AROMA; AURA; NOSE; POSY
bout JAG
bovine OX

bovver boy SKIN

bow ARC; ARCH; BEND; FRONT; PROW; STEM; YIELD; can also refer to something to do with a violin or violinist

bowl FONT; HOLLOW; WOOD

bowl over WOW

bowled B; OUT

bowler DERBY; HAT; TILE

bowler, type of SPIN

bowling OVER

bowman ARCHER

box ARK; BIN; CASE; CASKET; CHEST; COFFER; CRATE; CUFF; FIGHT; INRO; LOGE; SPAR; TIN; TREE; TUBE

boxer ALI; DOG; PUG

box, pill INRO

box of cards SHOE

boy LAD; PAGE; SON; SONNY; can signal a proper name eg. KEVIN, PETER; very often signals the diminutive of a proper name eg. AL, ED, HERB, JOB, NICK, NED, PHIL, RICK; STAN, TED, TIM, VIC; *see* MAN

boy, expectant PIP

boy of fifties TED

boycott, boycotted BLACK

boyfriend BEAU; DATE; FLAME; LOVER; STEADY

brace COUPLE; PAIR; STEEL; STRUT; TENSE; TWO

bract LEAF

brag BOAST; CROW

braid JOIN; LACE

brain rem: the giraffe has the most superior brain!

brainless DENSE

brains WIT

brains, bit of LOBE

brains, without DENSE; THICK

brainy BRIGHT

brake FERN; SLOW; STOP; THICKET

branch ARM; BOUGH; SPRAY; SPUR; STICK; SUB (as in sub-office); TINE; TWIG

brand CLASS; LINE; LABEL; MAKE; MARK; MARQUE; NAME; SEAR; SORT; TYPE; WAVE; WIELD

brandish WAVE; WIELD

brandy FINE; MARC

brass CASH; CHEEK; HORN; LIP; NECK; NERVE; *see* MONEY

brassy CHEEK; FRESH
brat IMP
brave BOLD; CREE; DARING; DEFY; DOUGHTY; FACE; GRITTY; STOUT; *see* AMERICAN INDIAN
brave person, type LION
bravo OLE
brawl ROW; SCRAP; SETTO (ie. set-to)
brawn BEEF; JELLY
brazen BOLD
breach RIFT; RUPTURE
bread CASH; DIME; LOAF; PITA; ROLL; PITA; *see* MONEY
break BUST; CRACK; CRUMBLE; LAPSE; KNAP (dial.); PAUSE; RENT; REST; RIFT; SHATTER; SHEAR; SNAP; STAVE; STOP; TRASH; anagram indicator
break down FAIL; STOP
break in electricity OUTAGE
break into song SING
break up anagram indicator; nesting indicator
breakable anagram indicator
breakdown anagram indicator
breaker ROLLER
breakfast can indicate some kind of cereal
breaking anagram indicator
breaks anagram indicator; nesting indicator
breakwater MOLE
breathe quickly PANT
breather BREAK; GILL; LUNG; PAUSE; REST
breed RACE; REAR; STRAIN
breeding establishment STUD
breeze WIND
breezing around anagram indicator
breezy AIRY
Brent GOOSE
brew BEER; MASH; anagram indicator
brewed, brewing anagram indicator
briar ROSE
bribe BUNG; SOP
brick BLOCK
bride WIFE
bridge ARCH; LINK; SPAN; TOWER

bridge (players, opponents, etc.) usually refers to various combinations of N,S,E,W
brief LETTER; NOTE; PRIME; SHORT; SPEC; TASK; TERSE; can indicate that something is of short duration, or concise in expression; abbreviation indicator; *see* SHORT
brief, not LONG
brief shower SPAT
brigand BANDIT
bright BRAINY; FAIR; LIT; LOUD; SHINY; SUNNY; *see* CLEVER
brightened LIT
brightened up LIT
brightness SHEEN; SUN
brill TOPPING
brilliance FLAIR
brilliant STAR
brim EDGE
bring FETCH
bring ashore LAND
bring down LAND
bring home STRESS
bring in EARN; IMPORT; NET
bring to light EXPOSE
bring up REAR; RAISE; reversal indicator
brink EDGE; VERGE
bristle AWN; TEEM
Brit POM
British B; BR; BRIT; UK
British Columbia BC
British control, rule RAJ
Briton, North PICT; SCOT
broaching anagram indicator
broad WIDE
broadcast AIR; ISSUE; OB; SEND; SHOW; SOW; SOWN; STREWN; anagram indicator; homophone indicator
broadcast, outside OB
broadcaster RADIO; SOWER
broadcasting AIRING; ON; anagram indicator
broke BUST; SMASHED; SKINT; TRASHED; anagram indicator
broken BUST; anagram indicator
bronze TAN
brooch CAMEO

brood ISSUE; LITTER; NEST; SIT
brooded SAT
brook ABIDE; BEAR; RILL; STAND; STREAM
brother BR; BRO; SIB
brothers BROS
brought LED
brought back reversal indicator
brought in nesting indicator
brought up BRED; reversal indicator
brown BAY; BEIGE; RUST; RUSTY; SIENNA; TAN; UMBER
Browning GUN
brown, purplish PUCE
bruised anagram indicator
brunette, not FAIR
brush BROOM; BUFF; SCUFF; SPAT; SWEEP; TAIL; TIFF; TOUCH
brutal person BEAST
brute BEAST
Brutus ROMAN
bubble BOIL; SEETHE; SIMMER
buck DEER; HIND; JUMP
bucks can indicate something to do with rabbits
Bucks town IVER
bud, buddy PAL
Buddhism ZEN
buff FAN; NUT; POLISH
Buffalo Bill CODY
buffet BAR; STRIKE
buffer can indicate someone who polishes eg. shoeblack
build FORM; FOUND
building BLOCK; HALL; HOUSE; HUT; anagram indicator
building material BRICK
building, part of large WING
built of anagram indicator
bulge SAG
bull OX; ROT; *see* RUBBISH
bullet ROUND; SHELL; SHOT; SLUG
bulletin NEWS
bully BEEF; HECTOR; anagram indicator
bum RUMP; anagram indicator

bump BARGE; BLOW; CRASH
bumpkin HICK; YOKEL
bun MOP; WAD (slang)
bunch CLUSTER; GANG; LOT; SET; WAD
bunch of documents FILE; WAD
bunch of keys some combination of A, B, C, D, E, F, G
bundle BALE; PACK; WAD
bung BRIBE; PLUG; STOPPER
bungle BOTCH
bungled anagram indicator
bunk BED; BERTH; COT; ROT; *see* RUBBISH
bunker SAND
bunting FLAGS
burden CROSS; HEAVY; LADE; LOAD; LUMBER; ONUS; WEIGHT
burgeon SPROUT
burial-place GRAVE; TOMB
burial mound BARROW
buried UNDER
buried in run indicator
Burlington House RA
burn BROOK; CHAR; FLARE; IGNITE; SCALD; SEAR; SINGE
burning HOT; IN
Burns can indicate something to do with rye
burrow HOLE; SETT
burst POP; anagram indicator
bury HIDE; INTER
busiest PEAK
business AGENCY; BIZ; CO; FIRM; HOUSE; TRADE; [PIGEON]; *see* COMPANY
business, agricultural FARM; HOLDING
business centre CITY
business community CITY
business, do DEAL; TRADE
business qualification MBA
businessman TYCOON
bust BREAK; BROKE; RAID; anagram indicator
busted anagram indicator
bustle ADO; FLAP; HUM; STIR
busy ENGAGED; PEAK; anagram indicator

busy person, type BEE
busybody PRY
but in Latin SED
butcher KILL; MANGLE; SLAY
butchered anagram indicator
butchers LOOK
butler SERVANT
butt CASK
butter FAT; GOAT; RAM
butter, portion of PAT
butterflies anagram of BUTTER
butterfly COMMA; SKIPPER; STROKE; with a capital letter can refer to something to so with the opera 'Madam Butterfly'; [ADMIRAL]
buttonhole ACCOST; COLLAR
Buttons PAGE
buttress PIER; PROP
buy GET; STAND
buy it DIE
buzz HUM; KICK; can indicate something to do with bee eg. drone
buzzing HUM
by AT; IN; NEAR; PER; VIA; X
by, French DE; DES
By God! EGAD
by means, or by way of PER; VIA
by mouth ORAL
by the way can indicate something to do with street furniture eg. gutter, lamp
by virtue of being QUA
by way of VIA
by-law RULE
bygone PAST
byre SHED
byway LANE

Cc

cabbage COLE; KALE
cabbage, some HEART
cabin CHALET; HUT
cable CORD; LINE; ROPE; WIRE
cache HIDE; STORE
cackle CHATTER; GAS
cacophony DIN; ROW
cad BOUNDER; HEEL; ROTTER
cadence CLOSE; FALL
caddis FLY; YARN
cadet L; SCION
cadre GROUP; UNIT
Caesar's last question ETTU (ie. et tu)
café DINER
cage COOP
cake ANGEL; BUN; CLOT; PASTRY; PUFF; ROCK; ROLL; SCONE; SPONGE; WAD;
cake mixture BATTER
cake, piece of EASY
cakes BAKING
calamitous anagram indicator
Caledonian PICT; SCOT
California CAL
Caligula ROMAN
call BID; CITE; CRY; DIAL; HAIL; HI; HOLLER; HOOT; NAME; PAGE; PHONE; RING; SHOUT; TERM; TIME(!); TITLE; YODEL
call for USE; WANT
call for help SOS
call names SLAG
call up ETIC (ie. cite reversed); EVOKE; RING
called CRIED; RANG; RUNG
called in French DIT
Calliope MUSE
calls for homophone indicator

calm COOL; EASE; EVEN; ; PEACE; QUELL; SOOTHE; STILL
calmness POISE
calorie allowance DIET
calumniate, calumny SLANDER; SMEAR
calumny SLANDER; SMEAR
camber BANK
came across FOUND; MET; READ
came down RAINED
came up AROSE; ROSE
camp BASE; TENT
campaign DRIVE; FIGHT
campanologist RINGER
can BILLY; GAOL; JOHN; LOO; MAY; PICKLE; PRESERVE; STIR; TIN; *see* PRISON
can be anagram indicator
can get can indicate that the synonym for the answer follows
Canada in a phrase such as 'in parts of Canada' can indicate a French word; *see* FRANCE, FRENCH
canal CUT; GUT
canal-boat BARGE
canal, stretch of LOCK
canary FINCH
cancel CUT; ERASE; REVOKE; SCRUB
cancelled OFF
candid FRANK
candidates FIELD
candle LIGHT; TAPER
cane BEAT; GRASS; REED; STAFF; STEM; STICK; THRASH
canine FANG; TOOTH; rem: can refer to a dog usually a specific breed
cannabis POT
canned a component to be nested within TIN
canny SHREWD; WISE
canoe-racing ROWING
canon LAW; ROUND; RULE; TEST
canons CHAPTER
canopy of sky DOME
cant HEEL; LIST; SLANG; SLOPE
Canterbury SEE
canvas SAIL; TENT; can indicate something to do with circus or circus artistes

cap COVER; CROWN; HAT; LID; TAN; TOP
cap decoration HACKLE
capacity ABILITY; CONTENT; G; GAL; GALLON; ROOM; VOL
cape C; CLOAK; HORN; NESS
caper LARK; LEAP; SKIP
capering anagram indicator
capital AI; GOOD; GREAT; HEAD; LEADING; MONEY; SUPER; initial letter indicator; can refer to a capital city: ADEN; LIMA; PARIS; RIGA; ROME
Capone AL [SCARFACE]
capricious anagram indicator
capsized anagram indicator; reversal indicator
captain CAP; CAPT; FLINT; HARDY; HOOD; KIDD; MORGAN; NEMO; SKIP; SKIPPER
captive POW
capture BAG; LAND; TAKE
captured TAKEN; TOOK
capturing nesting indicator
car AUTO; COUPE; ESTATE; GT; LIMO; can refer to a specific make or model: ETYPE; FORD; JAG; MAXI; MINI; ROLLS; UNO
car, leave PARK
car, old HEAP
car, US DODGE
car, dilapidated HEAP
carapace SHELL
carbonaceous rock COAL
card A; ACE; CLUB; COMB; COVE; DEUCE; DIAMOND; HEART; J; JACK; K; KING; Q; QUEEN; SPADE; TAROT; TREY; WAG
card game BANKER; BRAG; BRIDGE; LOO; NAP; OMBRE; POKER; SNAP; RUMMY; WHIST; associated words: DEAL; HAND; TENACE; TRUMP
card player E; EAST; N; NORTH; S; SOUTH; W; WEST
cardinal CHIEF; MAIN; RED; WINE; can refer to the cardinal points of the compass: N, E, W, S
cards DECK; HAND; HANDS; PACK; PAIR
cardsharp ROGUE
care CHARGE; MIND
care of CO
care of, take MIND

career DASH; JOB; LINE; RUN; RACE; SPEED; WORK
careful MIND
careless LAX; REMISS; SLACK; anagram indicator
caress BILL; STROKE
cargo FREIGHT; LADING; LOAD
caricature GUY
carnivore, small STOAT
carol SING; SONG; WASSAIL
carol singers WAIT
carol-singing WASSAIL
carousel can indicate something to do with luggage eg. cases
carp CAVIL; FISH
carpenter CHIPS
carpet RATE; RUG
carriage BRAKE; CHAISE; CAB; FLY; GAIT; GIG; PORT; POSTURE; PRAM; STAGE; SURREY
Caribbean WI
carried BORNE
carried away RAPT; SENT
carried by run indicator
carrier BAG; HOD; PORTER;TRAY; TRAIN;
carrot BAIT; BRIBE; LURE
carry BEAR; TOTE; nesting indicator
carry away SEND; TAKE
carry on FLIRT; LAST; RAGE; WAGE
carry out DO
carrying BEARING; anagram indicator
cart BARROW; DRAY; WAIN
cartoon STRIP
carve CUT; FORM; HEW; SHAPE
carved insertion indicator; anagram indicator
Casanova LOVER
case ACTION; APPEAL; BAG; BOX; COVER; CRATE; FRAME; HOLSTER; POD; SHEATHE; SUIT; TRIAL; grammatical case such as VOCATIVE or in abbreviated form – VOC, ACC, GEN, DAT, ABL; can refer to something to do with patient, illness, hospital etc.; can indicate something to do with the difference in letter case, ie. between upper and lower case, such as to express 'I' in lower case (i) requires a DOT; can indicate something to do with luggage eg. bellhop
case, in LEST

cash CHANGE; COIN; LUCRE; MONEY; NOTE; READY; TENDER; can signify a specific currency eg. ANNA, DIME, QUARTER etc; *see* CURRENCY

cash drawer TILL

casing COVER; SHELL; first and last letter indicator; nesting indicator

cask BUTT; KEG; PIN; TUN

cassette TAPE

cast ANGLE; FLING; FOUND; HEAVE; SET; SHAPE; SHED; SHIED; SLING; THREW; THROW; anagram indicator

cast down LOWER

cast light LIT

caste CLASS

castigated anagram indicator

Castilian, the EL

castle FORT; KEEP; PIECE; ROOK

castle, Englishman's HOME

casual ODD; anagram indicator

casual worker TEMP

casual workers LUMP

casually DOWN (as in dress down)

casualties DEAD

cat FLOG; LASH; LION; ; MOGGY; OUNCE; PANTHER; PUSS; PUSSY; QUEEN; TABBY; TIGER; TOM; WHIP [FURRY]

cat's paw PAWN; TOOL

catalogue LIST

catapult SLING

catastrophe RUIN

catcall BOO; JEER

catch BAG; COP; DETENT; ENTRAP; GET; HEAR; HOOK; LAND; NAB; NAIL; NET; SEE; SNAG; SNARE; TRAP; TRICK; TRIP; nesting indicator; can indicate something to do with angling, fish etc.

catch up TEN

cater FEED

catering for anagram indicator

cathedral DOM; ELY

cathedral precinct CLOSE

Catholic RC

cats and dogs BUCKETS; RAIN

cattle COWS; HERD; KINE; STOCK

cattle disease BSE
cattle food CUD
caucus CELL
caught C; CT; OUT; anagram indicator; nesting indicator
caught by nesting indicator
cause LET; MAKE; PROMPT; RAISE; REASON
caused by usually indicates that what follows are components of the solution
cause friction RUB
cause of ferment YEAST
cause of irritation RANKLE
caustic anagram indicator
caustic comment DIG
caution CARD
cautious LEERY; WARY
cavalry GREY
cavalry man LANCER
cave GROT; HOLE; WARNING (ie. Latin)
caviar, caviare ROE
cavity DENT; HOLE; SAC
cavort, cavorted, cavorting anagram indicator
cease DIE; DROP; HALT; STOP
cease to have LOSE
ceiling TOP
celebrate SING
celebrated NOTED
celebration DO; FAIR; GALA; MASS
celebratory FESTIVE; JOLLY
celebrities ALIST (ie. the A-list)
celebrity LEGEND; LION; NAME; STAR; VIP
cell EGG
Celtic IRISH
censor CATO; EDIT
censorship of anagram indicator
censure PAN; RAP; RATE
central MAIN; use middle letter(s) of associated word; run indicator
Central London ND (think about it)
centre CORE; HEART; HUB; MID; use middle letter(s) of associated word
centre, business CITY

century C; TON [TRECENTO]
century, half L
century, one short of OO (ie. first digit from 100)
ceramic POT; TILE
ceramic material CLAY
cereal BRAN; CORN; GRASS; OATS; RICE; SAGO; WHEAT;
cereal, bit of EAR
cereal head EAR
ceremonial POMP
ceremony FORM; MASS; RITE
cert CINCH; NAP
certain BOUND; SURE
certain, a SURE
certain amount SOME
certain, make ENSURE
certain, not MAY
certainly AY; AYE; SURE; YES
certainty NAP
certificate SCRIP; TICKET
cessation of hostilities TRUCE
chafe FRAY; FRET; RUB
chaff AWN; BANTER; RIB
chain BOND; LINKS; RANGE
chair HEAD; POST; RUN
chairman PROF; PROFESSOR
chair, took SAT
challenge CLAIM; DARE; DEFY; TACKLE
challenge for ball TACKLE
chamber PO
chamber room VAULT
champ CHEW; MUNCH
champagne BRUT
champion ACE; CHAMP; KNIGHT; VICTOR
champion, former ALI; LAVER
championship TITLE
chance BET; HAP; LOT; LUCK; RANDOM; RISK; STAKE; THROW; WAGER
chance, take a DICE
chances ODDS; *see* CHANCE
change ALTER; AMEND; CASH; EDIT; EMEND; SHIFT;

SWITCH; TURN; VARY; anagram indicator; can signify money (COIN) especially small coins; can indicate a verb form beginning with RE

change angle TURN

change book EDIT

change of NEW, as "change of players" can clue NEWCAST (to make NEWCASTLE for example)

change opinion SWING

changed NEW; anagram indicator; replacement indicator (eg. one letter for another)

changes PEAL; VARIES; anagram indicator

changing anagram indicator

changing places change-in-order indicator

changing sex substituting F for M or vice versa

changing sides within target word R to replace L or vice versa

channel DITCH; DRAIN; DUCT; GUTTER; RIVER; SIDE (ie. TV channel); SINUS; SOUND

Channel Island HERM

Channel Islands CI

chant MANTRA; SING

chanted SANG

chaos MESS; PIE (from printing)

chaos, in anagram indicator

chaotically anagram indicator

chap BOD; COVE; FELLOW; GENT; GUY; HE; MAN; a man's name (usually shortened) eg. AL, BILL, DAN, DON, HERB, IAN, JOE, LEN, PHIL, RON, SID, STAN, TIN, TOM, TONY; *see* MAN, FELLOW

chap, greedy PIG

chap, old COVE

chap's HIS

chaps MEN

chaps, you say GUISE

chapter C

char BURN; DAILY; SINGE

character AIR; CARD; ETHOS; GIST; KIDNEY; LETTER; PART; ROLE; TONE; TYPE

characteristic PROPERTY; TRAIT

characters CASE (ie. printing); anagram indicator; run indicator

characters, in anagram indicator; run indicator

characters' limits AZ

characters, relating to old RUNIC

charge ACC; ACCUSE; BILL; C; CARE; CH; COST; DEBT; DUE; FEE; FILL; FREIGHT; INVOICE; ION; LEVY; ORDER; PRICE; RAP; RATE; RENT; RUSH; TAX; TOLL; WARD; can signify something to do with electricity, neutron, etc

charge, criminal RAP

charge, in IC; OVER

charge, not at a FREE

charge, was in LED

charged HADUP (ie. had up)

charged, not FREE

charged, one ION

charges DUES

charitable organisation LIONS

charity AID; ALMS

charity event RAG

Charles CHAS; CHUCK

Charlie ASS; MUG

charm AURA; ENCHANT; ENGAGE; OBI; SPELL

charming CUTE; SWEET

chart GRAPH; LIST; MAP; PLAN; PLOT; SURVEY; TABLE

charts ATLAS; MAPS

chase HUNT; ETCH; FOLLOW; FRAME; RUN

chat TALK

chatter GAS; PRATE; RABBIT; TALK

chatting homophone indicator

chauffeur DRIVER

cheap PALTRY

cheap stuff TAT

cheaper DOWN

cheat CON; DIDDLE; DO; DUPE; DUPER; FIDDLE; FLEECE; GYP; ROOK; TRICK; TWIST

cheated DID

check AUDIT; BAULK; CH; CURB; DAM; DETER; LEASH; REIN; STEM; STOP; TEST; VET; can indicate something to do with chess

check, final MATE

checked stuff PLAID

Cheddar CHEESE; GORGE

cheek BRASS; CHAP; LIP; MOUTH; NECK; NERVE; SAUCE

cheeky BRASH; PERT; FRESH

cheer ELATE; LIVEN; OLE; PLEASE; RAH; ROOT; SHOUT;
cheer up ELATE; LIVEN; PLEASE
cheerful CHIPPER; GLAD; HAPPY; HIGH; SUNNY
cheerless DISMAL; DRAB; DREAR;
cheers TA
cheese BRIE; EDAM; FETA
cheesecake PIN-UP
cheese, different from CHALK
cheese, French BRIE
Chelsea BUN
chemical ESTER; OXIDE; TIN; *see* CHEMICAL ELEMENT
chemical element when a chemical element is specified to be used as a component it usually signifies that the technical symbol for the element is to be used, such as AS for arsenic, etc.
chemical firm ICI
chemist CURIE; DAVY
chess, constricted position in PIN
chess player BLACK; WHITE
chessman B; K; KING; KNIGHT; KT; N; P; PAWN; PIECE; Q; QUEEN; R; ROOK
chest ARK; BOX; BUREAU; COFFER
Chester DIVA
Chesterton GK
chestnut GAG; SAW
chesty noise RALE
chew CHAMP; CHOMP; EAT; MUNCH; NIBBLE
chewed anagram indicator
chic SMART
chicken BROILER; SCARED; YELLOW
chief AGA; ARCH; BOSS; CAPO; CINC (ie. C-in-C); HEAD; KING; LEADER; MAIN; PRIME; THANE; TOP
Chief Education Officer CEO
chief executive DG
child BABE; BAIRN; BRAT; CH; ELF; IMP; INFANT; ISSUE; KID; LAD; MITE; SON; TOT
child-minder NANNY
child, mischievous ELF
child, naughty, precocious etc BRAT; IMP
child, Scottish BAIRN; WEAN
child's fare HALF
childless D (for daughter) or SON to be omitted

children ISSUE
chill COLD
chilled COLD; ICY
chilling ICY; RAW
chilly COLD; ICY; PARKY
chime RING
chimney FLUE; FUNNEL; LUM; STACK
china AMIGO; CH; COBBER; CROCKERY; FRIEND; MATE; MING; PAL; POT
China CATHAY
China, right in, (proper in) TAO
Chinese criminals, criminal society TONG
Chinese dish RICE
Chinese dynasty HAN; MING
Chinese port CANTON
Chinese vessel JUNK
chink CRANNY; GAP; RIFT
chip SILICON; SLIVER
chisel CARVE; CUT; TOOL; TRICK
chit DOCKET; NOTE
Chlorine CL
chock-a-block FULL
chock WEDGE
choice GOOD; PICK; OPTION; RARE; TOP; can indicate that OR (ie. signifying an alternative) is to be inserted between two components
choice, make a *see* CHOOSE
choir SINGERS
choke GLUT
choking nesting indicator
choleric CROSS
choose DRAW; ELECT; OPT; PICK; SELECT
chop AXE; CRACK; CUT; HACK; HEW; LOP; MINCE
Chopin's friend SAND
chopped CUT; HEWN
chopped up anagram indicator
chopper, US AX
choppers TEETH
choppy anagram indicator
chore JOB; TASK

chosen DRAWN; ELECTED; ELITE; NAPPED; PICKED
christen NAME
Christian can indicate something to do with Fletcher Christian, Bounty, mutiny, Hans Christian Andersen
Christmas NOEL [CRACKER: HOLLY; WISHBONE]
Christmas, around CED; DEC
Christmas decoration HOLLY
Christmas offering CARD
Christmastime DEC
chuck THROW
chuffed GLAD
chum BUD; PAL; MATE
chunk LUMP
church ABBEY; CE; CH; MINSTER; ORATORY; RC
church dignitary CANON; DEAN
church land GLEBE
church official ELDER; USHER
church, part of APSE; CHANCEL; NAVE
church, Scots KIRK
church, underground CRYPT
churchman CLERIC; ELDER; REV
churchwarden PIPE
chute TROUGH
cicatrice SCAR
CID man DI; *see* POLICEMAN
cigarette FAG
cinch CERT
circle BAND; BELT; HOOP; LOOP; O; RING; ROUND; anagram indicator
circles OO; nesting indicator
circling anagram indicator; nesting indicator
circuit LAP; ROUND; can indicate something to do with motor-racing
circular ROUND
circulate FLOW
circulated ROUND
circulating anagram indicator
circulation can indicate a palindrome as “Old foreign coin retained in circulation” clues ANNA (ie. simply a foreign coin which reads the same both ways)
circumnavigator FOGG
circumscribed nesting indicator

circumstance STATE

circumstances. existing ASIS (ie. as is)

circus rem: as well as the 'big top' this includes the Roman circus, gladiators, etc

cistern TANK

cite NAME

city ADEN; BATH; DERRY; EC (abbreviation for Empire City, one of New York's nicknames); ELY; HULL; LA (ie. Los Angeles); NANCY; NY (New York); PARIS; RIO; ROME; STOKE; TOWN; UR; URB; WEN; *see* CAPITALS

City SMOKE; WEN

city, ancient (old) ILIUM; ROME; TROY; UR

City area a London postcode, NI, SE, EC, etc

city in Kansas DODGE

city of the Angels LA

city, going to UP

city outskirts CY

City Road pub EAGLE

city, way to UP

civil disorder RIOT

civil engineer CE

civil service CS

civil wrong TORT

claim ACTION; ALLEGE; ASSERT; AVER; AVOW; PLEAD; RIGHT; TITLE; can indicate a word beginning with IM (ie. I'm) as "Tense claim by paragon" clues IMPERFECT

claim, justified RIGHT

clamber CLIMB

clamour DIN

clan SEPT (Irish)

clanger BELL; ERROR; GAFFE

claptrap ROT

claret RED

clarify REFINE; RENDER

clash FIGHT; SCRAP; WAR

clasp GRIP; HOLD; LOCK

class BRAND; CL; CASTE; FORM; GRADE; GROUP; KIND; LESSON; ORDER; RANK; RATE; RATING; SECT; SET; SORT; STREAM; TEACHING; TYPE;

Class A UPPER

class, one of MEMBER

classic OAKS; can indicate word or phrase taken directly from Latin and usually unaltered in its modern use
classical GREEK; LATIN; TRAD
classical art ARS
classical character see Greek letter
classical style ATTIC; DORIC; IONIC
classical theatre ODEON
classification RANK; RANKING; STATUS
classify GRADE; RATE
claw NAIL
clay LUTE; TILL
clean BATHE; DUST; GROOM; PREEN; PURE; SCRUB; SWEEP; WASH
clean-cut NEAT; TRIM
clean up HOOVER; MOP
cleaner CHAR; DAILY; MOPPER; SCRUBBER; SWEEP
cleanse WASH
clear FREE; NET; NETT; OPEN; LUCID; PATENT; PLAIN; RID; SHEER; STARK; VAULT; WIPE; anagram indicator
clearing omission indicator
cleave SUNDER
cleft SPLIT
clergy CLOTH
clergymen CANON; CURATE; CURE; DEAN; PARSON; PASTOR; RECTOR; REV; REVD
clergymen CLOTH
cleric CANON; MINISTER; PARSON
clerics CLOTH; CHAPTER
clever ABLE; BRAINY; BRIGHT; CUTE; DEFT; FLY; NIFTY; SHARP; SMART
cleverness GUILE
cliche CORN
cliff BLUFF; CRAG
climb CLAMBER; SCALE; SHIN; reversal indicator; can indicate a verb followed by UP
climbed ROSE
climber IVY; LIANA; PEA; VINE
climbing reversal indicator
cling STICK
Clio MUSE
clip BLOW; HIT; PIN; PEG

clipped CUT; SHORN; indicator for first and last letters of associated word to be omitted

clippers SHEARS

clique SECT

cloak CAPE; HIDE; TOGA

clobber BASH; GEAR

cloche HAT

clock DIAL; FACE; SEE; STRIKE; TIMER

close DEAR; END; FOLD; HANDY; LOOMING; NARROW; NEAR; NIGH; SEAL; SHUT; WARM; last letter indicator (of adjacent word)

close, come LOOM; NEAR

close-fitting TIGHT

close to BY; NEAR; last letter indicator

close up PURSE

closed can indicate a word beginning with NO as "Negative consequences of gym being closed" (4) clues NOPE (ie. no PE)

closely follow DOG

closet PRESS

closing END; LAST; NET

clot ASS; DOPE

cloth LINEN; RAG; SATIN, TOWEL; TWEED

cloth, man of the DRAPER

clothes DUDS; GARB; GEAR; KIT; SLOPS; WEAR

clothing ATTIRE; COAT; DRESS; GARB; GEAR; HABIT; JACKET; KIT; REEFER; SUIT; *see* GARMENT

cloud NIMBUS; RACK

cloudy DIM; DULL

clout MIGHT; POWER

clown ANTIC; PIERROT

club BAT; BRASSIE; BRASSY; C; CARD; DRIVER; HIT; IRON; MACE; MASHIE; PASTE; PUTTER; SIDE; SPOON; TEAM; WOOD; WEDGE; can refer to pregnancy; or a specific football club eg. SPURS

clue HINT; KEY; LIGHT (ie. the technical term for a crossword clue); SIGN; TIP

clue for - - - (sometimes followed by ?) reverses the role of solver and setter, requiring the solver to produce an appropriate clue for the word or phrase given. Examples: 'Clue for PORE' (8-4) gives SKIPPING-ROPE, 'Clue for FIDEL' (7-5) gives PLAYING-FIELD

clue, this ACROSS; DOWN (ie. the direction of the clue itself in the grid)

clumsy, clumsily anagram indicator

clumsy person APE; OAF

cluster SWARM

clutch BROOD; GRAB; HOLD; SITTING

clutch, part of EGG

clutching nesting indicator

coach BUS; SCHOOL; STAGE; TEACH; TRAIN

coaches TRAIN; TRAINS

coal EMBER

coal-skuttle HOD

coalesce FUSE

coarse CRUDE

coarse person LOUT; OAF; SLOB

Coast, East, West rem: can refer to countries other than UK, usually US

coast, part of BEACH; CAPE; SHORE

coast, not near INLAND

coastal area, region BAY; COVE

coat ARMS; BATTER; COVER; FILM; FUR; HIDE; JACKET; LAYER; MAC; PLASTER; PLATE; REEFER; TAILS

coat, expensive FUR

coat, kind of ARMS

coat-of-arms *see* HERALDRY

coating COVER; FILM; FLAMBE; LAYER; LINING

cobbled anagram indicator

cobbler can indicate something to with 'last' ie. cobbler's tool'

cobblers NUTS; ROT

cocaine C

cocaine, dose of LINE

cocked READY; SET; reversal indicator

cockfight MAIN

cockney usually the cue to drop initial 'h from a word, as "tough Cockney" clues ARD

cockney lady ER (ie. 'er)

cockney man IM (ie. 'im)

cockney pal CHINA

cocktail anagram indicator

cod FOOL

code LAW

coded anagram indicator
coffee, style of French NOIR
coffer ARK; BOX; CHEST
coffin KIST
coffin nails usually indicates something to do with cigarettes, smoking etc
cohere GEL
coil HANK; SPRING; TWINE; WIND
coin BIT; CENT; CROWN; CHANGE; DIME; DINAR; NICKEL; P; PENNY
coin, old AS; BIT; CROWN; D; DUCAT; GROAT; JOEY; S; SOU; TANNER
coins CHANGE; PENCE
coins, make MINT
cold C; CHILL; CHILLY; DANK; ICY; NIPPY; SNIFF
cold stuff FROST; ICE; SNOW
collaborator ALLY
collapse DROP; FAIL; FALL; FOLD; GO; SAG; anagram indicator
collapsed FELL; FLAT; anagram indicator
collapses anagram indicator
collar CATCH; NAB; PINCH; RING; RUFF
collared by nesting indicator
colleague ALLY; PARTNER
collect AMASS; GATHER; PRAYER
collected anagram indicator
collection BUNCH; LOT; SET; can signify amalgamation of elements to achieve solution
collection of books NT; OT
collection of stories ANA
collective wisdom LORE
college C; ETON; KINGS; LSE; MIT; POLY; TECH
college once POLY
colliery PIT
collision BANG; BUMP; HIT
colonel CO; COL
colonialist RHODES
colonise SETTLE
colonist ANT
colonnade STOA
colony GIB; HIVE
colony, old, former ADEN

colophony RESIN
Colorado CO
colour AQUA; BLUE; DYE; FLAG; FLAME; GREEN; HUE; OCHRE; ORANGE; PAINT; RED; TAN; TEAM; TINGE; TINT; TONE; YELLOW
colour, add DYE; PAINT; TINGE; TINT
colour, light ECRU
colour, lose FADE; PALE
colourless ASHEN; PALE; WHITE
colours FLAG; *see* COLOUR
column FILE; LINE; LIST; PILLAR; POST; SPINE; SPIRE
comb CARD; CREST
combat, scene of ARENA; LIST; LISTS
combine MERGE
combination anagram indicator
come ENSUE
come down DIP; DROP; LAND; LIGHT; RAIN; *see* FALL
come in ENTER
come out FLOWER
come round ROUSE; TURN; WAKE; ; nesting indicator; reversal indicator
come through WEATHER
come to ROUSE; TOTAL; WAKE
come up ARISE; RISE
come upon FIND
comeback RETURN; reversal indicator
comedian CARD; DODD; TATI; WAG; WIT; *see* COMIC
comes round nesting indicator; reversal indicator
comfort CHEER; EASE; RELIEF; SOOTHE
comfortable COSY; EASY; WELL;
comfortable, get NESTLE
comfortable, more COSIER
comfortable place BED
comforter SCARF
comfortless BLEAK
comic CHAPLIN; DANDY; DROLL; FOOL; anagram indicator; *see* COMEDIAN
comical DROLL; FUNNY
coming ADVENT
coming in nesting indicator
coming round nesting indicator; reversal indicator

coming up RISING; reversal indicator
comma can indicate something to do with insect
command BID; BIDDING; CHARGE; DECREE; EDICT; FIAT; MUSH; ORDER
command to accelerate GEE
commanded BADE; BID
commander AGA; CINC (ie. C-in-C); EMIR; OC; SHOGUN
commendation PRAISE; TRIBUTE
commandment RULE; *see* COMMAND
commandments, all the, number of TEN
comment OPINE; REMARK; SAY
comment, witty SALLY
commerce TRADE
commercial AD; ADVERT
commercial venture SPEC
commission APPOINT; CHARGE; CHARTER; ERRAND; ORDER
committed LIABLE
committee BOARD; COM
committee boss CHAIR
common BANAL; GREEN; TRITE
Common Market EC
common sense NOUS
commonly colloquialism indicator, eg. MATE; indicator for dropping initial 'h'
commonplace BANAL; TRITE; TRUISM
Commons CHAMBER
communicate CONVERSE; TALK
communication FAX; LETTER; LINK; MAIL; MEMO; NOTE; POST; SIGNAL
communication, intuitive ESP
communication, means of BLOWER; *see* COMMUNICATION
communist COM; COMM; MAO; RED; TROT
community CITY; NATION; TOWN; VILLAGE
Community EC
community, business CITY
compact DENSE; TRIM
companies, amalgamation of MERGER
companion CH; MATE; PAL
companion, honoured CH
company ACTORS; CO; COY; CREW; FIRM; CONCERN; GROUP; HOST; ICI; PLC; REP (ie. stage company); TWO;

THREE; TROOP
company, large ICI
company. theatre REP
comparatively can indicate a comparative adjective (ie. ending in -ER)
comparatively little LESS
compare LIKEN
compartment BAY; HOLE; PLACE; SPACE
compass RANGE
compassion PITY
compensate ATONE; EXPIATE
compel MAKE
compere HOST
compete BID; RACE; VIE
compete for possession TACKLE
competent ABLE; FIT
competition COMP; CUP; EVENT; HEAT; OPEN; RACE; RALLY
competition, be in RUN; VIE
competition, early stages of HEAT
competition, was in RAN; VIED
competitor RIVAL
competitors ENTRY
compile LIST
compiled anagram indicator
compiler ME; SETTER
compiler, this ME
compiling anagram indicator
complacent SMUG
complain BEEF; BITCH; CARP; GRIPE; GRUMBLE; RAIL; WHINE; WINGE;
complainant CARPER; GRIPER
complaint AGUE; BEEF; FLU; GRIPE; GROUSE; MALADY; MOAN; TB; YAMMER
complement CREW
complete ENTIRE; END; FULL; INTACT; OVER; RANK; ROUND; SHEER; TOP; UTTER; WHOLE
completed OVER; DONE; OUT; WHOLE
completely ALL; FULLY; QUITE; SHEER
complex anagram indicator
complex, not EASY; SIMPLE
compliant EASY

complicate RAVEL
complicated anagram indicator
complication HITCH; SNAG; TANGLE; anagram indicator
component BIT; PART; UNIT
components anagram indicator
compose PEN; SETTLE; WRITE
composed anagram indicator
composer ARNE; BACH; BERG; BLISS; CAGE; CHOPIN; DOWLAND; GLUCK; LISZT; PARRY; RAVEL; STAINER; VERDI
composite, not SIMPLE
composition DUET; ESSAY; NUMBER; PIECE; TRIO; TUNE; anagram indicator
compound PEN; can indicate some chemical eg. ESTER; anagram indicator
comprehends nesting indicator
comprehensible PLAIN
comprehensive coverage BLANKET
comprehensively ALL
compromises HAS
compromised anagram indicator
computer APPLE
computer accessory, equipment MOUSE
computer program text CODE
computer memory units RAM
computer program DOS
computer science IT
computer store ROM
computer studies IT
computer system DOS
con DO; FIDDLE; FOOL; HAVE; LAG; LIFER; ROOK; SCAM; SWINDLE
conceal BURY; HIDE; PALM; VEIL
concealed HID; run indicator
concealed at first initial letter to be omitted
concealing nesting indicator; omission indicator eg. "boat concealing bottom" clues PUN where 'bottom' refers to the last letter of 'punt'
concede ADMIT; ALLOW; CEDE; GRANT; OWN; YIELD
conceited VAIN
conceivably can indicate the compiler is stretching a point, so expect

something especially tricky
concentrated STRONG; THICK
concept IDEA; NOTION; THOUGHT
conception *see* CONCEPT
concern BUSINESS; CARE; FIRM; MATTER
concern, show CARE
concerned, be CARE
concerned with IN; ON
concerning ABOUT; ASTO (ie, as to); ON; RE
concert GIG; PROM; UNITY
concession SOP
concise TERSE
conclude END; CLOSE; INFER
conclusion END; FINDING; POINT; TAIL; Z; can indicate that the last letter(s) of a word should be used [OMEGA]
conclusion of game E; MATE
concoct HATCH
concocted, concoction anagram indicator
concupiscent RANDY
condemnation, condemned anagram indicator
condescend DEIGN; STOOP
condescension, show DEIGN; STOOP
condition COMA; IF; NICK; STATE
condition, hopeless DESPAIR
conditioned anagram indicator
conduct LEAD; USHER
conductor COPPER; EARTH; WOOD (ie. Sir Henry)
conduit GUTTER
confab CHAT; TALK; WORDS
confectionery CAKE; SWEET; TRUFFLE
confederate ALLY
confer AWARD; DISCUSS; GRANT
conference SESSION
confess ALLOW; SING
confession IAM (ie. I am)
confidence BOTTLE; TRUST
confident SURE
confident expectation TRUST
confine GATE; HOLD; INTERN; PEN;
confined IN; PENT; nesting indicator

confined space COOP
confined to quarters can indicate that a component is to be nested within two points of the compass as SE in 'always confined to quarters' gives SEVERE
confirm OK; RATIFY
conflab *see* CONFAB
conflict CLASH; FRAY; STRIFE; WAR
conflict, in anagram indicator
conform FIT; SUIT
confounded BEAT; anagram indicator
confront BEARD; FACE; TACKLE
confuse ADDLE; DAZE; FOX
confused anagram indicator
confused state *see* CONFUSION
confused with anagram indicator
confusing anagram indicator
confusion BABEL; FOG; MESS
confusion, in anagram indicator
congealed SET
congregate GATHER; MEET; anagram indicator
conifer FIR
conjecture GUESS
conjunction UNION
conjured up anagram indicator
connect LINK; TIE
connected TIED
connected to RE
Connecticut CT
connection EARTH; LINK; TIE
conned HAD
connoisseur EXPERT
conquer BEAT; ROUT
conscious AWARE
consecrate BLESS
consecutive letters can refer to the use of consecutive letters in the alphabet, eg. FGH; run indicator
consent OK
consequence EFFECT; END
consequently ERGO; SO
conservation body, conservationists NT

conservative C; CON; RIGHT; SQUARE; TORY
conservative, moderate WET
consider CASE; DEBATE; DEEM; FEEL; JUDGE; MULL; PONDER; RATE; SCAN; SEE; THINK; WEIGH
consider carefully NB
considerable TIDY
consideration CARE
consign SHIP
consigning nesting indicator
conspiracy CABAL; PLOT
conspirator BRUTUS
conspirators CELL
conspire PLOT
constable COP; PC; SPECIAL; can indicate an associated word, such as BEAT
constant C; PI
constantly EVER
constituency SEAT
constituent PART
constituents (in) anagram indicator; run indicator
constitution CHARTER; anagram indicator
constraint LET
constricted NARROW
construct BUILD; MAKE
constructed, constructing anagram indicator
construction MAKE; READING; anagram indicator
construction worker RIGGER
construed anagram indicator
consume DRINK; EAT; SWALLOW; USE
consumed ATE; DRUNK; EATEN; anagram indicator
consumer DINER; EATER
consumerism, end of FAST
contact RING
container BAG; BASKET; BIN; BOWL; BOX; CAN; CASE; CASK; CHEST; CRATE; CUP; DISH; DRAM; DRAWER; EWER; HOD; HOPPER; JAR; PAIL; PAN; POT; PURSE; SACK; TIN; TRAY; TUN; URN; VAT
containing nesting indicator; run indicator
contaminated anagram indicator
contemplate MUSE; PONDER; THINK
contemporary IN; MOD; NEW

contempt SCORN
contempt, show HISS
contemptible LOW
contemptible person CAD; CUR; HEEL; LOUSE; RAT
contemptuous expression ROT
contend VIE
contending VYING
content HAPPY; PLEASE; PLEASED; run indicator
contention WAR
contents INDEX
contents of use middle letters of the word that follows
contest BATTLE; BOUT; CUP; DUEL; FIGHT; GAME; HEAT; LISTS; MATCH; PLAY; ROUND; SCRAP; WAR
continent ASIA; CHASTE
Continental FRENCH
Continental, the DER; EL; IL; LE; LA; LES
continue LAST; RESUME; can indicate that a verb is required which is followed by ON to make another word or component eg. ACT/ON, BAT/ON, GO/ON, FLAG/ON
continued CONT
contract CATCH; DEAL; DEED; ENGAGE; GATHER; KNIT; LEASE; LESSON; MAKE; PACT; PURSE; SHRINK; TREATY; can indicate something to do with bridge, eg. TRICK
contracted TAUT; TENSE
contradictory response NO
contrary anagram indicator; can indicate a meaning opposite to the immediately preceding idea. Example: “Series with city setting? On the contrary” builds up to RUN-NY, providing the answer RUNNY ie. the opposite of setting
contrary, on the NO
contrary gardener MARY
contribute OFFER
contributing to component to be included; run indicator
contribution FACTOR; INPUT; WHACK
contrived, contriving anagram indicator
control BUTTON; CLUTCH; DIAL; HELM, HOLD; LEASH; LEVER; MASTER; POWER; REIN; RIDE; RULE; RUN; STEER; anagram indicator
controller, traffic LIGHT
controlling anagram indicator
controversial anagram indicator

construed anagram indicator
convalesce REST
convenience FAST (ie. food); LAV; LOO; WC
convenient HANDY
conventional SQUARE; STAID
conversation CHAT; CHATTER; PATTER; TALK; homophone indicator
conversation, superficial PATTER
conversion anagram indicator
convert ALTER
converted, converts anagram indicator
convey CARRY; FERRY; PASS; TRUCK
conveyance CAB; *see* VEHICLE
conveyed when in the context of something like 'what is conveyed by' can indicate the answer consists of consecutive letters in the rest of the clue ie. a run indicator
convict CON; CONDEMN; INMATE; LAG; LIFER
convinced SURE
convoluted anagram indicator
cook BOIL; BRAISE; DEVIL; DO; FRY; POACH; ROAST; SILVER (ie. Long John); SIMMER; STEAM; anagram indicator
cook, place to HUB; *see* COOKER
cooked DONE; FRIED; ROASTED; anagram indicator
cooked lightly RARE
cooked, previously COLD
cooker AGA; APPLE; HUB; OVEN; RANGE; STOVE
cooking ON; anagram indicator
cooking pot WOK
cool CALM; FAN; HIP; ICE; ICY
cool down CHILL
cool guy CAT
cool-sounding PHAN
cooler CAN; FAN; PEN; STIR
coolness NERVE
cooperate PLAY
cooperative UNION
coordinate X; Y
cop CATCH; NAB; *see* POLICEMAN
cope DEAL
cope with STAND
copper CENT; CU; D (ie. old penny); P; PEELER; PENNY; PC; S;

see POLICEMAN
copper once D
coppice THICKET
copy APE; CRIB; FORGE; PRINT; REPRO; TRACE
copyist SCRIBE
coral PINK
coral ridge REEF
cord CABLE; FLEX; LINE; ROPE; STRING; TWINE
cordial TONIC; WARM
core HEART; WICK
cork BUNG; PLUG; STOPPER
corn CHAFF; EAR; can indicate something to do with foot
corn, some EAR; EARS
corner ANGLE; BEND; NOOK
cornet HORN
Cornish SW
Cornish resort LOOE
Cornwall's wife REGAN
corporal punishment CANE
corporation POT; TUM; can indicate something to do with stomach, waistline etc
corps CADRE; GROUP; UNIT
correct AMEND; DUE; EDIT; EMEND; IMPROVE; OK; REVISE; RIGHT
corrected anagram indicator
correctly RIGHT
correspond RELATE; SUIT; TALLY
correspondence MAIL; POST; RATIO
corrode RUST
corroded RUSTY
corroding anagram indicator
corrosion RUST
corrupt ROT; SPOIL; anagram indicator
corrupt activity VICE
corrupted anagram indicator
corruption ROT
cosmetic LINER; TONER
cosset PAMPER
cost CHARGE; FEE; PRICE; RATE; TOLL
cost, at a cost of FOR

cost, at a great DEAR
cost, high, large BOMB
costume HABIT; SUIT
cosy SNUG
cot BED; CRIB
cottage, small COT
cotton CHINO
couch BED
couched in nesting indicator
cough CROUP
could MAY; MIGHT
could be anagram indicator; can also indicate that the idea that immediately follows is an example of the word (or words) required as the solution. Example: "Copper's weapon could be bloody" (4,4) which clues CUSS WORD (ie. cu's sword)
could have, make anagram indicator
counsel ADVICE
counsel, old REDE
count ADD; NOBLE; POLL; RATE; SUM; TALLY; TELL [CENSUS]
count, start of ONE
counter BAR; BOARD; CHIP; DISC; FISH; MEET; TOKEN; can indicate something to do with accountant, adding machine, abacus, shop, shopkeeper
counterfeit DUD; FAKE; MOCK
counterfoil STUB
counterpart TWIN
counties NI
country LAND; REALM; STATE; short-named countries are often used as components eg. CHILE, EIRE, MALI, OMAN, WALES, and abbreviations especially eg. UK, US, USA
country, another ABROAD
country house GRANGE; HALL; MANOR; SEAT; VILLA
country man PEASANT
country, old RUS
country, open HEATH; MOOR
country pursuit HUNT; HUNTING; RAMBLE
country walk RAMBLE
countrywoman can indicate a nation personified as female eg. BRITANNIA
county AVON; BEDS; BUCKS; CLARE; DORSET; DOWN;

GLAM; HUNTS; KENT; MAYO; MEATH; SHIRE; STAFFS; SURREY; YORKS

couple BRACE; DUO; HITCH; ITEM; LINK; LOVERS; PAIR; TIE; TWAIN; TWO; UNITE; YOKE; can indicate two words (or components) with AND in between as "couple for a Cockney chap" clues ME-AND-ER ie. meander

couples beginning first two letters of succeeding words to be used

courage BOTTLE; DARING; GUTS; HEART; NERVE; PLUCK; RESOLVE

courageous BRAVE; PLUCKY

course CURRENT; DISH; ENTREE; LAP; LINKS; MEAT; PATH; PPE; RAN; RIVER; ROAST; ROUTE; RUN; STARTER; SWEET; TACK; TENOR; WAY; can refer to something to do with a meal (eg. SOUP, TABLE) or eating, for example "takes courses" clues EATS; can refer to a race-course eg. ASCOT, EPSOM; *see* RIVER, CURRENT

course (as 'in course of') nesting indicator

course, change of TACK

course, in due SO

course, main LIVER; ROAST

course, of NATCH (ie. colloquialism for 'naturally')

course of action LINE; TACK; TRACK

course of treatment CURE

course, part of TEE

course, state of GOING

courses MEAL; MENU

court CT; DATE; QUAD; ROTA; SEEK; WOO; YARD; can signal something to do with tennis

court case TRIAL

court, go to SUE

court, in UP

court official MACER; USHER

court, person in SUER

courtyard GARTH

couturier DIOR

cove BIGHT; BAY; CHAP

cover BURY; CAP; CAPE; CASE; COAT; DRESS; FILM; FUR; HAT; HIDE; HOOD; INSURE; LID; MASK; PALL; RUG; SCREEN; SHEET; SHUTTER; SPAN; TOP; VEIL

cover, temporary TENT

cover, took HID

cover-up can indicate an item of clothing
covered in, with nesting indicator
covering BARK; CAP; CAPE; CASE; COWL; CRUST; FOIL; HAT; HOOD; LID; LINO; MAT; MANTLE; RUG; TYRE; can indicate that an anagram is following; *see* COVER; CASE
cow AWE
coward MOUSE
cowardly CRAVEN; YELLOW
cowards MICE
cowboy, film WESTERN
cowl HOOD
cows HERD; KINE; STOCK
cowshed BYRE
coy SHY
crack ACE; CRANNY; CHOP; DIG; DRUG; GIBE; GO; QUIP; RAP; RIFT; RENT; SHOT; SOLVE; STAB; TOP; TRY; TURN
crack troops SAS
crack up PRAISE
cracked CLEFT; anagram indicator
cracked, become CHAP
crackers BARMY; MAD; NUTS; anagram indicator
cracking SPLIT; anagram indicator
crackpot NUT
cracksman, amateur RAFFLES
craft ARK; ART; BARGE; BOAT; JET; PLANE; PUNT; SHIP; SKILL; TRADE
craft, old ARGO
craftsman ARTISAN; COOPER; POTTER; SMITH
crafty ARCH; FOXY; SLY; WISE
crag ROCK
cram JAM; STUFF; SWOT
crank HANDLE; LEVER; LOON; WINCH
cranny CRACK
crash BANG; PRANG; RAM; RUIN; SLAM; anagram indicator
crashed, crashing anagram indicator
crate BOX; CAGE; CASE; HEAP
crater HOLE
crawl CREEP; can indicate something to do with swimming
craze FAD; RAGE; WHIM
crazy BARMY; BATS; LOCO; MAD; NUT; NUTS; RAVING; WACKY; WILD; anagram indicator

cream BEST; PLUM; SKIM
creamy RICH
crease FOLD; PLEAT; RUCK
create MAKE; RANT
create difficulty STIR
created MADE
creation anagram indicator
creative work ART
Creator GOD
creature EFT; MOLE; *see* ANIMAL, BIRD, FISH
creature, miserable WORM
creature, nocturnal BAT; BADGER
creature, stubborn MULE
creature, troublesome MIDGE
creatures, lot of ZOO
credible REAL
credit CR; TICK
credit card VISA
creditor CR
credulous NAIVE
creek COVE
creep EDGE
crest COMB; RIDGE
crevice NOOK
crew FOUR; EIGHT; HANDS; ISIS; MAN; MEN; SQUAD; TEAM
crewman, crew member HAND; TAR; *see* SAILOR
crib COT
cricket GRIG (insect); [cricketing terms are very popular among compilers, associated words: BAT; BAIL; IN; LEG; OFF; ON; OUT; OVER; POINT ; TEST]
cricket ball BOUNCER; YORKER
cricket match TEST
cricket side LEG; OFF; ON
cricketer BAT; BOWLER; GRACE; KEEPER; SLIP
cricketer's position CREASE
cricketer's protection BOX; PAD
cricketers CC
cried WEPT; *see* CRY
crikey COR; MY
crime ARSON; OFFENCE; SCAM; SIN; VICE

crime squad CID
criminal BAD; BENT; CON; CROOK; FELON; FENCE; FORGER; HOOD; LAG; THUG; anagram indicator
criminal activity RACKET; SCAM
criminal charge RAP
criminal group TRIAD
criminal, possible SUS
criminals TONG
crimson RED
crimson-clad component to be nested within RED
crisis HEAD
critical GRAVE; VITAL
critical, be KNOCK
critical remark BARB; DIG
criticise CHIDE; FLAY; KNOCK; PAN; RATE; ROAST; SLAG; SLAM; SLATE; SNIPE
criticism FLAK; PANNING; STICK
crockery CUP; PLATE
crony *see* PAL
crook BEND; CON; STAFF; STICK; anagram indicator
crooked AWRY; BENT; anagram indicator
crooks anagram indicator
crooned, one who BING
crooner BING
crop CORN; CUT; ETON; GORGE; MILLET; OATS; RICE; RYE; YIELD; anagram indicator
crop, part of STOCK
crop up ARISE
crops SEED
Crosby BING
cross FORD; GEORGE; IRATE; MAD; MULE; PLUS; ROOD; STERN; TESTY; X
cross, make ANGER; MARK
crossed anagram indicator
crossing FORD; nesting indicator
crossing point STILE
crossword, tackle SOLVE
crosswords anagram of WORDS
crowd ALL; DROVE; FLOCK; GANG; GATE; HERD; HOST; HOUSE; JAM; LOT; MASS; MOB; PACK; PARTY; PRESS; RUCK; SET; THREE

crowds MANY
crown CAP; CR; ER; HEAD; NUT; PEAK; TOP
crucial KEY
crucial point *see* CRUX
crucible POT
crucifix ROOD
crude BASE; COARSE; EARTHY; GROSS; OIL; RAW; ROUGH; anagram indicator
cruel anagram indicator
cruel emperor NERO
cruise TRIP
crumble, crumbled, crumbling anagram indicator
crumpled anagram indicator
crush BREAK; SCOTCH; STAVE; SWAT; anagram indicator
crushed anagram indicator
crust PASTRY
crux GIST; KEY; NUB
cry BAWL; CALL; CAW; KEEN; MEW; OH; OW; PULE; SCREAM; SOB; SHRIEK; WAIL; WEEP; YELL; YELP; *see* CRY, EXPRESSION OF PAIN, *etc.*
cry of alarm O; OH
cry of exultation HO; WHOOP
cry of pain OUCH; OW
cry of surprise COR
cry of triumph AHA
crypt VAULT
Cuba C
cube SOLID
cube-shape DICE
cubist LEGER
cubs PACK
cuckoo-pint ARUM
cuddle HUG
cudgel CLUB
cue TIP
cuff CLIP; SMACK
cult FAD; SECT
cultivate COURT; TILL; anagram indicator
cultivated REFINED; TILLED; anagram indicator
cultivated, poorly RUDE

cultivating TILLING; anagram indicator
cultivation anagram indicator
culture TASTE
cultured ARTY
cummerbund SASH
cunning ARCH; ART; FLY; GUILE; SHREWD; SLY; TRICKY; WILE; WILY
cunningly anagram indicator
cup TROPHY
cupboard ARK; LARDER; PRESS
cupholder SAUCER
cupola DOME
curative waters SPA
curb BIT; CHECK; REIN; STOP
cure HEAL; PRESERVE; SMOKE; TAN
curious NOSY; ODD; RUM; STRANGE; anagram indicator
curiosity RARITY
curiosity, show PRY
curiously anagram indicator
curl COIL; TWINE
currency COIN; TENDER; *see* CASH, MONEY, FOREIGN CURRENCY
currency charge AGIO
currency, foreign ANNA; CENT; DM; DOLLAR; ECU; EMU; EURO; FRANC; KRONA; LIRA; MARK; RAND; ROUBLE; SOU; YEN; YUAN
current AC; AMP; AMPS; DC; DRIFT; EDDY; IN; LIVE; NOW; PRESENT; RECENT; RIVER; STREAM; TIDE; TOPICAL; an old standby to indicate the name of a river; *see* RIVER; or otherwise indicative of running water, sea, etc.
current measure AMP
currently NOW
curry BALTI; COMB; DRESS; GROOM; anagram indicator
curse BAN; BLIGHT; CUSS; DAMN; HECK; HEX; OATH; SWEAR
cursorily anagram indicator
curtailed indicator for the omission of last letter
curtain NET; VEIL
curtsey BOB
curvaceous anagram indicator
curve ARC; ARCH; BEND; CAMBER

curve downward SAG

curve inshore BAY; BIGHT

curved BENT

curvy figure (shape) S

cushion EASE; PAD

cushy JAMMY

custody officer JAILER

custom HABIT; USE; USAGE; WAY

customary STOCK

customer SHOPPER

customers TRADE

customised anagram indicator

cut AXE; AXED; BARON; BOB; CHASE; CHOP; CHUNK; CLIP; DICE; DOCK; ELIDE; EXCISE; GASH; HACK; HEW; HEWN; LANCE; LASH; LOP; LOPPED; MILL; MINCE; MOW; MOWED; MOWN; NICK; NOTCH; PARE; PARED; POLL; PRUNE; REAP; SAW; SAWN; SEVER; SHAPE; SHEAR; SHORN; SLASH; SLIGHT; SNIP; STAB; TRIM; insertion indicator; anagram indicator; omission indicator; *see* CUT OF MEAT

cut down FELL; REAP; *see* CUT

cut of meat LOIN; ROUND; RUMP; SHIN; TOPSIDE

cut, power OUTAGE

cut, short BOB; CREW

cut up anagram indicator

cute TAKING

cutter BLADE; SAW; SWORD

cutting CLIP; SHARP; SLIP; TART ; nesting indicator

cutting edge BLADE; SWORD

cutting remark BARB; DIG; JAB

cycle AGE; MOPED; O; ROUND; SERIES; TRIKE

cycle inventor OTTO

cycling anagram indicator

cynic SCEPTIC

Cyprus CY

cyst SAC

Dd

Dad PA; POP; PATER
Dad's PAS
daily CHAR; HELP; PAPER; *see* NEWSPAPER, PAPER; [ASSOCIATED WORD: TREASURE]
dam BLOCK; CHECK; MOTHER; SMOTHER; WIER
damage BILL; CHIP; COST; CRACK; HARM; LAME; LOSS; MAR; PRICE; SCAR; SLUR; SPOIL; TOLL
damaged anagram indicator
damn CURSE; DARN
damp DANK; MOIST
dance BALL; BALLET; BOP; CONGA; DISCO; FLING; GALOP; HAY; HEY; HOP; JIG; JIVE; LAMBADA; LIMBO; MORRIS; PASS (ie. step); REEL; STEP; STOMP; TANGO; TRIP; TWIST
dance music SWING
dancer PRIMA
dancing TAP; anagram indicator
dandy BLOOD; BUCK; DUDE; FINE; FOP; OK
danger PERIL
danger, posing no SAFE
danger, sign of RED
dangerous TIGHT
dangerous, electrically LIVE
dangle HANG
dank MOIST
daring BRAVE; NERVE
daring manoeuvre STUNT
dark BLACK; DUN; GREY; NIGHT
dark, after LATE
dark hue NOIR
darkness BLACK; GLOOM; NIGHT; can indicate something to do with MOON
darling DEAR; LOVE; SUGAR; TOOTSY; *see* DEAR
Darling pet NANA
darn DASH; SEW
darts, line of fire for OCHE

dart ARROW; LUNGE; RACE; SHOOT; TUCK
dash BRIO; CAREER; DARN; DART; ELAN; HASTEN; HINT; RUN; RUSH; SPOT; SPRINT; TINGE; TROT
dashed RAN
dashing, was RAN
data FILE; GEN; INFO; INPUT
data transmission DT
date DAY; ERA; TIME; YEAR
date, fateful IDES
date, usual STEADY
dated OLD
daughter D; MISS
daughter, treacherous REGAN
dawdle POTTER
day D; DATE; LIGHT; IDES; day of the week in abbreviated form: MON, TUE, WED, THUR, FRI, SAT, SUN
day before EVE
day, fateful IDES
day in Rome DIES
day of victory VE
daybreak DAWN; anagram of DAY
days DD; WK (abbreviation of 'week)
days of fasting EMBER
days, these AD; LATELY; *see* NOW
daze STUN
dazzle BLIND
dead FLAT; GONE; LATE; NUMB
deal ALLOT; CONTRACT; COPE; DATE; HAND; SALE; SHARE; WOOD; can indicate something to do with playing cards eg. CARD; can indicate something to do with plank, carpentry
deal, a good BAGS; LOT; LOTS; MANY; OODLES
deal incompetently with MUFF
deal with ADDRESS; COVER; TACKLE
dealer AGENT; COSTER; PEDDLER; TRADER [PACK]
dealer, crooked FENCE
dealing with RE; anagram indicator
dealings TRUCK
dealt anagram indicator
dean INGE; SWIFT
Dean can indicate something to do with forest; *see* DEAN
dear HONEY; LOVE; PET; PRICY; SWEET; *see* DARLING

dear French CHER
dear, my LOVE; PET
dearth LACK; WANT
death BANE; END; EXPIRY; PASSING
death notice OBIT
deathly PALE
debatable MOOT
debate MOOT; TALK
debate, place for FORUM
debauched IMMORAL
debauchery, place of DEN; STY
debt IOU
debt, in OWING
debt, was in OWED
debtor OWER
debts IOUS
decade TEN
decant POUR
decapitated initial letter to be omitted
decay ROT; RUST; anagram indicator
decayed BAD; OFF; ROTTED; ROTTEN; anagram indicator
deceased DEAD; EX; LATE
deceit LIE
deceive CON; DUPE; FOX; HAVE
deceived HAD
deceiver CHEAT; LIAR
decent CLEAN; PROPER; RIGHT
deception FRAUD; LIE; SCAM; STING; TRICK
deceptive LYING; anagram indicator
deceptive appearance FRONT
decide on CHOOSE; PICK; SELECT
decided AGREED
decision VOTE
decisive move MATE
deck ADORN; BOARD; COVER; FLOOR; GROUND; PACK
declaration homophone indicator
declare ASSERT; AVER; STATE; SWEAR
declared homophone indicator
decline DIE; DOWN; DROOP; DROP; DWINDLE; EBB; FADE; FALL; FLAG; LAPSE; REFUSE; ROT; SAG; SET; SINK; WANE

declined AGED; FELL
decomposed anagram indicator
decorate ADORN; ICE; TRIM
decorating, start PRIME
decoration GARNISH; OBE; SEQUIN; *see* MEDAL, HONOUR
decorative anagram indicator
decorative band SASH
decorous DEMURE
decrease FALL; *see* DECLINE
decree ACT; EDICT; LAW
decrepit anagram indicator
dedication can indicate TO followed by a name as 'dedication for a Scot" clues TOKEN (ie. to Ken)
deduct, deducted omission indicator
deduction CUT; DISCOUNT
deed ACT; ACTION; FEAT; rem: can indicate something to do with land ownership, mortgage, etc
deem JUDGE; RATE
deep BASS; LOW; MAIN; SEA
deer BUCK; DOE; ELK; GNU; HART; HIND; PRICKET; RED; ROE; STAG
defamation, defame LIBEL; SMEAR
defeat BEAT; BEST; FAULT; HAMMER; KO; LICK; LOSS; ROUT; RUIN; WORST
defeated BEAT; LICKED; OUT
defeated party LOSER
defect SPOT; STAIN; VICE
defected, defection omission indicator, usually of immediately preceding element(s)
defence ALIBI; GROYNE; WALL
defender ALLY; BACK
defender of the faith HENRY
defenders, our MOD
defer DELAY
deficiency GAP; LACK; LOSS; omission indicator
deficiency disease RICKETS
deficient BELOW; SHORT; UNDER; omission indicator
deficit LOSS
defile PASS; SOIL
Defoe's creation MOLL
deform STUNT

deformed anagram indicator
defraud CON; STING
defy BRAVE; FACE
degenerate FALL; SINK
degree BA; BED; C (ie. Centigrade, Celsius); F (ie. Fahrenheit); MA; PASS; PHD; PPE; RATE; *see* GRADUATE
degree course MBS; PPE *see* DEGREE
degree, of small SLIGHT
degree of soil acidity PH
degrees, higher HEAT
deity GOD; RA; SOL
delay DALLY; DEFER; HINDER; LAG; PAUSE; TARRY; WAIT
delayed LATE
delete DROP; OMIT; STRIKE
deliberate PONDER
delicacy CAKE; ICE; SWEET
delicious TASTY; YUMMY
delight ELATE; GLEE; GUSTO; JOY; PLEASE; REVEL
delighted GLAD
delightful person GAS
deliver CARRY; FREE; HAND; RID; SAVE; SERVE; SUPPLY; anagram indicator
deliver ball BOWL; SERVE
delivered FREED; RID
deliveries BALLS; OVER (ie. from cricket); *see* DELIVERY
delivery BABY; BALL; BOUNCER; YORKER; can indicate something to do with birth (eg. storks)
delivery, make a BOWL; SERVE
delivery route, service ROUND
delude CON
delve DIG
demand ASK; BID; BILL; CALL; DUN; MARKET; ORDER
demand, in HOT
demand payment DUN
demanding HARD; TRYING
demands, make TRY
demeanour AIR; FRONT
demise END
demo MARCH
demolish RUIN; WRECK

demolished anagram indicator
demolition anagram indicator
demon IMP
demonstrate MARCH; PROVE; SHOW
demonstrating often immediately precedes the synonym for the solution
demonstration MARCH; PROOF; SHOW
den LAIR; HOLT; RETREAT; STUDY
denarius D
denial NO
denial, old-fashioned NAY
denigrate ABUSE
denomination CLASS
denouement END; ENDING; can indicate the last letters(s)
dent MARK
depend LEAN
dependable STAUNCH
dense THICK
depart DIE; GO; LEAVE
departed DEAD; LATE; LEFT
department AREA; DEPT; FIELD; can also refer to a French administrative district
departure EXIT; GOING
depleted LOW
deplorable, deplorably anagram indicator
deployed USED; anagram indicator
deployed by anagram indicator; run indicator
deployed in nesting indicator; run indicator
deployment USE
depose OUST; USURP
deposed anagram indicator
deposit LAYER; LODGE; ORE; STORE; SUM
depravity EVIL; SIN; VICE
depressed BLUE; DOWN; LOW; LOWER
depressed area DELL; GLEN; TROUGH; *see* DEPRESSION
depressing GREY
depressing event DOWNER
depression COL; DELL; DENT; DIP; GLEN; HOLLOW; LOW; RECESS; RUT; TROUGH; VALE
deprive of TAKE; *see* CUT

deprived BEREFT; NEEDY; anagram indicator
deputy DEP
deranged MAD; anagram indicator
Derby CHEESE; CLASSIC; HAT; RACE
derelict anagram indicator
derision SCORN
derisive sound BOO; YAH
derogatory SLIGHTING
Descartes THINKER ("I think therefore I am")
descend DROP; FALL
descendant SCION
descent DIVE
description SPEC
desert ARID; DEFECT; LEAVE; QUIT; RAT; SAND; WASTE
deserted LEFT; omission indicator
deserter RAT
deserve EARN; RATE
design ART; END; DECOR; PLAN; anagram indicator
designed anagram indicator
designer, fashion DIOR; QUANT
desirable DES; PLUM
desirable, most BEST
desire DREAM; FANCY; GREED; ITCH; LONG; LUST; URGE; WANT; WHIM; WISH; YEN
desist STOP
desk AMBO; TABLE
desolate LORN
desolation RUIN
despatch SEND
despatched SENT
desperate anagram indicator
desperate, character who's DAN
despicable BASE; LOW; VILE
despicable person TOAD
despise CONTEMN
dessert AFTERS; APPLE; FLAN; FOOL; FRITTER; ICE; KISS; MOUSSE; PIE; PUD; PUDDING; SWEET; TART; WHIP
dessicated DRY
destabilised anagram indicator
destiny FATE; KARMA; LOT

destroy DISH; END; RASE; ROUT; RUIN; WRECK; anagram indicator
destroyed GONE; anagram indicator
destroyer KILLER
destroying anagram indicator
destruction RUIN
detach PART
detached anagram indicator
detached territory ISLE
detachment UNIT
detail FACT; ITEM; PIECE; SPEC; last letter of a word to be omitted (ie. de-tail)
detailed last letter of a word to be omitted (ie. de-tailed)
detailed description SPEC
detect CATCH; NOSE; SENSE; TRACE
detective DI; DICK; DS; EYE; HOLMES; MARPLE; MORSE; PI; TEC
Detective Inspector DI
Detective Sergeant CLUFF; DS
detectives CID; PIS; TECS; YARD
deter HAMPER
deterioration RUST
determined SET
detest HATE
develop GROW; anagram indicator; can indicate something to do with photography
developed GREW; READY; RIPE; anagram indicator
developed, not fully can indicate that a large section of word is omitted
developing, development anagram indicator
deviant anagram indicator
deviate ERR; SWERVE; SWITCH; WANDER; YAW
device LASER; LOGO; TOOL; TRICK; WINCH
devices FANCY; WILL
device, electronic TIMER
devil BOGLE (Sc.); DICKENS; HECK; IMP; NICK; SATAN
devil, little IMP
devious, deviously anagram indicator
devise PLAN; SET
devised SET; anagram indicator
devoted AVID; KEEN

devotee BUFF; FAN
devotion LOVE; PIETY
devour GORGE
devoured nesting indicator
diabolical anagram indicator
dial CALL; CLOCK; FACE; RING
dialogue EXCHANGE; LINE; TALK
diamond D; STONE; can indicate something to do with baseball
diamonds DD; ICE; ROCKS; SUIT
diary LOG
diary item ENTRY
diatonic note C
diatribe TIRADE
dice CUT
Dickens HECK; HELL
Dickensian character (hero, herione) DODGER; NELL; PIP; OLIVER; RUDGE
dicky DODGY; IFFY; anagram indicator
Dicky see dicky
dictate ORDER
dictated homophone indicator
dictator DUCE; FRANCO; IDI; SHOGUN; TITO
dictionary DICT; OED
die BLOCK; END; EXIT; FADE; FALL; GO; LONG; STAMP; YEARN; [TESSERA]
died D; FELL; OB
died out D to be omitted
diesel oil DERV
differ VARY; anagram indicator
difference SPAT; TIFF; anagram indicator
different CHANGE; ELSE; OTHER; anagram indicator
different one OTHER
difficult HARD; HELL; STICKY; TRICKY; anagram indicator
difficult job GRIND
difficult position, situation LURCH; *see* DIFFICULTY
difficulties MIRE; anagram indicator
difficulties, in anagram indicator
difficulty ADO; BIND; CORNER; FIX; HARDNESS; HOLE; LURCH; MESS; PASS; PLIGHT; RUB; SCRAPE; SNAG; SPOT; anagram indicator
difficulty, create STIR

difficulty, in some anagram of SOME
difficulty, minor BUG; GLITCH; KINK
diffident COY; SHY
dig CRACK; DELVE; MINE; NUDGE
digger MINER
digging MINE
digit FINGER; NUMBER; THUMB; TOE
digital equipment FINGER; THUMB; TOE
dignitary LION; VIP
dignity FACE
digress RAMBLE
dilapidated SHABBY; TATTY; anagram indicator
dilapidated car BANGER; CRATE; HEAP
dilemma PLIGHT; SCRAPE; *see* DIFFICULT POSITION, DIFFICULTY
dim FADE; LOWER; *see* THICK.
diminished omission indicator
diminutive person SQUIT
din NOISE; RACKET; ROW
dine EAT; SUP
dined ATE
diner EATER
dinner MEAL
diocese SEE
dip DROP; DUCK; DUNK; FALL; SAG; RAMP
diplomacy TACT
dire BAD; EVIL; anagram indicator
direct CAST; FRANK; LEAD; OPEN; POINT; RUN; SHOW; STEER; STRAIGHT
direct steering CON
directed LED; RAN
direction BEARING; TACK; WAY; a compass bearing in full: EAST; NORTH; SOUTH; WEST, or abbreviated: E; N; NE; NW; S; SE; SW; W
directions several compass bearings, usually as letters
directions, in both palindrome indicator
directly DUE
director BOSS; DIR; HEAD
directors BOARD; D
dirt FILTH; GRIME; SCUM
disable SCOTCH

disadvantage MINUS
disagreeable BAD
disagreement RIFT; SPAT; TIFF
disappear GO; MELT
disappeared WENT
disappointed, very GUTTED
disappointing OFF; POOR
disapproval ODIUM
disapprove soundly BOO; TUT
disapproval, audible (express, voice, voiced, etc) BOO; TUT
disarray anagram indicator
disaster ROUT; RUIN; anagram indicator
disastrous FATAL; LETHAL; anagram indicator
disastrously anagram indicator
disc COUNTER; O; TOKEN; *see* RECORD
discarded SHED; omission indicator
discarding omission indicator
discern SPY
discharge MATTER; PUS; SACK; SHOOT; SHOT
discipline ORDER
disciplined CANED; anagram indicator
disclosure LEAK
discomfort ACHE; PAIN
disconcert RATTLE; THROW
disconcerted THREW; anagram indicator
disconnect CUT; SEVER
discontented anagram indicator
discontinue END
discontinued OFF
discordant anagram indicator
discount CUT; omission indicator
discount, initial omission indicator for initial letter
discourage DETER; UNMAN
discovered FOUND
discreet WISE
discretion TACT
discrimination TASTE
discuss AIR; CHAT
discussing ON; can require that ON is used in conjunction with its subject as "doctor discussing" clues MOON

discussion AIRING; CHAT; PARLEY; TALK
disease GOUT; TB
disease, bird GAPES
disease, evidence of RASH
disease, flu-like ME
diseased ILL; SICK
disembark LAND
disfigure MAR; SCAR; SPOIL; anagram indicator
disfigured anagram indicator
disgrace TAINT
disgraceful anagram indicator
disguised, disguising anagram indicator
disgust APPAL; REPEL
disgusted expression UGH
disgusting SICK; anagram indicator
dish ASHET; CRUMBLE; FOOD; MEAL; PEACH; PIE; PLATE; PLATTER; RUIN; can refer to some aspect of a woman; anagram indicator
dish out ALLOT; DOLE
disheartened omission indicator for middle letter(s) of associated word
dishonest BENT; CROOK; LYING
dishonest, be LIE
dishonour STAIN
dishonourable man CAD; ROTTER
disinfectant BLEACH
dislike HATE; ODIUM; RESENT
disloyalty TREASON
dismal DREAR; DREARY; POOR
dismantled anagram indicator
dismay APPAL; DREAD
dismiss CASHIER; SACK; SPURN; YORK; omission indicator
dismissal SACK; omission indicator
dismissed BOWLED; OUT; UP; omission indicator
disorder MUDDLE; anagram indicator
disordered MUDDLED; anagram indicator
disorderly ILL; anagram indicator
disorderly character TED
disorderly scene RAG
disorganised anagram indicator

disparage DECRY
dispatch KILL; SEND; anagram indicator
dispatched SENT
dispense with CHUCK; DROP; DUMP; JUNK; omission indicator
dispersed anagram indicator
display AIR; HANG; POMP; SHOW; STAND; anagram indicator; can imply a word beginning with BE followed by an appropriate adjective as "Display humour, producing requisite for retiring camper" clues BED-ROLL (ie. be droll)
display, vain POMP
displayed AIRED; HUNG; anagram indicator
displayed in nesting indicator
displaying anagram indicator; nesting indicator
displaying, some nesting indicator
disposal SALE
dispose of DROP; DUMP; EAT; SELL
disposed, disposal, disposition anagram indicator
disposed of SOLD
disposing of anagram indicator
disposition MOOD; PENCHANT
disprove REFUTE
dispute ROW; SPAR; SPAT; TIFF; WAR; WRANGLE
disregard MISS; OMIT; omission indicator
disreputable person RIP
disreputable newspaper RAG
disrobe BARE
disrupted anagram indicator
disruption RUFFLE
disruptive anagram indicator
disseminate, disseminated SPREAD; anagram indicator
disseminating, dissemination anagram indicator
dissent DEMUR
dissenter REBEL
dissenters, group of SECT
dissident anagram indicator
dissipate WASTE
dissipates, dissipated, dissipating anagram indicator
dissolute LOOSE; anagram indicator
dissuade DETER
distance CUBIT; METRE; MILE; *see* LENGTH, MEASURE

distance, at a BACK
distance, short FOOT; FT; INCH
distant COOL; CHILLY; FARAWAY (ie. far away); REMOTE; STRANGE
distilling anagram indicator
distinctive atmosphere AURA
distort BUCKLE; MANGLE; TWIST; anagram indicator
distorted anagram indicator
distortion BUCKLE; anagram indicator
distraught DOWN; LOW; anagram indicator
distress PAIN; REND; anagram indicator
distress call SOS
distressed as well as being an anagram indicator, like other words of the root 'distress', can refer to having hair cut
distressing anagram indicator
distribute ALLOT; DEAL; SHARE; SOW
distributed anagram indicator
distributes cards DEALS
distributing anagram indicator
distribution SHARE; anagram indicator
distribution of papers ROUND
distribution of power GRID
district AREA; PATCH
District Commissioner DC
disturb MOVE; RATTLE; ROCK; SHAKE; anagram indicator
disturbance RIOT; anagram indicator
disturbed MOVED; SHAKEN; anagram indicator
ditch DROP; DUMP; DYKE; TRENCH
dithering anagram Indicator
ditty SONG
dive DUMP; JOINT; SINK; STOOP
diver PEARLER; can indicate something to do with a bird eg. grebe
diversified, diversifying anagram indicator
diversion TRICK; SPORT
diversion, active SPORT
diverted anagram indicator
Dives Latin for rich man, so can indicate something to do with the legendary rich eg. Midas, Croesus [PLUTOCRAT]
divide FORK; PART; REND; SPLIT
divided RENT; SPLIT; TORN

divider RULER
divine DD; HOLY
division CLASS; SPLIT; RENT
division in church AISLE
divorcee EX
Dixie SOUTH
dizzy GIDDY; LIGHT; anagram indicator
do ACT; APE; BASH; CON; COPY; FARE; PARTY; PAY; TURN
do battle FIGHT; WAR
do business DEAL; TRADE
do something ACT
do without FAST
do wrong ERR; SIN
dock BERTH; CUT; LAND; PEN; PORT; MOOR; TRIM; WEED; last letter to be omitted
docked CUT; last letter to be omitted
docket CHIT
doctor ALTER; D; DOC; DR; FIX; GALEN; GP; INTERN; MB; MD; MO; PHD; RIG; TREAT; VET; WHO; anagram indicator
Dr Arnold HEAD
doctor's time MOST
doctors' army RAMC
doctored anagram indicator
doctrine ISM
docudrama FACTION
document DEED; FORM; MS; PAPER; LIST; RECORD; SCREED; SLIP; VISA; WILL; WRIT
documents MSS
doddery AGED; OLD; anagram indicator
dodge DUCK; ELUDE; PLOY; RUSE; SCAM
dodging anagram indicator
dodgy ICKY; IFFY; anagram indicator
does ACTS; DEER
does (old, Shakespearian) DOTH
dog BARKER; BITCH; BITER; CHOW; COCKER; CUR; FIDO; FOLLOW; HOUND; HUSKY; MUTT; PET; PLUTO; POM; POOCH; POODLE; PUG; PUP; REX; ROVER; SETTER; STRAY; TAG; TAIL; TRACK; TRAIL; YAPPER
dog, little D; PUP
dole METE; UB
dole money UB

dollar BUCK
dollars, lots of G
dolly SITTER
dolphins SCHOOL
domestic animal CAT; DOG; PET
domesticated TAME
dome can indicate something to do with the top of the head
dominant CHIEF; MAIN
dominate BOSS; RIDE
domineering BOSSY
don DRESS; FELLOW; SENOR [ASSUME]
Don can indicate something to do with Don Quixote eg. windmills, Sancho Panza; *see* DON QUIXOTE
Don Quixote can indicate the use of a Spanish word, as "Don Quixote's goodbye" clues ADIOS
donations ALMS; GIFTS
done AGREED; OVER; UP
done, not RAW
donjon KEEP
donkey ASS; JENNY; MOKE
donor GIVER
dons can indicate something to do with Spaniards, eg. armada or some other aspect of Spanish history, or a Spanish word
don't give up GOON (ie. go on)
don't let on SH
doodah, all of a anagram indicator
doomed FATED
door ENTRY; EXIT
door, part of HINGE; JAMB
doorkeeper *see* DOORMAN
doorman BOUNCER; USHER
doorway PORTAL; *see* DOOR
dope ASS; CLOT; DRUG; GEN; INFO; SAP
Dorothy DOT
dorsal BACK
dosh *see* MONEY
dosser TRAMP
dossier FILE
Dostoevsky (Dostoyevsky) can indicate something to do with IDIOT, CRIME, PUNISHMENT etc
dot SPOT

dotty anagram indicator

double DRINK; DUAL; FETCH (naut.); TWIN; RINGER; TWICE; can indicate that a letter or component should be repeated

double-barrelled can indicate something to do with a hyphen

double bend S

double first AA; II

doubled can indicate double letters

doubles can signal the repetition of an element

doublet can indicate double letters

doubt QUESTION

doubt, no CERTAIN; SURE

doubter SCEPTIC

doubtful IFFY; anagram indicator

doubtless CERTAIN; SURE

dough PASTA; PASTE; can indicate something to do with money eg. CASH, BREAD, TENDER

dour GRIM

dowdy DRAB

down BELOW; BLUE; D; DRINK; FEATHER(S); FELL; LOW; OVER; OWING; PEAKY; SAD; SINK; SWALLOW; UNDER; when used with a verb can indicate a word-combination or phrase incorporating LESS (eg. "cut down" signals DO LESS)

down, cast LOWER

down, go DIP; DROP; FALL

downfall DROP; RUIN

downgrade DEMOTE

downright SHEER

downstairs BELOW

doze NAP

dozen DOZ

drab DOWDY; DULL

draft BILL; MS; PLAN; SKETCH

drag DRAW; HALE; HAUL; LINGER; LUG; PUFF; PULL; TOW; TRAIL

drain EMPTY; SAP; SEWER; SPEND; SUCK; TIRE

drained ALLIN (ie. all in); DRY

dram NIP; TOT

drama FUSS; PLAY; NO; NOH

dramatic piece SCENE

dramatist PINTER; SHAW; WILDE; YEATS

draped anagram indicator

draught SWIG; TOT; WIND; can indicate something to do with a draught animal eg. DRAY; can indicate something to do with beer as 'draughtsman' might clue TAPSTER
draughthorse DRAY; PUNCH; SHIRE
draw DOODLE; DRAG; ENGAGE; LURE; PULL; SKETCH; STRETCH; TAKE; TIE; TOW; can indicate something to do with a cigarette, smoking
draw up FRAME; WARD
drawer, cash TILL
drawer, top U (ie. social status)
drawers can indicate something to do with western gunfighters
dray CART
dread AWE; FEAR; TERROR
dreadful BAD; DIRE; anagram indicator
dreadfully anagram indicator
dream FANCY; TRANCE; WISH
dreamer BOTTOM (from 'Midsummer Night's Dream')
dreary DULL
dreary experience DRAG
dress ALIGN; DECK; DON; FROCK; GARB; GEAR; GOWN; GROOM; HABIT; ORDER; RIG; ROBE; SACK; SARI; SHIFT; SKIRT; SMOCK; SUIT; TOG
dressed CLAD; DECENT
dressed (up) anagram indicator
dressing GAUZE; LINT; SALVE; SAUCE; TOPPING
dress up DECK
drew TIED; TOWED
dribble SLAVER
dried up SERE
drier SPINNER; TOWEL
drift DUNE; GIST; ROAM; YAW
drill BORE; GYM; PE; PT; SCHOOL; TEACH; *see* EXERCISE
drill, army BULL
drill pioneer TULL
drilling can indicate something to do with a WELL
drink ALE; BEER; BEVVY; BRANDY; BREW; BOTTLE; CHA; CHAR; CHASER; CIDER; COLA; CUP; DOUBLE; DOWN; DRAM; FLIP; GROG; HALF; HOCK; JAR; LAGER; LASSI; LAP; LIQUOR; MAIN; MALT; MEAD; MED; NIP; NOG; PEG; PERRY; PINT; POND; PORT; PORTER; POSSET; POTION; PUNCH; QUAFF; ROSE; SACK; SAKE; SEA; SHANDY;

SHERRY; SHORT; SIP; SLING; SNIFTER; STOUT; SUP; TEA; TENT; TIPPLE; TOAST; TOPE; TOT; WATER; WINE; *see* WHISKY

drink, amount of GILL; HALF; PINT; *see* DRINK, LITTLE

drink, avoiding DRY; TT

drink, little D; DRAM; DROP; HALF; NIP; PEG; SHORT; TOT

drinker SOT; TOPER; *see* DRUNKARD

drinking bout BENDER; BINGE

drinking den BAR

drinking establishment, place etc BAR; INN; PUB

drinking session BENDER; BINGE; BOUT

drinks ROUND

drip FALL; WIMP

drive EGG; IMPEL; FORCE; PUSH; RAM; THRUST; TRIP; SPIN; URGE

drive aimlessly TOOTLE

drive away, out, out CHASE; ROUT; SHOO

drive, prepared to FEED

drivel PAP

driver CLUB; ENGINE; HERD (as in shepherd); MOTOR; WOOD

driver(s) can indicate something to do with golf as "driver's place" clues TEE

drivers AA; RAC

droll FUNNY; MERRY; WITTY; WRY

drone HUM; IDLER

droop FLAG; SAG; WILT

drop BEAD; DIP; DRAM; DUMP; FALL; HANG; JUNK; LOWER; OMIT; RAIN; SAG; SCRAP; SHED; SPOT; TEAR; TOT; omission indicator

drop, little CC

drop off KIP; NAP; NOD; SLEEP

dropped FELL; anagram indicator; omission indicator

dross SCUM; SLACK

drove FLOCK; HERD; HOST

drub BEAT

drudge HACK; SERF; TOIL; TOILER; can indicate something to do with Dr Johnson

drug ACID; COKE; CRACK; CURE; DOPE; DOWNER; E; GRASS; H; HEMP; HORSE; POT; SMACK; SPEED; UPPER

drug agent NARC

drug, hard CRACK

drug, instance of E; *see* DRUG
drug, soft POT
drug supplier PUSHER
drugs, on HIGH
drugs, use of TRIP
drum TAP; TUB
drunk BLIND; BLOTTO; CANNED; GONE; HAPPY; HIGH; LIT; LOADED; LUSH; MERRY; OILED; PICKLED; RIPE; SODDEN; SOT; SOUSED; SQUIFFY; STONED; TIDDLY; TIGHT; TOPER; anagram indicator; can indicate that a word is slurred
drunkard BINGER; BOOZER; LUSH; SOT; SOUSE; TOPER
drunken *see* DRUNK
dry AIR; ARID; BARREN; BRUT; SEC; SERE; THIRSTY; TT
dry, become PARCH
dryer *see* DRIER
dual DOUBLE; can indicate that a component is to be repeated, or two components of similar meaning are to be used, probably consecutively
dubious IFFY; anagram indicator
dubiously anagram indicator
duck DIP; DODGE; ELUDE; FABRIC; O; NIL; NOUGHT; SCAUP (bird); TEAL; TERN; ZERO
duct FLUE
dud *see* FAILURE
dude CAT; DANDY; TOFF
Dudley LEICESTER
duds can indicate something to do with clothes
due COMING; FIT; FITTING; FOR; OWED; OWING
duff FAKE; PUDDING; anagram indicator
dug DELVED; MINED; TEAT
duke D; FIST
dull BLAND; DENSE; DREARY; DRY; FLAT; GREY; LAME; MAT; MATT; SLOW; THICK; TRITE
dullard DUNCE
dumb MUTE; THICK
dumbstruck AWED
dump CHUCK; DROP
dun DEMAND; HORSE
dunce ASS
Dundee CAKE
dunderhead ASS; D

dune SAND
dunk DIP
dupe GULL; STING; SUCKER
Durham COW
during IN; ON; WHILE; WHILST; nesting indicator
dusky UMBER
dust CLEAN; DIRT
Dutch D; DU; WIFE [MISSUS]
Dutch coast HOOK
duty CHARGE; FEE; OFFICE; TAX; TOLL; ROLE; can indicate something to do with Customs and Excise
dwarf DOC; HAPPY; SLEEPY; STUNT; TROLL
dwell ABIDE; LIVE; LODGE; RESIDE; STAY
dwelling ABODE; CABIN; FLAT; HOME; HOUSE; SEMI; TENT
dye COLOUR; HENNA
dyke DITCH; WALL
dynamic DRIVING
dynamite TNT
dynasty HOUSE; MING; *see* HOUSE

Ee

each EA; EVERY; PER
'eadgear AT (ie. 'at)
eager AGOG; AVID; HOT; KEEN; PANTING
eagre BORE
ear INTEREST
ear, on the homophone indicator
ear, part of DRUM; LOBE
ear-piece MUFF
earl E; PEER
earlier AGO; BACK; PRIOR; preceding indicator
early AM; RATHE (from A.S.); consider the word 'early' carefully

even when it is used in what appears to be its ordinary sense, for instance "early transport" may call to mind penny-farthings etc but it may be referring to the early years of its users eg. PRAM, PUSH-CHAIR; similarly an "early bird" can refer to a flying creature from the dinosaur age

early light DAWN

early part of day AM; MORN

early stage of competition HEAT

early, very IAM (ie. one am.)

earn MAKE; MERIT; NET; PULL

earnest GRAVE; INTEREST

earner PRO

earnings PAY; WAGE

earshot homophone indicator

earth CLAY; EA; GROUND; SOD; SOIL; WORLD

earthwork builder OFFA

earthy COARSE; CRUDE; LUSTY

ease RELENT; REST

easel STAND

easily anagram indicator

east E; can indicate a component is to be used reading from right to left (ie. east to west)

East End D; T; can also indicate that the initial H should be omitted from a word, or the final G from an -ing word (ie. supposed East Ender's pronunciation)

East European CROAT; SLAV

east, from the reversal indicator, as "American marksman watched a man from the east" clues DEADEYE (ie. EYED-A-ED reversed)

East German OST

East London DON

east to west reversal indicator

Eastcheap can refer to a Shakespearean character associated with the area eg. PISTOL

Eastender T (ie, end of 'east')

Easter, first Sunday after LOW

Easter, seventh Sunday after WHIT

Easter, some time before LENT

Eastern E

eastern game GO

easy LIGHT; LOOSE; SIMPLE

easy catch SITTER

easy pace AMBLE
easy, take it REST
easy target SITTER
easy thing PIE
easy victory ROMP
eat DINE; FEAST; GOBBLE; GORGE; SUP; nesting indicator
eat, a little to BITE
eat a lot PIG
eat grain PECK
eat greedily GORGE; SCOFF; WOLF
'eated OT (ie. 'ot)
eater APPLE; DINER
eating-house CAFE; CAFF
eating-place MESS
eccentric CARD; CASE; CRANK; DOTTY; NUT; ODD; OUTRE; RUM; anagram indicator
eccentric Oxford don can signify a spoonerism (after The Rev. Spooner, see Introduction)
eco-friendly GREEN
ecological GREEN
economist KEYNES; MILL
ecstasy E
ecstatic SENT; anagram indicator
Eden GARDEN
edge BRIM; BRINK; END; HEM; LINE; LIP; MARGIN; RIM; SIDE; VERGE; first or last letter indicator
edge, give HONE
edged nesting indicator
edges first and last letters indicator
edges of first and last letters indicator; rem: it may be necessary to insert the implied AND as "edges of high" clues HANDH (eg. on the way to building up HANDHOLD)
edging nesting indicator
edgy JUMPY; TENSE
edit anagram indicator
edited anagram indicator
edition BOOK; ED; ISSUE; PRINT; VERSION; anagram indicator
edition, special EXTRA
editor ED; can indicate something to do with LEADER
educate TEACH; TRAIN
educated ED; TAUGHT; TRAINED

education ED; LEARNING; TRAINING
educational establishment LSE; POLY; *see* COLLEGE, SCHOOL, UNIVERSITY
educational publication TES
educationalist, trained BED
Edward ED; NED; TED
Edward, King SPUD
effect CAUSE; END; TONE
effect, general TONE
effect, had an BIT
effect, lasting SCAR
effective NEAT; NET; TELLING
effective, was, were BIT
effectual SOUND
effeminate type PONCE
effervescent anagram indicator
efficient GOOD
effigy BUST
effort PUSH; STRAIN; TRY
efforts TRIES
'efty UGE (ie. 'uge)
egg DUCK; GOAD; NIT; O; POKE; PROD; PRESS; SPUR; URGE
egg-head E
egg-part SHELL; WHITE; YOLK
egg-shaped OVOID
egg, size of an GLAIR (ie. viscous substance)
eggs OVA; ROE
Egypt ET
Egyptian god RA
Egyptologist CARTER
eight CUBE
eight German ACHT
eight short OCT
eighteen, under MINOR
either way can indicate the answer is a palindrome (see introduction)
eject OUST; OUT
ejected OUT
elaborate, elaborating anagram indicator
elan DASH
elapse PASS

elastic YIELDING
elation LIFT
elbow NUDGE
elder SENIOR; TREE
elderly relative GRAN
Eleanor ELLIE
elect PICK; VOTE
elected IN
election POLL; VOTE
electoral division WARD
electoral system PR
electric SHOCKING
electrical device FUSE; PLUG; SWITCH
electrical fault SHORT
electrically dangerous LIVE
electrician SPARKS
electricity JUICE; POWER
electricity, break in OUTAGE
electricity supply AC; DC
electronic device BUG; CHIP; TIMER
elegance GRACE
elegant CHIC; SMART
elegant, make REFINE
element AS; IRON; PART; RADON; RESPECT; TIN; U; when a chemical element is specified, it usually calls for the use of the technical symbol for the element, AS for arsenic etc.
element, noble ARGON
elementary can indicate a chemical element
elevate RAISE
elevated HIGH
eleven SIDE; TEAM; XI
eleven abroad XI
eleven, first K (ie. position in the alphabet)
eleventh hour LATE
elf TROLL
eliminate END
elite BEST; CREAM; PICK; SAS; TOP
Elizabeth BETTY
elsewhere OUT
elusive anagram indicator

embankment DAM; DYKE
embargo BAN; BLACK; BLOCK; STOP
embark BOARD; ENTER
embarked OFF
embarrass ABASH
embarrassed RED
embarrassment, show BLUSH
embarrassment, sign of BLUSH; FLUSH
embassy MISSION
embed SET
embellish LARD
embellishments DECOR
emblem BADGE; MARK
emboss CHASE
embrace HUG
embraced by run indicator; nesting indicator
emcee HOST
emerge ARISE
emergency appeal SOS
emigre EXPAT
eminence MOUNT; TOR; or can refer to a particular mountain
emit SEND
emotion HATE; IRE; LOVE; PANG
emperor NERO; TSAR
emphasis ACCENT; STRESS; TONE
emphasise ACCENT; STRESS
employ USE
employed USED
employee HAND
employees STAFF
employer BOSS; USER
employment JOB; PLACE; POST; TASK; USAGE; USE
employment, in USED
emptied omission indicator, all but first and last letters of associated word to be omitted, as "emptied bottle" clues BE
empty BARE; DRAIN; IDLE; omission indicator where all but first and last letters of associated word to be omitted as "empty container" clues CR; can also indicate the inclusion of O within a word or component, as "Chap's empty complaint" clues MOAN (ie. M-O-AN)
emulsion PAINT

enable ALLOW
enchant CHARM
enchantress CIRCE
enclosed ENC; nesting indicator
enclosure CAGE; CIRCLE; FOLD; PEN; RING; YARD
encomium PRAISE
encounter FACE; INCUR; MEET
encounter, brief can indicate something to do with Noel Coward
encountered MET
encountered in nesting indicator
encourage EGG; PRESS; PROD; PUSH; SPUR; URGE
encouragement FILIP; NUDGE; PUSH
encrypted a component to be nested within CODE
end AIM; BACK; BOUND; CHECK; CLOSE; DEATH; DIE; EDGE; EXPIRE; FINIS; GOAL; LAST; STOP; TAIL; TIP; indicator of first or last letter(s)
end, came to an DIED; STOPPED
end of book FINIS
end up LAND
endeavour ATTEMPT; TRY
ended DONE; OVER; UP
ending last letter indicator
ending, game's MATE
endless, endlessly EVER; last letter(s) to be omitted from associated word
endorse BACK; RATIFY
ends indicator of first and last letters
endure LAST; WEAR
enemy FOE; TIME
energetic person DOER; GOER
energy DRIVE; E; ELAN; GO; LIFE; PEP; STEAM; VIM
energy, amount of KW
enfold HUG
engage BOOK; CHARM; DRAW; ENLIST; HIRE; LOCK; SIGN
engaged in AT; nesting indicator
engagement DATE; can indicate something to do with battle, fighting, etc
engaging nesting indicator
engender BREED
engine, increase speed of REV
engine, part of SUMP

engineer CE; ENG; SAPPER; WATT
engineering graduate BE
engineers CES; RE; REME
England E; ENG; REALM
English E; ENG
English in Spain INGLES
English, Old OE
Englishman abroad POM
engrave CHASE; ETCH
engraving PRINT
engrossed RAPT
engulf SWAMP
enjoin ORDER
enjoy DIG; LIKE; LOVE
enjoy book READ
enjoy life BE
enjoyment FUN; KICK
enormous HUGE; MEGA; OS; VAST
enough AMPLE; ENOW
enough, not UNDER
enquire ASK
enraptured SENT
ensemble anagram indicator
ensue COME
ensnares nesting indicator
ENT specialism EAR
entangled, entangling anagram indicator
enter LOG; START
entered nesting indicator
entering nesting indicator; run indicator
enterprise DRIVE; GO
enters nesting indicator
entertain AMUSE
entertain lavishly FETE
entertained nesting indicator
entertainer ARCHIE (Osborne character, first name); COMIC; HOST; RICE (Osborne character, second name)
entertainer, radio DJ
entertaining FUN
entertainment FAIR; PLAY; PORT (Gael.); REVUE; SHOW

entertainment, place of (venue etc) CLUB; FAIR
enthralled by nesting indicator
enthusiasm GUSTO; MANIA; RAGE
enthusiast BUFF; FAN
enthusiastic HOT; KEEN; MANIC
entice DRAW; LURE
enticement BAIT; LURE
enticed LED (ON)
entire FULL; WHOLE
entire range AZ
entirely ALL
entitled can indicate something to do with the peerage, or a book title
entrance ADIT; DOOR; ENCHANT; GATE; nesting indicator; initial letter indicator
entrance hall FOYER; LOBBY
entrance to initial letter indicator
entranced RAPT
entrap CATCH; NET
entreat BEG; PRAY
entreaty PLEA
entries GATE
envious GREEN
environment HOME; nesting indicator
environment, concerned with GREEN
environmental GREEN
environmentally-friendly GREEN
environmentalist GREEN
environs of first and last letters indicator
epic SAGA
episode EVENT; PAGE; STORY
epistle ELI; LETTER; TIM
epistler PETER
epitaph RIP
equal EVEN; LIKE; PEER
equal outcome DRAW; TIE
equality PARITY
equally AS
equestrian RIDER
equip KIT; RIG
equipped KITTED; RIGGED

equipment GEAR; KIT; RIG; TACKLE
equipment, riding TACK
equitable FAIR; JUST; RIGHT
eradicate omission indicator
Eric AMBLER
ermine STOAT
erode ROT
eroding anagram indicator
erotic STEAMY
err FALL; SIN; SLIP
errant anagram indicator
error BUG; FLAW; GAFFE; LAPSE; OUT; SIN; SLIP; TYPO
error in AMISS; anagram indicator
erroneously anagram indicator
ersatz FAKE
erstwhile EX
erupt anagram indicator
eruption RASH; SPOT
escape AVOID; FLEE; FLIGHT; FLY; GO; LEAK; RUN
escape (US) LAM
escape, narrow SQUEAK
escaped FLED; FLEW; GONE; WENT
escort BEAU; LEAD; SQUIRE; TAKE; USHER
escorted LED; TOOK
escorting nesting indicator
especially ESP
espionage activity BUGGING
espionage device BUG
esprit WIT
espy SPOT; NOTE
essay GO; TRY
essayist ELIA (pen-name of Lamb); STEELE
essence CORE; GIST; HEART; NUB; POINT; ROOT
essential KEY; MUST; ROOT
essential for (in, to) run indicator
essential element PITH; *see* ESSENCE
essentially this can mean that the middle of a word is to be used; more rarely, and a little more complicated, it can mean that the middle run between two words constitutes the necessary set of letters as "Essentially Royal Society rescheduled party" cues an anagram of ALSOCI leading to SOCIAL

establish FOUND; DEFINE; FIX; FORM; SET; SETTLE
established E; EST; FIXED; HARD; SET
established actor, performer STAR
establishment, anti- RED
Establishment SYSTEM
establishment, small COTTAGE
estate CAR; EST; LAND; MANOR
esteem RATE; RESPECT
estimate ASSESS; COST; RATE
estuary HUMBER
ethics, of MORAL
etiquette FORM
euphoric HIGH; anagram indicator
Europe EU
European E; EC; can indicate a European nationality eg. DANE, POLE, SLAV, ROMAN
European city PARIS; ROME; TURIN
European Union EU
evade DODGE; PARRY
evaluate ASSESS; APPRAISE; MARK; RATE; SCORE
evaluation MARK; RATING; SCORE
evangelist JOHN; LUKE; MARK
evasion PARRY
evasive COY
even EEN; FLAT; IRON; LEVEL; FLUSH; SQUARE; YET
even if THOUGH
even though IF
even up ALIGN
evening LATE; NIGHT
event DO; FETE; HEAT; PARTY; RACE; RALLY
ever AY; AYE (Mid. Eng.)
Everest MOUNT; PEAK
every EACH; PER
every one PER
every year PA
everybody ALL
everybody else REST
everyone ALL; E; EACH
everything ALL; SUM; TOTAL
evidence GROUND; GROUNDS; PROOF; SIGN; TRACE

evidence of disease RASH
evident CLEAR
evident in, among, etc run indicator; anagram indicator
evil BAD; ILL; MALIGN; SIN; VICE; VILE
evil doer IMP
evil event CRIME
evil woman WITCH
ex- FORMER
ex-PM *see* PRIME MINISTER
ex-rail BR
exact RIGHT
exactly DUE
exaggerate can signpost a word beginning with OVER
exalt PRAISE
exalted HIGH; RAISED; UP; can indicate something to do with a means of being elevated eg. being on stilts
exalted, not LOW
exam *see* EXAMINATION
exam, take SIT
exam, took SAT
examination MEDICAL; MOT; ORAL; PPE; PRELIM; SCAN; SEARCH; STUDY; TEST; TRIAL; VETTING; VIVA
examine CASE; EYE; READ; SCAN; TEST; TRY; VET
examine judicially HEAR; TRY
example CASE; IDEAL
example, fine ONER
example, following AFTER
example, for AS; eg.; SAY
excavation MINE; PIT; QUARRY
excel BEAT; CAP; SHINE; STAR; TOP
excelled LED
excellence CLASS
excellent ACE; AI; BEST; CLASS; DIVINE; FAB; FINE; GOOD; GRAND; GREAT; SUPER; TOP; TOPPING
excellent thing PEACH
except SAVE
exception of BUT; SAVE
exceptional RARE; SUPER
exceptionally anagram indicator
excess OTT

excessive HIGH; UNDUE; can indicate the use of TOO
excessively OTT; TOO; can indicate an element to be repeated
excessively large OS
exchange BARTER; SWAP; SWITCH; SWOP; TRADE; TRUCK
exchange, Parisian stock BOURSE
excising omission indicator; can indicate something to do with tax
excite INFLAME; ROUSE; WOW
excited HOT; SENT; anagram indicator
excited, get WHET; WOW
excited state FLAP; TIZZY; WHIRL
excitement BUZZ; FERMENT; FLAP; HEAT; HUM; KICK; STIR; THRILL; ZING
excitement, in a state of AGOG
exciting HOT; anagram indicator
exclamation AH; AW; CRY; GOSH; HA; MY
exclamation of disapproval BOO; TUT
exclamation of distaste UGH; YUCK
exclamation of joy WHEE
exclamation of surprise, pleasure AH; BOY; COR; GEE; MY
exclamation, Spanish OLE
exclude BAN; BAR; DEBAR
excluded ALONE
exclusive SCOOP; SOLE
exclusive group ELITE; SET
excursion OUTING; TRIP
excuse ALIBI; PLEA; REASON
execute DO; HANG; KILL; TOP
executed initial letter omission indicator
executive SUIT
executive, chief DG
exercise APPLY; DRILL; EXERT; PE; PT; TRAIN; USE; WIELD
exercise choice PICK; SELECT
exercising anagram indicator
exert influence ACT
exertion, show PANT
exhaust DRAIN; TIRE; WEAR
exhausted ALLIN (ie. all-in); DEAD; SHOT
exhibit SHOW
exhibited in run indicator
exhibition EXPO; FAIR; SHOW; SPECTACLE

exile DEPORT
exist AM; ARE; BE; LIVE
existed previously WAS
existence LIFE
existence, have *see* EXIST
existing circumstances ASIS
exists IS; LIVES
exit DIE; GO; LEAVE; LEAVING; OUT
exotic anagram indicator
expand GROW; PAD
expansive WIDE
expect AWAIT; HOPE
expectant AGOG; in relation to a person (eg. hero) can indicate something to do with Dickens' 'Great Expectations' eg. PIP
expectantly AGOG
expectation HOPE
expected DUE; PAR
expected time of arrival ETA
expedition DESPATCH; HASTE; MISSION; QUEST; TRIP
expedition, with FAST; can indicate that something is done quickly eg. 'move with expedition' can clue RUN
expel OUST; OUT
expelled RID
expense COST
expensive STEEP
expensive coat FUR
expensive, now more UP
experience FEEL; HAVE; SEE; SUFFER; TASTE; USE
experience, brief SAMPLE; TASTE
experience, dreary BIND; CHORE; DRAG; FAG
experience life BE
experience, short of GREEN; RAW
experienced ABLE; FELT; HAD; PROVED; SAW
experiment PILOT; TEST; TRIAL
expert ABLE; ACE; BUFF; DAB; DEFT; MASTER; ONER; PRO
expertise ART; SKILL
expertly ABLY; WELL
expire DIE; LAPSE; PASS
expired DEAD; GONE; OVER; UP
explain TELL

explanation KEY
expletive BLAST; DAMN
exploded, explodes, exploding anagram indicator
exploit DEED; FEAT; MILK; USE
exploited USED; anagram indicator
explorer COOK; CABOT; OATES; PARK; ROSS; SCOTT
explosion anagram indicator
explosive H; HE; SHELL; TNT; *see* EXPLOSIVE DEVICE
explosive device BOMB; CAP; MINE; SHELL
explosive, use BLAST
export omission indicator as "ice, one for export" clues CE (ie. 'i' to be omitted)
expose AIR; BARE; OUT; STRIP
express PUT; SAY; UTTER; VENT
express annoyance TUT
express disapproval BOO; HISS; TUT
express glee CROW
express pleasure PURR
express view OPINE
express weariness SIGH
expressed homophone indicator
expressed glee CREW
expression TERM
expression of aggression SNARL
expression of amazement WOW
expression of derision BOO; YAH
expression of disapproval AHEM
expression of disgust FIE; UGH; YUCK
expression of dismay HECK
expression of exultation WHOOP
expression of gratitude TA
expression of impatience PSHAW; TUT
expression of joy AH
expression of pain AGH; OW
expression of relief PHEW
expression of suffering GROAN
expression of surprise COR; EH; GOSH; LOR; MY; WELL
expression of sympathy THERE
expression of triumph AHA
expression of weariness SIGH

expression, relieved SIGH
exquisitely anagram indicator
extempore, extemporised anagram indicator
extend SPREAD
extend loan RENEW
extended LONG
extended (Scottish) LANG
extensive LONG; HIGH
extent AMBIT; LENGTH; SIZE; SCOPE; *see* SCOPE
extent (to some extent) run indicator
exterior nesting indicator
exterior, tough SHELL
extort WRING
extortionate anagram indicator
extra BYE; GASH; MORE; ODD; OVER; RISE; SPARE; WIDE
extra fifty changes an L to a C
extra, five changes a V to an X
extra five hundred changes a D to an M
extra note PS
extra payment BONUS
extract DERIVE; DRAW; EXT; MILK; PRESS; PUMP; run indicator
extracted DREW; OUT; TOOK; omission indicator
extraction DESCENT
extraordinary, extraordinarily anagram indicator
extractor MINER
extravagant FANCY; OTT; anagram indicator
extreme END; POLE; POLAR; UTTER; first or last letter indicator
extremely MOST; ULTRA; VERY; first and/or last letter indicator
extremes *see* EXTREMES OF
extremes of indicator of first and last letters of associated word(s); can also require AND to be inserted between the end letters of indicated word eg. "extremes of rascality" gives RANDY, "extremes of paranoia" gives PANDA; can indicate something to do with fingertips, nails, toes, etc
extreme characters *see* EXTREMES OF
extremis, in OTT; *see* EXTREMES OF
extremity END
exudes anagram indicator
exult CROW; GLOAT
exultation, cry of WHOOP
eye LOOK; OGLE; ORB; SEE

eye protector VISOR
eyesore SIGHT
eyewash SALVE; ROT; *see* RUBBISH

Ff

fabric CHINO; DIMITY; DUCK; LACE; LAME; LINEN; LISLE; NINON; RAYON; REP; SATIN; SERGE; TOILE; TWILL
fabrication LIE; LYING; MYTH
fabulous GREAT
fabulous bird ROC
facade FRONT; SHOW
face CLOCK; DIAL; FRONT; MEET; MUG; PAN; can refer to coal-face
face of initial letter indicator
face-saving device VISOR
faceless initial letter omission indicator
faced MET
faceless initial letter to be omitted
facet SIDE
facial feature BROW; CHIN; CHEEK; LIP; NOSE; *see* FEATURE
facial hair BEARD; GOATEE; TACHE
facile LIGHT; WEAK
facility EASE; ROOM
fact DEED; TRUTH
faction SET; SIDE; TEAM; WING *see* GROUP
factor PH
factory MILL; PLANT; WORKS
faculty FLAIR
fad CRAZE; RAGE
fade DIE; FLAG; PALE; TIRE
fade away DIE
faded PASSE; RUSTY

fading DYING; *see* FADE
fail DIE; FLUNK; LAPSE; LOSE; MISS; can indicate a verb beginning with UNDER
fail to see MISS
fail to win DRAW; LOSE
failed LOST
failing DYING; ERROR; FLAW; LAPSE
failing to see BLIND
failure DUD; FLOP; LAPSE; LOSER
faint DIM; PALE; WEAK
fair BRIGHT; EVEN; FINE; HONEST; JUST; LIGHT; PALE; RIGHT; SALE; WELL
fairly PRETTY
fairy ELF; PERI; PUCK
fairy tale LIE
faith BELIEF; TRUST
faithful TRUE
faithful woman NUN
fake BUM; COD; ERSATZ; FRAUD; SHAM
falcon SAKER
Falkland Islands FI
fall DIE; DIP; DRIP; DROOP; DROP; ERR; LAPSE; MISS; RAIN; SIN; SNOW; SPILL; STUMBLE; TRIP; TUMBLE
fall out FIGHT; SCRAP
fallen reverse indicator
fallow IDLE
false SHAM; anagram indicator; *see* FAKE
false impression LIE
falsified anagram indicator
falsify LIE
falter FLAG
fame NAME; REPUTE
familiar OLD; PAL; *see* FRIEND
family BLOOD; CLAN; FAM; HOUSE; KIN; RACE; SEPT
family member AUNT; GRAN; RELATION; SON; UNCLE; *see* FATHER, MOTHER
family, royal ORANGE; HOUSE
famine DEARTH
famous NOTED
famously WELL
famous horse ARKLE; BESS

fan BUFF; COOL
fancied to win HOT
fancy DREAM; FAD; GUESS; IDEA; LIKE; LOVE; NOTION; WHIM; anagram indicator
fanfare TUCKET
fantastic anagram indicator; can indicate something to do with a well-known legend or myth
far from REMOTE
far, too OVER
fare CHEER; CHOW; DO; EATS; FOOD; MEAL; TABLE; can indicate a specific food; *see* MEAL, FOOD
fare, child's HALF
farewell ADIEU; VALE
farm HOLDING; RANCH; SPREAD; STUD
farm animal BULL; COW; EWE; GOAT; PIG, RAM; SHEEP; SOW; STEER
farm building BARN; BYRE; STY
farm policy CAP
farmhouse BREAD; LOAF
farming scheme, European CAP
fascinated SMITTEN
fascinated by INTO
fascist leader DUCE
fashion CULT; DRESS; FORGE; FORM; MODE; RAGE; SHAPE; STYLE; TON; TONE; TREND; VOGUE; WAY; anagram indicator
fashion designer DIOR
fashion, man of RAKE
fashion, people of TON
fashionable CHIC; HOT; IN; SWELL; anagram indicator
fashionable crowd TON
fashioned anagram indicator
fast FIRM; LENT; NIPPY; PACY; SPEEDY; STUCK; can indicate something to do with Lent, Ash Wednesday
fast days EMBER
fast, held STUCK
fast, move DART; HASTEN; RACE; RUN; RUSH; SPEED
fast, moved RAN; SPED
fast, went RAN; SPED
fasten BIND; CLIP; CLOSE; FIX; LASH; LOCK; NAIL; PIN; SCREW; SEAL; TAPE; TIE; ZIP
fastener CLIP; HASP; LOCK; NAIL; NUT; PIN; SCREW; STAPLE;

STUD; ZIP

fastening KNOT; TIE

fastidious CHARY; NICE; PICKY

fat BUTTER; DRIPPING; DUMPY; ESTER; GROSS; LARD; PLUMP; STOUT; SUET

fat, very OS

fatal DIRE

fate DOOM; LOT

fateful day IDES

father DA; DAD; FR; PA; PATER; POP; SIRE

Father, Old usually refers to the Thames

fatigue TIRE

fatigued DRAWN; TIRED; WEARY

fault BLIP; BUG; ERROR; HITCH; PRIDE; SHORT (ie. elec.); SIN; SLIP; VICE

fault, at anagram indicator

fault, find CARP

faulty DUFF; anagram indicator

faulty item DUD; REJECT

faux pas SLIP

favour BOON; GRACE; HELP; LIKE

favour, in FOR; PRO

favour of, not in AGIN; ANTI; CON

favourable PRO [BOON]

favoured IN; PET; POPULAR

favouring FOR; PRO

favourite PET

FBI agent FED

fear ALARM; AWE; DREAD; TERROR

fearful anagram indicator

fearless BRAVE

feast JUNKET

feat DEED

feather PLUME

feathers DOWN

feathery accessory BOA

feature MARK; PROPERTY; STAR; TRAIT; often indicates a facial feature commonly CHIN, EAR, NOSE; also can indicate a distinctive part of anything (eg. with reference to a limb can indicate a particular bone) or something essential (eg. as a ball is to snooker); when related to a place (eg. as a geographic feature) can refer to a specific river, mountain, etc

feature, geographic PLAIN; *see* FEATURE

feature of run indicator

featured BILLED (ie. as on a poster)

features MOVIES; STARS; *see* FEATURE

February FEB; within the context of the clue (with some reference to omission) can indicate FIVE or FIFTH (ie. it is the month usually missing the fifth week!)

fed-up BLUE; BORED; DEF; FULL; LOW

federal agents CIA; GMEN (ie. G-men)

federation FED

fee SUM

feeble FRAIL; LAME; LIMP; SAD; WEAK; WET

feeble individual WIMP

feed STOKE

feel GROPE; SENSE; TOUCH

feel bad AIL; RESENT

feel ill AIL

feeling HEART; HUNCH; MOOD; SENSE

feeling, bad ODIUM

feet HOOVES; IAMBI

feet, several YARD

feline CAT; LYNX; *see* CAT

fell DIED; DOWN; MOOR; SKIN; anagram indicator

felled DOWN

fellow BOD; CHAP; CO (ie. co- as in co-worker); COVE; DON; F; GENT; GUY; MAN; MATE; PEER; can refer to a man's name; *see* MAN

fellow, Aussie SPORT

fellow, that HIM

fellows FF; MEN

felony CRIME

female DOE; F; HEN; MISS; MS; SHE; SISTER; can refer to a woman's name; *see* GIRL, WOMAN; can indicate that a word ends in -ESS

female, a French UNE

female, characterised as DISTAFF

female dress, gear DRAG

female teacher MISS

female's HER

fence PALE; PICKET

fencing KENDO; PALING
fend off WARD
ferment BREW; anagram indicator
ferment, cause of YEAST
fermented, fermenting anagram indicator
festival EASTER; FETE; WHIT
festive JOLLY
festive meal SPREAD
festive season NOEL; YULE
festivity GALA
fetch BRING; DOUBLE; GET
fetch up LAND
fetish TOTEM
fever AGUE
feverish HECTIC; anagram indicator
few SOME; small number, TWO, THREE, FOUR
few words NOTE
Fiat UNO
fib LIE
fibre ISTLE; JUTE; STRING; *see* FILAMENT
fibrous STRINGY
fiction FIB; LEGEND; LIE; NOVEL; STORY; TALE
fiddle BOW; CON; FIX; RIG; SCAM; SCRAPE; STRAD; TINKER; anagram indicator
fiddle cash LAUNDER
fiddle, part of NECK; STRING
fiddle with FIX; RIG
fiddled, fiddling anagram indicator
field AREA; ENTRY; DOMAIN; GROUND; LAND; LEA; PITCH
field event HAMMER
field, one in *see* FIELDER
field, part of OFF; ON
fielder POINT; SLIP
fielding OUT
fielding position COVER; GULLY; MIDON (ie. mid-on); POINT; SLIP
fiend DEMON; DEVIL
fiery HOT
fifties, boy of TED
fifty L

fifty cards DECK; PACK
fifty extra changes an L to a C
fifty-one LI
Figaro BARBER
fight BOUT; BOX; BRAWL; CLASH; FENCE; MELEE; MATCH; MILL; ROW; SCRAP; SETTO; SPAR; TIFF; TILT
fight, prepare to ARM
fighter BOXER; FENCER; ZERO
fighter, old VET
fighters ARMY; WING
fighting ACTION; FRAY; WAR
fighting force TA; *see* ARMY
fighting man BOXER; FENCER; *see* SOLDIER
figure BUILD; CIRCLE; CONE; FIG; FORM; M; NUMBER; OBLONG; PRICE; SHAPE; SQUARE; TRIANGLE; *see* NUMBER
figure-head F
figures, set of TABLE
filament HAIR; STRAND; THREAD
file LINE; LIST; MARCH; RASP; ROW
fill CHARGE
fill up BRIM; TOP
filling nesting indicator
filling, sandwich HAM
film CINE; COAT; COVER; EPIC; ET; FLICK; GREASE; LAYER; LOOP; MIST; MOVIE; PANC; PIC; PSYCHO; REEL; ROLL; SHINE; SHOOT; SKIN; SPOOL
film actress GARBO; LOREN
film extra EXTRA
film, make SHOOT
film, piece of CLIP
film shot TAKE
film star COOPER; GABLE
filter STRAIN
filth DIRT; GRIME; SMUT
filthy place STY
final END; LAST; NET; NETT; ULT; last letter(s) indicator
final check MATE
final letter Z
final piece CODA
final words PS
finale END; last letter(s) indicator

finalist last letter indicator
finally last letter(s) indicator
finally going last letter to be omitted
finance BACK
finance house BANK
financial adviser CA
financial centre NY; N
financial obligations IOUS
find LOCATE; TRACE
find answer CRACK; SOLVE
find fault CARP
find not guilty CLEAR
find out anagram of FIND
fine AI; DANDY; F; FAIR; GOOD; OK; OKAY; RIGHT; SHEER; THIN
fine fabric LACE
fine one PEACH
fine rain, spray MIST
finest BEST
finger on, lay a TOUCH
finish AMEN; CEASE; CLOSE; EDGE; END; ENDING; KILL; STOP; last letter indicator
finish off END
finish off, something to ENDER
finished DEAD; DONE; OVER; PAST; THROUGH; UP
finishing END; last letter(s) indicator
Finland, Finnish SUOMI
fir PINE
fire FLAME; INGLE; LOB; PYRE; SACK; SHOOT
fire to, set LIGHT; TORCH
firearm GUN; GAT; RIFLE
fired LIT; anagram indicator
fired again RELIT
fireplace INGLE
firework CRACKER; SQUIB
firm CO; CONSTANT; COY; FAST; HARD; SET; SOLID; STABLE; STEADY; STIFF; STRONG; SURE; TIGHT
firmness STEEL
firm hold CINCH; GRIP
first A; ALPHA; ARCH; I; IST; LEADING; ONE; PRIME; PROTO; TOP; initial letter(s) indicator; ordering indicator

first, be B; LEAD; WIN
first class AI; C; GRAND; TOPS
first couple of first two letters of subsequent word to be used
first eleven E; K (ie. position in the alphabet)
first, go G; LEAD
first, gone G; LED
first lady EVE; L
first light DAWN; L
first man ADAM; M
first person ADAM; I; P
first rate A; ACE; AI; AONE (ie. AI); CLASS; CRACK; PRIME; R
first thirteen letters ATOM (ie. A to M)
first sixteen letters ATOP (ie. A to P)
first, was LED; W
first week W; can refer to Genesis
first woman EVE; W
fish ANGLE; BASS; BIB; BREAM; BRILL; BRIT; DAB; CARP; CATCH; CHAR; CHARR; CHUB; COD; DORY; EEL; FLOUNDER; GAR; GOBY; HAG; HAKE; IDE; KIPPER; LING; LOACH; PARR; PERCH; PIKE; PLAICE; POUT; RAY; ROACH; RUFF; RUFFE; SCAD; SCHOOL; SHAD; SHINER; SMELT; SOLE; SPRAT; SWIMMER; TENCH; TOPE; TRAWL; TROLL; TROUT; TUNA; TUNNY
fish basket CREEL
fish, bit of FINGER
fish eg.gs ROE
fish, part of, piece of GILL; FIN; SCALE
fisherman ANGLER; WALTON
fishing-spear GAFFE
fishy ODD; RUM
fishy, something CRAN (a measure of fish catch)
fissure CRACK; RENT
fist DUKE; PUNCH
fit ABLE; AGUE; AI; APT; BOUT; HALE; HEALTHY; MOOD; PET; RIGHT; SOUND; SUIT; TRIM; WELL;
fit out EQUIP
fitfully anagram indicator
fitly ABLY
fitness FORM
fitted ABLE
fitter BETTER

fitting APT; PROPER; RIGHT
Fitzgerald ELLA
five V
five centavos COLON
five dollar bill FIN
five extra changes a V to an X
five hundred D; MONKEY; THOU (ie. half a thousand!)
five hundred extra changes a D to an K
five hundred pounds MONKEY
fix AMEND; CLAMP; CLIP; CURE; EMBED; FASTEN; NAIL; PICKLE; PIN; PLACE; REPAIR; RIG; RIVET; SCREW; SET; SPOT; STAPLE; STEW; WANGLE; anagram indicator; *see* PICKLE
fixed PRESET; SET; STABLE; STUCK; SURE; anagram indicator
fixer HYPO
fixing anagram indicator
fixing device CLIP; NAIL; PIN; RIVET; SCREW
fixture AWAY; DATE; HOME; TIE; VENUE
fixture, part of LEG
fizzle out DIE
flag COLOUR; DROOP; ENSIGN; FADE; FALTER; HAIL; IRIS; JACK; PAVE; PENNON; PIN; SAG; STANDARD; STREAMER; TAG; TIRE; WAVE; WILT; can indicate something to do with pavement [associated word: POLEJ]
flagrant GROSS
flame BEAU; FIRE; LOVER
flame, old EX
flaming HOT
flan TART
flanks first and last letters indicator
flanks, both LR; RL
flap BUSTLE; COVER; TAB; TODO (ie. to-do)
flapping anagram indicator
flash GLEAM; LINE; SECOND; STREAK; STRIP
flashy JAZZY; SHOWY
flat BANAL; DULL; EVEN; LEVEL; MAT; MATT; PAD; PLAIN; PRONE
flatfish PLAICE; SKATE
flats can indicate something to do with theatrical scenery
flatter TOADY
flattery SOAP; UNCTION

flaunting anagram indicator
flavour SPICE; TANG; TASTE
flavouring ANISE; SPICE
flaw BLEMISH; *see* BLEMISH
flay SKIN
fleck SPOT
fled RAN
flee BOLT; FLY; RUN
fleece COVER; HAIR; ROB; SHEAR; STRIP; WEB; can indicate something to do with the Golden Fleece, Jason, Argonauts etc
fleet ARMADA; FAST; NAVY; RAPID; SWIFT
flesh, loose WATTLE
fleshly CARNAL
flex CORD
flexible LIMP
flew FLED
flier BADER; BAT; PILOT; TIT; WING; *see* BIRD
fliers RAF
flies JETS
flight FLOCK; LAM; TRIP; can indicate something to do with stairs eg. CARACOLE, NEWEL, STAIR, STEP; can require that a word is to be followed by UP eg. 'catch flight' can clue TRIP UP
flight, put to ROUT
flight, short HOP
fling CAST; HURL; SHY; THROW; TOSS; *see* PARTY
flip anagram indicator
flirt SPOON
flirtation DALLIANCE
flit FLEE
flitted FLED
flock DROVE
flog LICK; SELL
flood SPATE; can indicate something to do with Noah's Ark
flooded AWASH
floodland FEN; MARSH
floor DECK; DOWN; STOREY
floozie TART
flop BOMB; TURKEY
florid RED
Florida town TAMPA

flounder DAB; WALLOW
floundering anagram indicator
flourish SHAKE; TUCKET; WAVE
flourished, flourishing anagram indicator
flow CURRENT; RUN; STREAM
flowed RAN
flower ASTER; BELL; BLOOM; FLAG; GLAD; PICK; POPPY; PRIME; ROSE; TULIP; *see* PLANT; *also an old standby to signal a river; see* RIVER
flower, blue NILE
flower-part PETAL; STAMEN; STEM
flower, white NILE
flowery can indicate something to do with flowers, see flower-part
flowing RUNNY; anagram indicator
flue DUCT; VENT
fluent GLIB
fluff BOTCH; BUNGLE; DOWN
fluent, insincerely GLIB
flunk FAIL
flush SCOUR; SWILL
flushed RED
flustered anagram indicator
flutter BET; can indicate something to do with a bird or a flag
fluttering anagram indicator
fly BOT; CADDIS; FLEE; FLIT; GLIDE; GNAT; HACKLE; HOVER; JET; RACE; RUSH; SOAR; WING; ZOOM
fly-by-night BAT; MOTH; OWL
flyer AD; PILOT; can indicate a bird; *see* BIRD, FLIER
flyers' decoration AFM
flying anagram indicator
flying ace BADER
flying, one can indicate a bird see bird
flying saucer UFO
Flynn ERROL
focus AIM; HUB
fog FRET; MIST
fold BEND; CLOSE; CREASE; PEN; PLEAT
folder BINDER
folio LEAF; PAGE
folk KIN; MEN

folks KIN
follow DOG; SHADOW; STALK; TAG; TAIL; TRACK
follower, a B
followers SCHOOL
following F; NEXT
following example AFTER
food BRAN; BREAD; BUN; CAKE; CHOP; CHOW; DIET; DISH; eg.G; ENTREE; FARE; FODDER; GRUB; HAM; MEAL; MEAT; NOSH; PASTA; RICE; STEAK; TABLE; TART; TOAST; TUCK; WAFFLE; *see* COURSE, MEAL, MEAT
food, Australian TUCKER
food, health BRAN
food, invalid PAP
food, selection of DIET
food, soft PAP
food, sweet JAM
food store DELI
fool ASS; CHUMP; CLOT; COD; DUMMY; DUNCE; DUPE; GIT; GOOSE; JESTER; KID; LOON; MUG; NERD; NIT; NOODLE; NUT; NUTTER; PRAT; PUDDING; SAP; SUCKER; TWERP; TWIT; rem: can also mean a dessert
fool, Australian DILL
foolhardy RASH
foolish DUMB; MAD; RASH; SILLY; SIMPLE; anagram indicator
foolish person ASS; *see* FOOL
foolishly anagram indicator
foot BASE; FT; HOOF; PAD; PAEON; PAW; SPONDEE; TOOTSY; TROTTER
foot, part of ARCH; SOLE
football team FOREST; SPURS; UNITED
footballer BACK; FORWARD; KEEPER; PELE; STRIKER; WING
football match TIE
footer can indicate a dancer
footing, on equal PAR
footwear BOOT; CLOG; HOSE; OXFORD; SHOE; SLIPPER; SOCK
for PER; PRO; TO; can indicate that the definition follows
for each PER
for example EG; SAY
for French AU; POUR
for instance EG; SAY

for me MY
for sale GOING
for us OUR
for, Spanish POR
forbidden OUT
forbidding DOUR; GRIM; STERN
force COERCE; CRAM; DRIVE; DYNE; F; G; JAM; MAKE; MIGHT; MUSCLE; POWER; PRESS; PRISE; RAF; RAM; RUC; STRESS; TA; can indicate something to do with the police
force, elite (British, special) SAS
force, fighting TA etc; *see* ARMY
force, in ING (ie. in + g); VALID
force of law POSSE; *see* POLICEMEN
force, remove by OUST; REAVE
force to flee, fly ROUT
forced MADE; anagram indicator
forceful HARD; PUNCHY; STERN; TELLING
forcing anagram indicator
ford CROSS
Ford's preferred colour BLACK
fore FRONT; VAN
foreign ALIEN; ODD; STRANGE; anagram indicator
foreign, a EIN; UN, UNE
foreign article DER; EIN; EL; IL; LA; LE; LES; UN; UNE
foreign articles UNDER
foreign city AIX; ROME; PARIS
foreign coin *see* FOREIGN CURRENCY
foreign currency COLON; DM; FRANC; GUILDER; LIRA; LIRE; MARK; ROUBLE
foreign friend AMI
foreign hotel PENSION
foreign language LANGUE
Foreign Office FO
foreign private GI
foreign royalty ROI
foreign soldier GI
foreign, the DER; EL; IL; LA; LE; LES
foreign title PASHA
foreigner ALIEN
foreman GAFFER

foremost BEST; TOP; first letter(s) indicator
forepart FRONT; PROW
forest ARDEN; BLACK; DEAN; JUNGLE; WOOD
Forester's book GUN (ie. 'The Gun')
forged MADE; anagram indicator
forget MISS
forgetful ABSENT
forgotten LOST
fork Y
forked, something Y
form BED; BENCH; CAST; CLASS; MAKE; SEAT; SHAPE; anagram indicator
form of anagram indicator for the words that follow
formal DRY; STIFF
formal attire TAILS
formal gathering BALL; DANCE; MEET
formality ICE; STARCH
formation anagram indicator
formed MADE
formed in run indicator
former EX; LATE; ONCE; OLD; PAST
formerly EX; LATE; NEE; ONCE; can indicate that a component is to be placed at the front
former pupil OB
former pupils OBS
formidable GRIM
formulated anagram indicator
fortepiano FP
forth ON
forthcoming, not COY; SHY
forthright BLUNT
fortress CASTLE; TOWER
fortune BOMB; DOOM; LOT; LUCK; MINT; PILE
fortification CAMP; KEEP; REDAN; WALL
fortified place KEEP
fortitude COURAGE; GRIT
forty XL
forty-nine IL
forty ponies GRAND
forty winks NAP

forward AHEAD; ON; PERT
foul EVIL; VILE
fouled anagram indicator
found BASE; CAST; START; run indicator; anagram indicator
found, are LIE
found everywhere COMMON
found here run indicator
found in run indicator; nesting indicator
found out nesting indicator
foundation BASE; CAUSE; FOOT; REASON; ROCK; START
founded anagram indicator
founder SINK
foundered SANK
foundering anagram indicator
four IV
four pints GAL
fourth-rate D
fowl HEN; SULTAN
fractured anagram indicator
fragment BIT; CHIP; PIECE; SHRED; SNATCH
fragrance AROMA
frame CASE; CHASE; PLAN; nesting indicator; run indicator
frame (under skirt) BUSTLE
frame of mind MOOD; TEMPER
framed, frames nesting indicator; run indicator
France (formerly) GAUL
France in EN
France in, or OU
France, that in QUE
France, well in BIEN
Francis DRAKE
frank BLUNT; HONEST; PLAIN; STAMP
frantic MAD; anagram indicator
frantically anagram indicator
fraud CON; FAKE; SCAM; STING
fray RUB
free DELIVER; LOOSE; OPEN; RID; UNTIE; anagram indicator; can indicate a phrase beginning with NO (eg. NO CHARGE)
free play VENT
free transport LIFT

freedom EASE
freeloader SPONGE
freely LIEF; anagram indicator
freewheel COAST
freezing BITTER; GELID
French F; FR; the use of a French locality in a clue, commonly Paris, Nice, can indicate that a French word is required; *see* BELOW
French actor TATI
French alternative OU
French are ES
French art ES
French author *see* FRENCH WRITER
French authoress SAND
French beach PLAGE
French bed LIT
French biography VIE
French book ROMAN
French, by DE
French city NANCY
French coin, old SOU
French collaborator PETAIN
French company CIE
French dear CHER
French department OISE
French drink VIN
French fashion TON
French for POUR
French, first person in JE
French friend AMI
French good BON
French house MAISON
French husband MARI
French, in DE; EN
French is EST
French island ILE
French kiosk TABAC
French nobleman DUC
French novel ROMAN
French novelist SAND
French, of DE; DES; DU

French or OU
French plainsong CHANT
French port BREST
French pussy CHAT
French refusal NON
French resort NICE
French, second person in TU
French she ELLE
French, some DES
French, speaks in DIT
French state ETAT
French street RUE
French, the LA; LE; LES
French, this CE
French to A; ALA (ie. a la); AU; AUX
French town BREST; NANCY; NICE; TOUR
French trip TOUR
French, very TRES
French what QUOI
French where OU
French wine VIN
French writer CAMUS; GIDE; SAND
Frenchman FROG; M; RENE
frenzied MAD; anagram indicator
frenzy, in a anagram indicator
frequency, high OFTEN
frequent COMMON
frequently FR; OFT; OFTEN
fresh BRACING; CLEAN; CHEEKY; CHILLY; FORWARD; IMPRUDENT; LATE; NEW; PERT; anagram indicator
fresh, not OFF; STALE
fret BAR; CHAFE; FOG; MIST; MOPE; WORRY
Freudian concept ID
friction, cause RUB
friend ALLY; AMI; BUD; BUDDY; CHINA; CHUM; COCK; CRONY; MATE; PAL
friend, American BUD; BUDDY
friend, familiar COCK
friend, French AMI
friendly KIND; PALLY

friendly AFFABLE; GESTURE; PAT
friendship AMITY
frighten COW; SCARE
frightening SCARY
frigidity ICE
frill RUFF
fringe BORDER; EDGE; *see* HAIR; can indicate something to do with Edinburgh (ie. via The Fringe)
fringe benefit PERK
frisky anagram indicator
fritter away time POTTER
frivolous LIGHT; SHALLOW
frock DRESS
frolic CAPER; LARK
from EX; OFF; OUT; run indicator; can indicate that the definition precedes (i.e. before the word 'from')
front BOW; FACE; FACADE; FORE; HEAD; LEAD; PROW; SHOW; VAN; first letter/word indicator; preceding indicator; can indicate something to do with weather, meteorology
front, in AHEAD; HEADING; LEADING
front, was in LED; WON
frontage first letter indicator
frontal first letter/word indicator
fronted first letter/word indicator; preceding indicator
frontier BORDER; MARCH
frost RIME
frozen FRIGID
frozen, more NUMBER (one of the classic chestnuts)
fruit ACORN; APPLE; BERRY; CONE; DATE; FIG; GRAPE; HAW; HIP; ISSUE; LIME; MAST; NUT; OLIVE; PEACH; PEAR; PLUM; PRUNE; SLOE
fruit cake NUT; NUTTER
frumpish DRAB; DOWDY
frustrate BAFFLE; DASH; FOIL; SCOTCH
FT PAPER; can indicate something to do with PINK (as the newspaper)
fudge COOK
fuel COAL; COKE; DERV; FIRE; GAS; OIL; PEAT; PETROL; STOKE
fuel, add STOKE
fugitive RUNNER

full FAT
full range AZ (ie, range of alphabet)
full set BEARD
fulminate RAGE
fumbled anagram indicator
fun JEST; LARK; PLAY; SPORT
function DO; EVENT; GO; JOB; PART; PARTY; ROLE; USE; WORK; can refer to a mathematical function, commonly COS, LOG, SINE
functioning ON
fund KITTY; SUB
funding *see* FUNDS
funds AID; BACKING; PURSE
funerary receptacle URN
funnel HOPPER
funnily anagram indicator
funny COMIC; DROLL; ODD; STRANGE; RUM; anagram indicator
funny fellow FISH
funny, very KILLING
fur NAP; SABLE
furious CROSS; MAD; anagram indicator
furious, become SEERED (ie. see red)
furiously anagram indicator
furnish EQUIP
furniture BED; BUNK; CHAIR; COT; COUCH; DRESSER; PRESS; SOFA; STAND; STOOL; TABLE
furniture, old LUMBER
furrow RIDGE; RUT
further ELSE; MORE; SERVE; in conjunction with verb can indicate the use of RE as a prefix
furtiveness STEALTH
fury ANGER; IRE; RAGE; anagram indicator
furze GORSE; WHIN
fuse SOLDER; WELD
fuss ADO; DO; DUST; LATHER; POTHER; RANT; ROW; STINK
fuss, make a CREATE
fusing, fussy anagram indicator
future can indicate something to do with tense ie. future tense in grammar

Gg

gad WANDER
Gael SCOT
Gaelic ERSE
gaffe BLUNDER; ERROR
gag VOMIT
gain WIN
gain access HACK
gaiter SPAT
gale BLOW; WIND
gall ANGER
gallery GODS; TATE; can indicate something to with rogue ie. via rogue's gallery
gallery, contents of ART
gallery, modern ICA
gallop CANTER
galloped RAN; SPED
gamble BACK; BET; CHANCE; DICE; LAY; PLAY; PUNT; SPEC; STAKE; WAGER
gambled LAYED
gambler BETTER; PUNTER; STAKER; TAKER
gambling LOTTO
gambling centre RENO
gambol PRANCE; ROMP
gambolling anagram indicator
game BINGO; BOWLS; BRIDGE; DARTS; FARO; FOOTER; FOWL; FRAME; GO; LAME; LOO; LOTTO; MATCH; NAP; NIM; POLO; RAG; RU; RUGGER; RUSE; SOLO; SPORT; TAG; TRICK; WHIST; *see* CARD GAME; can indicate something to do with hunted animal
game, board GO
game, card *see* CARD GAME
game taken BAG
game's ending MATE
games FE; PT; RUBBER; SET; SPORT
games, number of RUBBER; SET

gammon ROT
gander LOOK; PEEK
gang BAND; CREW; CROWD; HORDE; LOT; MOB; RING; SQUAD; SWARM; TEAM
gang-leader G
gangster AL; CAPONE; HOOD
gap VENT
garb DRESS
garbled anagram indicator
garden BED; EDEN; HOE; PARK; PATCH; PLOT; WEED
garden equipment FORK; HOE; MOWER; SPADE
garden suburb KEW
garden tool *see* GARDEN EQUIPMENT
gardener, contrary MARY
gardens HOES; KEW
garish LOUD
garland LEI
garlic ALLIUM
garlic, segment of CLOVE
garment BRA; CAPE; CLOAK; COAT; DRESS; GOWN; HABIT; LUNGI; MINI; MAXI; ROBE; SKIRT; SLIP; STOLE; VEST; *see* CLOTHING
garment, old TOGA
garment, scant MINI; THONG
garment, tiny THONG
garret ATTIC
garter ORDER
gas A; ARGON; CHAT; CL; CS; H; HE; N; NE; NEON; O; RADON; SPEECH; TALK; WAFFLE; XE
gash CUT
gasp PANT
gat ROD
gate CROWD; PORTAL; WICKET
gatehouse LODGE
gatekeeper PORTER
Gateshead G
gateway DOOR; PORTAL
gather AMASS; CONTRACT; DRAW; GLEAN; HEAR; INFER; MARSHAL; MEET; MUSTER
gathering CROWD; DO; MASS; MEET; PARTY; RALLY; anagram indicator

gathering, formal BALL
gauge METER; TIMER
gave birth BORE
gave off SHED
gay, openly OUT
gave up QUIT
gaze EYE; GLARE
gaze at EYE;
gear COG; DRESS; KIT; RIG; can indicate something to do with clothes, or engine
gear, female DRAG
geese GAGGLE
Geller URI
gem AGATE; GARNET; OPAL; PEARL; RUBY; STONE
gemstone *see* GEM
gen DOPE
gender SEX
general AVERAGE; BROAD; COMMON; CUSTER; G; GEN; LEE; RIFE; THUMB; WOLFE
general effect TONE
general, small THUMB
general's assistant ADC
generate CAUSE; START
generous AMPLE; LARGE; NOBLE
Genesis BIRTH
genetic material DNA
Genoa SAIL
gent NOB; TOFF; *see* MAN
gentle MILD; P; TAME; TENDER
gentleman G; GN; SIR
gentlemen LOO
gently P
gently wash LAP
genuine ECHT; HONEST; REAL; RIGHT; STRAIGHT; TRUE
genuine, not SHAM
genus BREED; SORT; TYPE
geological specimen ROCK
George can indicate something to do with automatic pilot
Georgia GA
germ SEED

German D; G; GER; HANS; HERR; HUN; VON
German, a EIN
German article DAS; DER; DIE; EIN
German car AUDI
German city EMS; ESSEN; TRIER
German consent JA
German currency DM; M; MARK
German east OST
German, famous GOETHE
German gentleman HERR
German how WIE
German is IST
German joiner UND
German, old FRANK
German poet HEINE
German quarter OST
German state LAND; REICH
German, the DER; DIE
German wine WEIN
German with MIT
German woman FRAU
German writer MANN
Germany D; GER
Gershwin IRA
gesture BECKON; SIGN
gesture of affection CARESS; KISS
get CATCH; COP; EARN; FETCH; TAKE; TWIG; inclusion indicator
get a load of COP
get a move on *see* RUN
get airborne FLY
get annoyed RILE
get beaten LOSE
get better RALLY; RISE
get better of BEAT; PIP
get by COPE
get excited ELATE; WOW
get from run indicator
get imprisoned INTERN
get lost SHOO

get money EARN
get off ALIGHT; LIGHT
get on AGE; BOARD; MOUNT
get on well CLICK
get over CLEAR; VAULT
get ready RIPEN; EARN
get rid of DELETE; DITCH; DROP; DUMP; EJECT; FIRE; KICK; OUT; PURGE; SACK; SCRAP; SHED; SLING; TRIM; ZAP; can indicate that the answer is a verb beginning with DE as 'get rid of shadow' clues DETAIL (ie. de-tail)
get rid of mess CLEAN
get to REACH
get to know LEARN
get together ALLY; BAND; UNITE
get up RISE; STAND; STIR; reverse order indicator
get very excited OVERHEAT
get weary FLAG; TIRE
get well CURE; HEAL
gets HAS
gets up reverse order indicator
getting on AGEING; AGED; LATE; OLD; OLDER
ghastly WHITE
ghetto SLUM
ghost SPIRIT
giant HUGE; OGRE; TITAN
gibe BARB; CRACK; GUY; MOCK; TAUNT
Gibraltar ROCK
giddy LIGHT
GI's shop PX
gift DOWER; PRESENT; TIP
Gilbertian princess IDA
gin TRAP
gipsy queen MEG
girder(s) can indicate something to do with a form of clothing around the waist
girl ADA; ANN; ANNA; AVA; BETH; CATHY; CHLOE; CLARE; CORA; DAM; DI; DAWN; DEE; DOLL; ELLA; EVA; EVE; GAL; HER; IDA; IRENE; ISLA; IVY; JO; JOY; KATE; KITTY; LASS; LILY; LISA; LULU; MAE; MAI; MARY; MAUD; MAY; MILLIE; MISS; MOLL; MOLLIE; NELL; NORMA; PAM; PENNY; POLLY; RITA; ROSA; ROSE; RUTH; SAL; SOPHY;

SUE; TESS; TRU; UNA; VAL; VERA; VI; VIV; use of 'girl' usually signifies the name is shortened; *see* LITTLE GIRL
girl, attractive DISH; DOLL
girl, good-time TART
girl, little DI; SAL; SIS; SUE; VAL; VI; *see* GIRL
girl, presentable DEB
girlfriend DATE; FLAME; STEADY; LOVER
girl's DIS; HER
gist DRIFT; POINT
give ALLOT; DOLE; HAND; PRESENT; RENDER
give a hand AID; CLAP; HELP
give details RETAIL; TELL
give instructions BRIEF; TEACH; TRAIN; TELL
give off, out EMIT
give pleasure TICKLE
give up CEDE; DROP; FORSAKE; KICK; QUIT; RESIGN
give voice SING
give way CEDE; DEFER; SAG; YIELD
given, be GET
given orders BOSSED
gives anagram indicator
glad HAPPY
glade ARBOUR
gladly LIEF
glamorous GLAM
glance LOOK
glare GAZE; GLOWER
glass JAR; LENS; PANE; PONY; TUMBLER
glasses SPECS
glaze SIZE
gleam FLASH; GLINT; SHINE; TRACE
glean GATHER
glee, expressed CREW
glib PAT
glide SKATE; SOAR
glimpse SIGHT
glittering GARISH
glitzy GLAM
globe EARTH; O; ORB
gloomy DARK; DISMAL; DULL; GREY; SABLE

gloomy dean INGE (one-time Dean of St Pauls)
gloomy type MOPER
glory PRAISE
gloss SHEEN; SHINE
glossy SLEEK
glove MITT; MITTEN
glower STARE
glowing coal EMBER
glue PASTE; SIZE; STICK
glum MOROSE
glut GORGE
glutton HOG; PIG
gnash GRATE
gnaw CHEW
gnome MORAL
go CRACK; EXIT; LEAVE; PEP; SCAT; SHOO; SHOT; STAB; TRY; TURN; WEND; WORK
go after CHASE; ENSUE
go ahead LEAD; LEAVE
go ashore LAND
go astray ERR; SIN; WANDER
go away SHOO
go back RETIRE
go down DIE; DIP
go down quickly DIVE
go fast BELT; HURTLE; NIP
go North of the Border GANG
go off ADDLE; ROT; SOUR; TURN
go out DIE
go over CROSS; OG; RECAP; VAULT
go over again RELIVE
go quickly BELT
go round EDDY; ROLL; SPIN; TURN
go round corner BEND
go slowly LINGER
go through RIFLE
go to BASH
go to court, law SUE
go to Paris ALLER
go up CLIMB; reverse indicator

go wrong ERR; anagram indicator
goad EGG; POKE; PRESS; PROD; PUSH; URGE
goal AIM; CROSS; END
goal, put ball into NET; SCORE
goalie SAVER
goat BILLY; KID; NANNY
god FAUN; IDOL; INDRA; KAMA; MARS; PAN; PLUTO; RA; THOR; TITAN
God, Thank DG
God Willing DV
goddess DIANA; HEBE; HERA; KALI; VENUS
gods can indicate something to do with theatre seats
goes across one element to span another
Goethe can indicate something to do with Faust
going EXIT; OFF; ON
going by VIA
going down DESCENT
going into nesting indicator
going off HIGH; TURNING
going out EGRESS
going round reversal indicator; nesting indicator
going through nesting indicator
going up reverse indicator
gold AU; BULL; OR; SPECIE
gold coin SOV
gold measure CARAT
gold-plated an element to be nested within O and R
golf GAME; SPORT; [BIRDIE; CLUB; EAGLE; GREEN; HOOK; IRON; PRO; TEE]
Golf CAR
golf-ball GUTTA
golf course TROON
golf club DRIVER; *see* CLUB
golf shot PUT; PUTT
golf tournament OPEN
gone BY; LATE; LEFT; PAST; WENT
gone ahead LED
gone back reversal indicator
gone first LED
gone off HIGH; LEFT; TURNED

gone round nesting indicator
gone through MET
Goneril's father LEAR
gong MC; MEDAL
good BON; FAIR; FINE; G; HIGH; OK; PI; PIOUS; RIGHT; can indicate some religious association as "good book" for Bible, "good man" for saint etc
good book AV; BIBLE; JER; JUDGES; *see* BOOK
good deal BAGS; LOT; MANY
good deal of, a most of a word to be used
good French BON
good hand FLUSH
good in Scotland GUID
good-looking DISHY
good man S; ST
good-natured NICE
good, not BAD; ILL; OFF
good queen BESS
good reason, with RIGHTLY
good result GAIN; WIN
good sort BRICK
good thing BOON
good time FUN
good time girl TART
good, very ACE; AI
goodbye VALE
goodness LUMME (contraction of 'Lord love me!'); MY (ie. exclamation)
goods FREIGHT; LINE; STUFF; WARES
goodwill AMITY
Goodwood COURSE
goody-goody PI; PRIG
goose BRENT; EIDER; MUTT; SAP
gorge EAT; GULCH; OVEREAT
gorse WHIN
gory BLOODY; RED
gosh COR; GEE; LORD; MY; OOPS
gospel can indicate a Biblical book eg. MARK
gossip CHAT; CHATTER; GAB; JAW; NOISE; RAP; RATTLE; TATTLE; YAP
Gotham NY; can refer to some aspect of New York

got TOOK
got rid of FIRED; SACKED; SHED
got up ROSE
governed, being UNDER
governed by UNDER
governess ANNA
governing body BOARD
government REIN; REIGN; RULE; STATE
government department FO; MOD
government, place in FO
government official WHIP
governor BEY; BOSS; DAD; HE; HEAD; PA; POP
gown ROBE
grab SNATCH
grab greedily HOG
grabbing nesting indicator; run indicator
grace POISE
grade A; B; C; CLASS; D; E; MARK; LEVEL
graduate BA; BE; BED; BSC; MA; MBA; PASS
graft SPLICE
grain CORN; GR
grain, remainder of BRAN
grain store SILO
grains SAND
grand BIG; EPIC; G; K
grandma *see* GRANDMOTHER
grandmother GRAN; NAN
granny KNOT; *see* GRANDMOTHER
grant ALLOW; CEDE; CONFER; DOLE; LET; YIELD
grape juice MUST
graph CHART
grapple with TACKLE
grasp HOLD; SEE; SEIZE
grasped GOT
grasping thing CLAW
grass BENT; CANE; CEREAL; HAY; JOINT; LAWN; NARK; OAT; OATS; PANIC; POT; REED; REEFER; RYE; SEED; SNEAK; SOD; SPILL; TALK; VERGE; WEED
grassland LEA; LEY
grate FRAME; RUB

grating GRID; HARSH
grave ACCENT; STERN; SAD; TOMB
gravel SHINGLE
graves STYLE
Graves WINE
graze FEED; SCRAPE
grazed FED
grazing area FIELD; LEA
grease SMARM
greasy WAXY
great FAB; GOOD; GRAND; HIGH; HUGE; MAIN; MOST; OLD; VAST
great deal LOT; LOTS; OODLES; SIGHT; TON; TONS
great many SLEW; *see* GREAT DEAL
great time BALL
greater MORE
grebe DIVER
greedy chap HOG; PIG
Greek ATTIC; GR; SOLON; TIMON
Greek character, letter 2 letters: EI, MU, NU, XI, OU, PI; 3 letters: ETA, RHO, TAU, PHI, CHI, PSI; 4 letters: BETA, IOTA, ZETA; 5 letters: ALPHA, GAMMA, DELTA, THETA, KAPPA, LAMBDA; SIGMA, OMEGA; 7 letters: EPSILON, OMICRON, UPSILON
Greek god ARES
Greek island COS
Greek maiden IO
green CALLOW; COURSE; LEAFY; LIME; NEW; OLIVE; RAW; SICK; TURF; VEG; VERT; YOUNG; can indicate something to do with GO (ie. traffic light); [GARDEN]
green, type of CROWN
greenkeeper can indicate something to do with COURSE
greens VEG
Greenwich, say TIME
greet FLAG; HAIL; KEEN; SALUTE; WAVE
greeting HAILING; HALLO; HELLO; HI; WAVE; YO
greeting, Indian HOW
grew ROSE
grey ASHEN; ASHY; DULL; DIN; OLD; PALE; SAD
grey-haired OLD
grey in Paris GRIS
greyish-brown DUN

grid GRATING
grief SORROW; WOE; anagram indicator
grief, come to anagram indicator
grief, evidence of TEAR
grievance BEEF; *see* GROUSE
grim DOUR; HARD; STERN
grime DIRT
grin SMILE
grind CHEW; GRATE; MILL
grinder MOLAR
grip BITE; HOLD
gripe BEEF; BITCH; GROAN; GROUSE; MOAN
gripped BITTEN; HELD; nesting indicator
gripped by nesting indicator; run indicator
grit GUTS; NERVE; SAND
gritty BRAVE; SANDY
grizzled GREY
groan GRIPE; SIGH
groom COMB; CURRY; DRESS
groove CHANNEL; RUT; SLOT
gross FAT; GR; RANK
gross, not NET
grotesque anagram indicator
grotto CAVE
ground CLAY; EARTH; LAND; LOT; PARK; TERRA; anagram indicator
ground, our HOME
ground, piece of LOT; SOD
grounds DREGS; DROSS; ESTATE; LEES
group BAND; BATCH; BEE; BLOC; BOARD; BODY; BRACKET; BUNCH; CASTE; CELL; CLASS; CLUSTER; FACTION; FORM; GANG; GENUS; GP; LOT; ORDER; PARTY; RING; SCHOOL; SECT; SET; SIDE; SORT; TRIBE; TRIO; TROOP; WING; as a run indicator can refer to a group of consecutive letters within the clue
group, management BOARD; TRUST
group of flags HOIST
group of girls BEVY
group of quail BEVY
group of players BAND; CAST; LSO; ORC
group of workers CREW; GANG; GUILD; SHIFT; STAFF; TU;

UNION

group, our US

group, political PARTY; CELL

group. small DUO; TRIO

grouse BEEF; BITCH; CRAB; GRIPE; GRUMBLE; MOAN; MUTTER

grove THICKET

grow BLOOM; RAISE; SWELL; THRIVE

grow old AGE

grow older AGE; RIPEN

grow large SWELL; WAX

growth BEARD; MOSS; POLYP; SPRIG; WART; WEN

growth potential EGG; SEED

grub CHOW; FOOD; LARVA; NOSH; ROOT; ROOTLE

grueling HARD; anagram indicator

grumble CARP; CRAB; CRIB; CHUNTER; GROUSE; MUTTER; YAMMER; *see* GROUSE

grumpy SURLY

Grundy *see* GRUNDY, MRS. GRUNDY, SOLOMON

Grundy, Mrs PRUDE (character in play); *see* GRUNDY, SOLOMON

Grundy, Solomon indicates an activity or its associated day stemming from the nursery rhyme: Born on Monday, Christened on Tuesday, Married on Wednesday, Took ill on Thursday, Worse on Friday, Died on Saturday

guarantee ENSURE; INSURE

guaranteed CERTAIN; SURE

guard KEEP; SENTRY; WATCH

guard's intended ALICE

guarded CAGY

guerrilla CONTRA

guerrilla leader CHE; G

Guevara CHE

guess DIVINE; FANCY; OPINE; RATE; THINK

guide GILLIE; LEAD; LEADER; MAP; RUDDER; SCOUT; SHOW; STEER; TRAIN; USHER

guided LED; SHOWN

Guiness ALE

gulf SPLIT

Gulf state OMAN

gull CHEAT; CON; DELUDE; DUPE; SUCKER

gullible GREEN

gum GLUE; STICK; PASTE
gumption NOUS
gun ARM; COLT; GAT; LUGER; MORTAR; PIECE; PISTOL; RIFLE; ROD; STEN; UZI
gun, pull a DRAW
gunman EARP; SNIPER
gunmen RA
gunners RA
gush SPOUT
gust BLOW; WIND
gusto SPIRIT
gusty anagram indicator
gut see gutted
guts GRIT
guts, some COLON
gutted middle letter(s) to be omitted
guttering CHANNEL; anagram indicator
guy CHAFF; MAN; RAG; RIB; ROPE; STAY; TEASE; can also signify a man's name eg. SAM, STAN; *see* MAN; can indicate something to do with tent, camping, etc
guzzler GANNET
gym PE; PT
gypsy TINKER
gyrate SPIN; TURN

Hh

habit DRESS; SUIT; WIMPLE; some item of clothing; can indicate something to do with holy orders, or riding
hack CHOP; HEW; HORSE; MANGLE; SEVER
hackneyed STALE
hackneyed idiom CANT
had D (ie. 'd usually clued with an abbreviation indicator eg. 'briefly'); TRICKED

had, I ID (ie. I'd)
hag FISH; WITCH
haggard DRAWN; GAUNT
hail AVE; CHEER; FLAG; WAVE
hair BEARD; BRAID; BRISTLE; BUN; CREW; DOWN; LASH; LOCK; MANE; MOP; ROLL; TACHE; TRESS; WIG
hair dye HENNA
hair of the dog usually indicates something to do with alcohol or where it is drunk
haircut TRIM; *see* HAIRSTYLE
haircut, short BOB; CREW
hairdo RINSE; *see* HAIRSTYLE
hairstyle AFRO; BANG; BOB; BUN; CROP; CUT; TRIM
hairy ROUGH; anagram indicator
Hal, like BLUFF
half DEMI; SEMI; half of indicated word to be used
half century L
half-cooked RARE
half-hearted, half-heartedly one of the two middle letters of an evenly-numbered word to be omitted as 'half-hearted shout' clues BELOW
half-hundred L
half-measure EN
half of F; O; half of the word that follows 'of' to be used
half-term two consecutive letters of TERM to be used
half-time two consecutive letters of TIME to be used
hall CHAMBER; LOBBY; ROOM; SEAT
haloed nesting indicator
halt CEASE; END; STOP
ham THIGH
Hamlet DANE; or can indicate something Danish eg. pastry [IDIOT; MADNESS]
hammer BEAT; DRIVE; GAVEL; TOOL; TROUNCE
hammer-blow, deal KNAP
hammered, hammering anagram indicator
hamper BAR; BLOCK; DETER
hampered nesting indicator
hand DEAL; DUMMY; E; EAST; GIVE; MAN; MEMBER; MITT; N; NORTH; PALM; PASS; PAW; S; SOUTH; W; WEST; WORKER
hand, good FLUSH; STRAIGHT

hand, on CLOSE; NEAR
hand, out of anagram indicator
hand over GIVE; PASS; PRESENT
handcart BARROW
handiwork DIY
handle CRANK; HILT; LEVER; NAME; STOCK; TACKLE; TAG; TITLE; TREAT
handle roughly MAUL; SCRAG
handler COACH; TRAINER
handout DOLE
hands CREW
hands, in both a component is to be nested between L and R
handy CLOSE; NEARBY
hang DANGLE; LYNCH; PEND; KILL; SAG; SWING
hang about, around HOVER
hang on TARRY; WAIT
hang-ups can indicate something to do with washing line eg. peg
hanger-on BURR
hanging can indicate something to do with paintings
hank COIL
hanker LONG
haphazardly anagram indicator
happen CHANCE; OCCUR
happened CAME
happening AFFAIR; EVENT
happens, as it LIVE
happiness BLISS; GLEE; JOY
happy GAY; GLAD
happy, not SAD
happy sound PURR
harbour BERTH; DOCK; HAVEN; HOME; PORT; SHELTER
harassed anagram indicator
hard FIRM; GRIM; H; HEAVY; RAW; ROUGH; SET; STERN; STIFF
hard area CALLUS
hard-fought CLOSE
hard-hearted AR; H to be the centre of an element
hard look GLARE
hard skin CORN
hard tissue BONE

hard-up BROKE; SKINT
hard wood EBONY; TEAK
hard work FAG; GRAFT; HOP (ie. H op.)
hard worker BEE
harden ENURE; INURE
hardliner DRY (ie. in politics as opposed to "wet")
hardship NEED
hardware, article of SCREW
Hardy sergeant TROY
Hardy's girl TESS
hare RUN
harm HURT; ILL; anagram indicator
harmful BAD; EVIL
harmonic ACCORD
harmonium ORGAN
harmonize TONE
harmony BLISS; ORDER
harness HITCH; REIN
Harrier FIGHTER
Harris ISLE; ROLF
harsh ROUGH; RUDE
harvest CROP; GLEAN; REAP
has OWNS; S (ie. 's abbr.)
has previously HATH
hash CHOP; anagram indicator
hasn't omission indicator, usually the following word to be omitted
haste HURRY; RUSH; SPEED
haste, make RUN; SURGE; TEAR
hasten HIE; RUN; TEAR
hastened RAN; TORE
hasty RASH
hat BERET; BONNET; CAP; DERBY; LID; MITRE; TILE; TOPPER
hating ANTI
hatred SPITE
haughty PROUD
haul DRAG; LUG; PULL
haul up HOIST
haulier CARTER
have CON; KEEP; OWN; TRICK

have a word with SEE
have existence ARE
have fun PLAY; SPORT
have, I IVE
have importance COUNT
have life BE
having WITH
having potential ABLE
having spoken SAID
Hawaiin greeting ALOHA
hawk CRY; COUGH; SELL; TOUT
Hawthorn MAY
hay COCK; DANCE; RICK
hay, make TED
haymaker BALER; PUNCH
haystack COCK; RICK
hazard BAR (ie. sandbar); BERG; CHANCE; RISK
hazard, maritime BAR; BERG; REEF
haze FOG; MIST
he can indicate a man's name, worker or occupation
he had HED
he in France IL
he will HELL
he would HED
head BEAN; BONCE; BRAIN; CAPE; CROWN; DOME; LEAD; LOAF; NAPPER; NESS; NOB; NUT; ONION; PATE; POLL; PRES (for President); PROW; TOP; initial letter indicator; can indicate something to do with head (eg. hair, hat); can refer to a particular geographic head eg. LIZARD
head, a EACH; PER
head of can indicate that the initial letter of the ensuing word is to be used
head, cereal EAR
head lowered initial letter to be relocated further back into the word as with "Imposing gaze with head lowered" changes GLARE (ie. gaze) into the solution LARGE (ie. imposing)
head of faculty DEAN; F
head of state KING; S
head over heels anagram indicator; reversal indicator
head, Scottish RECTOR
head to foot initial letter to be transposed to the end as 'Shook head

to foot' clues HOOKS

head-dress D; *see* HEADGEAR

headgear BERET; BONNET; CAP; CROWN; G; HAT; TOP; TURBAN; VEIL

heading BOUND (as 'heading East' clues EBOUND); initial letter indicator

headland CAPE; L

headless first letter(s) to be omitted

headlight HALO

headmaster HM

heads (all the) only the initials of indicated words to be used

heads off initial letters to be removed from adjacent words

headwind W

heal CURE

health TOAST

health, propose TOAST

health centre AL; HYDRO; SPA

healthy FIT; GOOD; HALE; SOUND; TRIM; WELL

healthy, appearing less PALER

healthy, not AILING; PEAKY; SICK

heap CRATE; HILL; MOUND; PILE; STACK

hear CATCH; GATHER; TRY; homophone indicator; can indicate a word of phrase sometimes uttered by the subject; similarly; can indicate a sound associated with the subject (BARK for dog, MEW for cat and so on)

hear, we homophone indicator

heard TRIED; homophone indicator

hearing SESSION; TRIAL; homophone indicator

hearing, in homophone indicator

hears TRIES

heart CENTRE; CORE; GIST; MIDDLE; NUB; PITH; TICKER; the middle letter(s) of a word is to be used

heart, at *see* AT HEART

heartbreak anagram of HEART

hearted indicates an element to be inserted in middle of a word

hearth INGLE

hearth-frame FENDER

heartily the middle letter(s) of a word to be used

heartless omit the middle of a word, usually one letter but can be several

heartlessly *see* HEARTLESS

hearts H; *see* HEART
heat ANGER; BAKE; BOIL; EVENT; H; MULL; RACE; WARM
heated HOT; WARM; ANGRY
heath MOOR
heathen PAGAN
heather LING
heats H; RACES
heave LIFT; PUSH; RAISE
heaven BLISS; SKY
heaven, in ABOVE
heavenly body EARTH,; MOON; STAR; SUN
heavenly body's LUNAR; SOLAR
heavens GOSH; SKY
heaviness WEIGHT
heavy BOLD; HARD; WEIGHTY
heavy demands, make TAX
heavy metal LEAD; PB
heavyweight TON
Hebrew measure COR
hectic, hectically anagram indicator
heed RECK; WATCH
heel BOUNDER; CAD; CANT; LEAN; LIST; LOUSE; ROTTER; ROGUE
height ALTITUDE; HILL; MOUNT; TOR
heighten RAISE
heiress, Venetian PORTIA
heist STEAL
held HAD
held by nesting indicator
held fast STUCK
held in run indicator; nesting indicator
held on CLUNG
held up HUNG; LATE; PENT; reversal indicator
Helen's mother LEDA
Helium HE
hell DIS
hellish anagram indicator
helot SLAVE
help ABET; AID; ASSIST; AVAIL; FAVOUR; SERVE; SOS
help, request for SOS

helper AID; AIDE; HAND; MATE
helping RATION; SHARE
helter-skelter anagram indicator
hence SO
henpeck NAG
Henry H; HAL; HY; can indicate something to do with the Martini-Henry rifle
heraldic band, device FESS
heraldry [associated words: ORDINARY, SINISTER, CHEVRON]
herb FENNEL; PARSLEY; SAGE; SIMPLE; THYME
Herbert LOM
herd DROVE; FLOCK
here GRID (ie. the puzzle itself); PRESENT; NOW
here in France ICI
here in Germany HIER
hereditary element GENE
heretic ARIUS (ancient priest)
hermit CRAB
hero FAUST; LEAD; STAR
heroic EPIC
heroin H; HORSE
heroine BECKY; BESS; DIDO; MOLL; NELL; NORMA; TESS
hesitant utterance ER; UM; UR
hesitate FALTER; HOVER; TEETER; WAVER
hesitation DOUBT; ER; UM; UR
hew CHOP; *see* CUT
hi-fi, piece of AMP
hidden DOGGO
hidden by run indicator
hide BURROW; CACHE; COAT; COVER; DEN; FELL; KID; LAIR; LEATHER; PELT; SCREEN; SKIN; SUEDE
hideout DEN; HOLE; LAIR
hides run indicator
hiding-place HOLE
high GREAT; MANIC; OFF; STEEP; STONED; TALL; UP; anagram indicator; can indicate something to do with being drunk or on a drug-trip; can refer to an elevated location as 'high water' can clue TARN; similarly with regard to the body eg. 'high level habit' can indicate some kind of headwear
high class U
high cost BOMB

high explosive HE
high-flier *see* BIRD
high frequency OFTEN
high, get RISE
high, got ROSE
high-level RIDGE; ROOF
high living can indicate a national or animal living in mountainous region
high place MOUNT; STATUS; TOR
high-rise RIDGE
high shot LOB
high tension HT
highball LOB
higher degrees HEAT
higher in price UP
highest BEST; TOP
highest place TOP
Highland area ROSS
Highland dress KILT
Highland town WICK
Highlander SCOT; *see* HIGH LIVING
hike RAISE; RAMBLE
hiker RAMBLER
hiking club YHA
hilarious person RIOT
highlight VERY (ie. from Very pistol)
hill BRAE; FELL; HEAP; MOUND; PEAK; RISE; TOR
hill top H
hillside BRAE
hilltop H; RIDGE
hind BACK; REAR; STERN
hindered LET
hindquarters HAUNCH
hindrance LET
Hindu goddess KALI
hint CUE; CLUE; DASH; TIP; TRACE; can signal that only a small part (usually one letter) of indicated word is to be used
hip COOL
hire LEASE; LET; RENT
hired LEASED; LET; RENTED

hired man HAND
hires LET
hirsute HAIRY
his or her ONES
historian BEDE; LIVY
historic OLD
historic city TROY; UR
history PAST
hit BAT; BELT; BLOW; BUTT; BUTTED; CLUB; CUFF; LAM; PAT; RAP; SLAP; SLOG; SMASH; SMITE; SOCK; STRUCK; SUCCESS
hit, big ACE; SIX
hit out anagram of HIT
hitch can indicate a knot; *see* SNAG
Hitler's men, some of SS
hitting, keep FLOG
HM ER
hoard SAVE; STOCK; STORE
hoarse HUSKY
hoax CON; DUPE; KID
hobby rem: this is a bird as well as meaning 'pastime'
hobby-horse can indicate something to do with morris dancing
hock POP; WINE
hoe WEED
hog SWINE
hold BIND; GRIP; HAVE; KEEP; LOCK
hold back DEFER; DELAY; WAIT
hold in run indicator
hold out OFFER
hold tight CLASP; CLING; GRIP
hold up BLOCK; DEFER; DELAY; PROP
hold-up GLITCH; HEIST; HITCH; SNAG
holder HOD; *see* CONTAINER
holds HAS
hole CELL; CORNER; CRATER; DEN; GORE; JAM; LAIR; MINE; O; PIT; POCK; PORT; SLOT; SPACE; SPOT; VOID
hole, make a BORE; DRILL; GORE
holiday BREAK; CRUISE; EASTER; FEAST; HOL; LEAVE; PACKAGE; RECESS; REST; VAC; WHIT [OFF]
holiday centre RESORT; SPA
holiday, Northern WAKE

holiday, on AWAY; OFF
holidaymaker CAMPER; TRIPPER
holler CALL
hollow CAVE; COMBE; COOMB; DELL; DIMPLE; DIP; CRATER; TOKEN
hollow sound BONG
Hollywood LA
Hollywood spectacular EPIC
Hollywood star COOPER; GABLE
holy PI
holy book KORAN; *see* BIBLE, BOOK
holy man MONK; SAINT; ST
holy person SAINT; ST
holy writ NT; OT
home DEN; EARTH; FLAT; HEARTH; HOUSE; IN; LAIR; NEST; PAD
home, bring STRESS
Home Counties SE
home improvement DIY
home of monster LOCH
home, stately HALL; PILE
Homer rem: despite the capital letter, can refer to the pigeon as well as the poet
homework PREP
homosexual GAY
honest FAIR; FRANK; TRUE; UPRIGHT; WORTHY
honesty TRUTH
honey COMB; DEAR; LOVE; MEL
honour CBE; CE; CROWN; DBE; LAUD; MBE; OBE; OM; can refer to an honour card ie. ACE, JACK, QUEEN, KING
honoured companion CH
hood BONNET; COWL; COVER
hook GAFF
hooligan LOUT; ROUGH; TED; THUG; YOB
hooter HORN; NOSE
hope TRUST; YEARN; YEARNING
hop SPRING
Hope can refer to the author and his work
hopeful ROSY
hopelessly anagram indicator
hopelessness DESPAIR

Horace, characteristic of his poetry ODIC
Horatio can indicate something to do with philosophy (ie. from 'Hamlet')
horde ARMY; GANG; MASS; MOB; SWARM
horizon KEN
horn CORNET; HOOTER; LUR
horn, sound TOOT
horribly anagram indicator
horrific anagram indicator
horrify APPAL
horse ARAB; ARKLE; BARB; BAY; BESS; CHARGER; CHASER; COB; COLT; COURSER; DUN; FILLY; FOAL; GG; GREY; H; HACK; HUNTER; MARE; NAG; PACER; PINTO; PONY; PUNCH; ROAN; SHIRE; *see* RACEHORSE
horse, black, dark BESS
horse-dealer COPER
horse sure to win CERT
horse-trader *see* HORSE-DEALER
horseback GAN (ie. nag reversed)
horseback, on UP
horseback, travel on RIDE
horseman RIDER
hospital BARTS; ENT; GUYS; H; MASH
hospital department ENT
hospital, military MASH
hospital, part of ENT; WARD
hospital room WARD
hospital unit ENT; WARD
hospitality CHEER
host ARMY; CROWD; LOT; MASS; MC; SWARM; nesting indicator [ENTERTAIN]
hostilities STRIFE; WAR
hostility MALICE
hot CROSS; H; IN; STOLEN
hot-headed RASH
hot meal CHILLI
hot potato ISSUE
hot spot OVEN
hot, very RED
hot weather SUN
hotel HYDRO; INN

hotel employee PAGE
hour H; HR; can indicate any figure up to twelve
hour of prayer SEXT
house BINGO; BULL (ie. Taurus); CASTLE; CO; CROWD; DRUM; FIRM; GRANGE; HANOVER; H; HO; HUT; INN; LEO; LODGE; LOTTO; MANOR; MANSE; ORANGE; SEMI; TUDOR; VILLA; WINDSOR; YORK; can indicate something to do with theatre; also rem: other astrological houses eg. Taurus, Leo
house. big GRANGE; MANOR; MANSE
House, European, French MAISON
house, little COT; H
house, part of big WING
housing nesting indicator
housing complex ESTATE
housing development CITY; ESTATE; TOWN
hovel HUT; SHACK; SHED; STY
however BUT
how German WIE
howl WAIL
HQ BASE; DEPOT
hub FOCUS
hue TINCT; TONE
hug ENFOLD; nesting indicator; run indicator
huge BIG; TITAN
hugs nesting indicator; run indicator
Hull rem: as well as a town can refer to a boat
hum PONG
hum, humming can indicate something to do with smell
humble ABASE; LOW; LOWER
humble person HEEP (ie. from Dickens)
humble place HOVEL; HUT; SHED
humbug SHAM
humdrum BANAL; TRITE
humiliate TEASE
humming NIFFY
humorist CARD; LEAR; WAG; WIT
humorous COMIC; DROLL; FUNNY; WITTY
humorous material, feeble CORN
humour MOOD; WIT
hunch CLUE; HINT; HUMP
hundred C; TON

hundred, one short of OO
hundred pence POUND
hundreds CC
hunger GREED
hungry NEEDY; if a person is involved in the clue, 'hungry' can signify the insertion of O into the person (ie. 'has nothing inside'!)
hunt CHASE; MEET; QUEST; SEARCH; SCOUR; SHOOT
hunt illegally POACH
hunt protester SAB
hunter HORSE; MOUNT; WATCH
hunting party SHOOT
huntsman PEEL
hurdle JUMP
hurl LOB; PITCH; THROW; TOSS
hurled anagram indicator
hurried RAN; RACED; SPED; TORE
hurry BELT; HASTE; HIE; NIP; RACE; RUN; RUSH; SPEED
hurt ACHE; HARM; PAIN; SMART; STING
hurts, that OUCH
husband CONSERVE; H; MAN; MATE; SAVE; SPOUSE
husband, French MARI
hush money BRIBE; BUNG
husk AWN
husky HOARSE
husky, sounds HORSE
hut CABIN; HOGAN; HOVEL; SHACK; SHED
hybrid ASS
hymn-writer DAVID
hyphen DASH
hypocrisy CANT
hypocrite PRIG

Ii

I EGO; ONE; rem: first person 'I' can itself be an element in the answer
I am IM
I had ID
I have IVE
I, in Paris JE
I'm IM
I reported EYE
I shall ILL
I will ILL
I would ID
Ibsen can indicate something to do with his plays eg. BRAND, GHOSTS
Ibsen heroine GABLER
Icarus can call for something to do with sun, wax
ice BERG; RINK; can indicate something to do with diamonds
ice, kind of BLACK; CREAM; PACK
ice-cream CHOC; CONE; SCOOP; TUB
ice, quantity of BERG; CONE; SCOOP; RINK
ice venue RINK
icebox FRIDGE
Iceland IS
ID NAME
idea NOTION; PLAN; THOUGHT
identical SAME
identification ID
identify FINGER; NAME; PLACE
identity ID
idiot ASS; NIT; SAP; TWIT; anagram indicator; *see* FOOL
idiotic anagram indicator
idle FALLOW; LAZE; LAZY; SLACK; VAIN; anagram indicator
idle fellow *see* IDLER
idle talk GAS; PRATTLE
idler DRONE; WASTER

idling LAZING; SLACKING
idol BAAL
ignite BURN; LIGHT
ignited LIT
ignoble BASE; LOW; MEAN
ignore CUT; OMIT; PASS; omission indicator
ignored omission indicator
if CONDITION
ill AILING; POORLY; anagram indicator
ill-advisedly anagram indicator
ill-assorted anagram indicator
ill-bred type BOOR; CAD; OAF; LOUT; YOB
ill-gotten anagram indicator
ill-gotten gains LOOT
ill-humour BILE; PET; SPLEEN; TEMPER
ill, taken anagram indicator
ill-used anagram indicator
illegally record BUG
illicit BLACK; anagram indicator
illicitly anagram indicator
illiterate anagram indicator; homophone indicator; *see* ILLITERATES, FOR
illiterates, for can indicate a deliberate misspelling as "school for illiterates brought back" clues LOOKS
illness BUG; FLU
illness, minor COLD
illuminated LIT
illumination BEAM; LIGHT; RAY
illumination, form of LED; SPOT
image ICON
imaginative American POE (recalling his 'Tales of the Imagination')
imbued with nesting indicator
imitate APE; COPY; FORGE
imitation COPY; SHAM
immaculate PURE
immature CALLOW; EARLY; GREEN
immediate PROMPT
immediately NOW
immediately after ON
immense HUGE; STEEP

immerse BATHE; DIP
immoral woman TART
imp BRAT; SPRITE
impact, have an TELL
impale SPEAR; SPIKE
impartial FAIR; JUST
impassioned STORMY
impassive STOLID
impatience in driving, show HOOT; TOOT
impatient AGOG
impatient, be ITCH
impecunious BROKE; POOR; SKINT; can indicate that an associated word is to lose a money-related letter/component such as P, L
impediment LET; RUB
impend LOOM
imperceptible, almost SLIGHT
impersonate APE
impertinent COOL; FORWARD; LIPPY
implausible TALL
implement AWL; SPADE; SPIKE; TOOL; USE; *see* INSTRUMENT, TOOL
implore BEG; PLEAD; ENTREAT
imply MEAN
import GIST; MEAN; NUB; POINT; WEIGHT
importance WEIGHT; can indicate something to do with Wilde's play eg. ERNEST; *see* IMPORT
importance, have COUNT
important BIG; HIGH; KEY; VITAL
important, are MATTER
imported MEANT; can indicate a foreign word as "imported article" clues LE, UN, etc
importune BEG; PLEAD; PRESS
impose LEVY
impound nesting indicator
imprecise VAGUE
impress STAMP
impression AIR; DENT; FEEL; PRINT; SEAL; SENSE; STAMP
impression, make an DENT; ETCH; PRINT; SEAL
imprison INTERN; CAGE
imprisoned nesting indicator; can indicate that a component is to be

nested within a synonym for prison eg.. PEN or GAOL as in "Doctor could be imprisoned for caper" which leads to GAMBOL (ie. GA-MB-OL)

imprisoned, get INTERN
imprisoned, not FREE; OUT
improbably anagram indicator
improper, improperly anagram indicator
improve BETTER; EMEND; MEND; REFORM
improve on CAP; TOP
improved BETTER
improvement REFORM
improvements DIY
improvise JAM
improvised, improvising anagram indicator
impudence CRUST; GALL; LIP
impudent CHEEKY; FRESH
impudent youngster BRAT; IMP
impulse INSTINCT; ITCH; URGE
impulses, set of ID
in HOME; LIT; TRENDY; nesting indicator; run indicator; can indicate that whatever follows is synonymous with the answer; rem: like all small innocent looking words, IN itself can be part of the answer as "Element unknown in club" gives ZINC (ie. Z-IN-C); used as a prefix can indicate NOT
in advantageous position UP
in care of nesting indicator
in case LEST
in charge IC; OVER
in court UP
in demand HOT
in difficulties anagram indicator
in extremis first and last letter indicator
in favour FOR; PRO
in French DE; EN
in French a UN; UNE
in front AHEAD
in good time EARLY
in hearing homophone indicator
in many cases OFTEN
in Paris a UN; UNE
in pieces anagram indicator

in place ON
in such a way anagram indicator
in the case of FOR
in the form of AS
in the manner of ALA (ie. a la); AS
in this way SO; THUS
inaccurate OUT; anagram indicator
inaccurate statement LIE
inadequate POOR; SLENDER; THIN; WEAK; anagram indicator
inadvertently anagram indicator
inattentive, be SKIP
inaugurate FOUND; LAUNCH; START
inbuilt nesting Indicator
incense ANGER
incensed, be FUME; RANT; RAVE
incentive BAIT; BUNG; CARROT; GOAD; SPUR
inch EDGE; IN
incise SCORE
incisive can refer to the incisor tooth
incisor TOOTH
incite BAIT; DRIVE; GOAD; TEMPT; SPUR
incited DROVE; SPURRED
inclination BENT; CANT; HUMOUR; LEAN; LIST; SLOPE; TILT; TREND; RAMP
incline BEND; LEAN; LIST; SLOPE; TEND; TILT; RAMP
inclined BENT; LEANED; TENDED; TILTED
include ADD
included HAD; nesting indicator
includes nesting indicator
income CUT; FEE; PAY; SCREW; TITHE; WAGE;
incomer SETTLER
incomplete PARTIAL; omission indicator; run indicator
incompletely omission indicator; run indicator
inconsistent FADDY
incorporated INC; anagram indicator; nesting indicator; run indicator
incorporates, incorporating anagram indicator; nesting indicator; run indicator
incorrect, incorrectly anagram indicator
increase ACCRUE; GROW; RAISE; RISE; UP
increase, pay RAISE; RISE

increase speed GUN
increased ROSE; UP
incredible TALL
incriminating factor PLANT
incur MEET; ENCOUNTER
indecent BLUE
indecision, position of FENCE
indefinite number N; X
indentation BIGHT
independent IN; IND
index AZ; LIST; TABLE
India I
Indian I; IN; INCA; can indicate something to do with tea; *see* AMERICAN INDIAN
Indian, American *see* AMERICAN INDIAN
Indian greeting HOW
Indian state, territory GOA
indicate MEAN; NOD; POINT; SHOW; SIGN
indicated MEANT
indication SIGN
indicating anagram indicator
indicator of weather COCK; GLASS; VANE
indifferent COLD; COOL
indigent POOR
indignant CROSS; IRATE
indisposed ILL
indistinct BLEAR; FAINT
individual ONE; OWN; PERSON; SINGLE; SOUL; UNIT
indolent IDLE; LAZY
induce GOAD; LEAD; LURE; SPUR; TEMPT; URGE
induced LED
inducement BRIBE; SOP
indulge PANDER; TREAT
indulgence BINGE; TREAT
ineffectual person PRAT; TWIT
inefficient anagram indicator
inept, ineptly anagram indicator
inexpensive CHEAP
inexperienced FRESH; GREEN; RAW
inexperienced person L

infant BABE; CHILD; TODDLER
infantry FOOT
infatuation PASH
infection BUG; FLU; STYE
inferior BELOW; CRUMMY; LESS; LOW; LOWER; POOR; ROPY; SUB; UNDER
infinite ALL
inflame ANGER; HEAT; RILE
inflammation BOIL
inflexible RIGID; STERN
inflict DEAL
influence AFFECT; CLOUT; DRAG; PULL; REACH; SAY; SWAY
inform GRASS; NARK; TELL; RAT; SING; SNITCH; TELL
inform on SHOP; SPLIT
informally anagram indicator
information DATA; DATUM; FILE; GEN; GRIFF; INF; NEWS; TIP
information, give TELL
information, inside TIP
information, provide GRASS; SHOP; TELL
Information Technology IT
information, try to get SNOOP; PRY
informed AWARE; HIP; RATTED; SHOPPED; TOLD
informed, be HEAR
informed, was HEARD
informer GRASS; NARK; RAT
infrared IR
infusion BREW
ingenious DEFT
ingenuity ART; CRAFT; SKILL
ingle HEARTH
ingredients anagram indicator
ingress ENTRY
inheritance GENE
inhibited SHY
iniquity, place of DEN
initial FIRST; SIGN; initial letter indicator; can indicate the initial state of something eg. 'initial child' can clue BIRTH
initially initial letter(s) indicator; adjacent word or element to go to the front of the other element
initiate SPARK; START

initiation initial letter indicator
initiative DRIVE; LEAD
injected nesting indicator
injection IV; JAB; SHOT
injure HARM; HURT; LAME; MAR; WOUND
injured HURT; LAME; anagram indicator
injury CUT; HARM; HURT; SPRAIN; WOUND
injury, leg LIMP
injury to anagram indicator
inlet BAY; COVE; CREEK; RIA; WASH
inner ENDO; RED (ie. target)
inner cover LINING
innings KNOCK; STAND
innocent CHASTE; WHITE
Innocent POPE
innocent, declare CLEAR
inordinately anagram indicator
input DATA
inquire ASK
inquisitive NOSY
insane *see* NUTS
inscribed nesting indicator
insecure anagram indicator
insect ANT; BEE; BUG; CRICKET; FLEA; FLY; GNAT; INSTAR; LOUSE; MIDGE; MITE; MOTH; WASP
insects LICE
inserts nesting indicator
inside run indicator; nesting indicator; can indicate a component is to be nested within SIDE
insignia CHAIN
insignificant SMALL; TINY; WEE
insincere FAKE; PHONY; SHAM
insincerely fluent GLIB
insipid BLAND; DULL; VAPID
insist DEMAND
insist on EXACT
insolent CHEEKY; LIPPY; RUDE
inspect CHECK; EXAMINE; SCAN; TEST
inspection CHECK; MOT; TEST; *see* EXAMINATION
inspection, make inspection *see* INSPECTION

inspiration MUSE
inspire FIRE; PUSH; URGE
inspired FIRED; LIT
installed in nesting indicator
instance, for AS; eg.; SAY
instant FLASH; MO; SEC; TICK; TRICE; TWINKLE
instinct DRIVE; EAR; ID; IMPULSE; URGE
institute FOUND; INST; LAUNCH; START
institution HOUSE; INST
instruct BRIEF; PRIME; TEACH; TRAIN
instruction BRIEF; LESSON; STET (from printing)
instruction, give TEACH; TRAIN
instructions BRIEF
instructor TEACHER
instrument AWL; CLOCK; LEVER; METER; PROBE; TOOL; *see* MUSICAL INSTRUMENT
instrument, surgical PROBE
instrument, textile CARD
instruments BAND; REEDS; STRINGS; ORC
insufficiently UNDER
insult ABUSE; AFFRONT; CUT; SLAG; SLIGHT; SNUB
insurance COVER; INS
insurance premium LOADING
intellect BRAIN; NOUS
intelligence CIA; MI; NEWS; NOUS; WIT
intelligence agency CIA
intelligence, U.S. CIA
intelligent BRIGHT; CLEVER; SHARP
intend AIM; MEAN; PLAN
intended FIANCE; MEANT
intense ACUTE; GREAT; STRONG
intent, intention AIM; END
intent, with MEANT
interest CUT; SHARE; SIDE; SLICE; SPICE; STAKE; USURY
interested in INTO
interfere with MEDDLE
interference STATIC
interferes FRIES
interior INNER
interior design DECOR

interminable last letter to be omitted (ie. unending)
intermission BREAK
internal run indicator
international CAP; INT; TEST
international group BLOC; EC; NATO; UN; WHO
international medical group WHO
international organisation *see* INTERNATIONAL GROUP
international peacekeepers UN
internet WEB
interment, place for GRAVE; TOMB; VAULT
interpret READ
interpreted READ
interrogate PUMP
interrupt HECKLE
interrupt movement PAUSE
interrupted nesting indicator
interrupting nesting indicator; run indicator
interval GAP; RECESS; REST; SPACE
intervening nesting indicator
interview ASK; SEE
interwoven anagram indicator
intestine GUT
intimate BOON; CLOSE; HINT; IMPLY; INFORM; STATE
intimation CLUE; HINT; WIND
intimidate AWE; COW
into nesting indicator
intoxicated anagram indicator; *see* DRUNK
intoxicating HEADY
intricacy WEB
intriguing character PLOTTER
introduce LAUNCH; PRESENT; START; nesting indicator
introduce oneself, attempt to can indicate a word beginning with ME (in the style of "Me, Tarzan") as "Physician's attempt to introduce himself to non-English tipple" clues the wine MEDOC (ie. Me, Doc)
introduced first letter indicator
introducing nesting indicator
introduction can indicate that the word alongside should be placed at the beginning
introduction for/to initial letter indicator
invader GOTH

invades nesting indicator
invading nesting indicator
invalid NULL
invariably ALWAYS; EER; EVER
invasion RAID
inveigh RAIL
inventor MORSE
invest ENDUE; SINK
investigate PROBE; STUDY; SUS
investigation CASE; PROBE; STUDY
investigator DC; DI; DS; EYE; PI; TEC
investigators CID
investing apart from the financial meaning, can indicate something to do with donning clothes
investment nesting indicator
investor ANGEL
invited BADE
invited person GUEST
inviting nesting indicator
invoice BILL
involved (in) anagram indicator; nesting indicator; run indicator
iodine I
Iranian, old MEDE
irascible CRUSTY; TESTY
irate MAD
Ireland EIRE; I
iridescent substance NACRE
iridium IR
Irish ERSE; I; IR; TEMPER; can refer to some aspect of Irish culture, history or language, such as CEILIDH, CONACRE, etc
Irish boy *see* IRISH FELLOW
Irish city DERRY
Irish county CLARE; CORK; DOWN; KERRY; MAYO
Irish fellow LIAM; PADDY; PAT; SEAN
Irish politicians DAIL
Irish town BALLA; BRAY; CORK
Irish water LOUGH
Irishman PAT; PADDY; with some reference to speech can indicate ‘H’ to be eliminated in ‘TH’, for example THREE to become TREE
irk ANGER

irksomely anagram indicator
iron CLUB; FE; MASHIE; PRESS; SMOOTH; SPOON
ironclad F and E to be placed either side of element or word
ironic DRY
irrational, irrationally anagram indicator
irrational number E
irrelevant TRIFLING
irreverent RUDE; *see* CHEEKY
irrigate WATER
irritability BILE
irritable EDGY; RATTY
irritate BUG; FRET; GRATE; IRK; RANKLE; RILE
irritated SORE; *see* IRASCIBLE
irritating GRATING; IRKING
irritation BUG; ITCH; PIQUE; PRICK
irritation, cause *see* IRRITATE
irregular, irregularly anagram indicator
is S (ie. 's); rem: IS can be innocently placed in clue while actually constituting an element in building up the solution
is able CAN
is French EST
is German IST
is, it TIS
is no longer WAS
Isaac IKE
isinglass MICA
island AIT; ARRAN; ATOLL; BARRA; COS; CRETE; CUBA; ELBA; I; INCH; IOM; IONA; IOW; IS; JAVA; KEY; MAN; MULL; SARK; SKYE; TIREE; *see* ISLE; note ELBA is very common with a reverse indicator because it usefully provides ABLE for the end of an adjective
islander ARIEL
islands CI; II
isle MAN; WIGHT; *see* ISLAND
Islington area NI
isn't AINT
Israel HANDS; ZION
Israeli city ACRE
issue BROOD; CAUSE; EDITION; EMIT; FLOW; MATTER; NUMBER; POINT; PRINT; SEED; SON; SPAWN; UTTER; YOUNG; can indicate something to do with children, offspring

it ARTICLE; SA (ie. sex appeal); THING; rem: although innocently placed, IT itself can be an element in constructing the solution; can refer to a drink as in 'gin and it'
IT design CAD
it is ITS; TIS
it's TIS
it's said homophone indicator
it, with COOL; HIP; SEXY
Italian I; IT; ITAL
Italian agreement SI
Italian article IL
Italian city GENOA; MILAN; ROMA; ROME; TURIN
Italian food PASTA
Italian leader (former) DUCE
Italian restaurant TRAT
Italian, the IL
Italian writer ECO
item BIT; COUPLE; IT; PIECE; POINT; THING; UNIT
item, auction LOT
item, faulty DUD; REJECT
item, newspaper CUTTING
item, per EACH
itemise LIST; TABLE
itinerary ROUTE; WAY
ivory WHITE

Jj

jab DIG; POKE; PROD; SHOT; STAB
jack AB; BALL; CARD; FLAG; HAND; J; KNAVE; LIFT; PIKE; RAISE; SPRAT; TAR; *see* SAILOR; can indicate something to do with (1) the nursery rhyme about Jack Sprat; (2) the proverb "All work and no play makes Jack a dull boy"; (3) money (U.S.)
jacket COAT; REEFER; TUX

Jacob can indicate something to do with Jacob having no hair eg. bare-faced
jade HACK; STONE
jag BINGE; BOUT; BENDER; PRICK
Jag CAR
jagged ROUGH; anagram indicator
jail CAN; GAOL; NICK; PEN; QUAD; QUOD; SLAMMER
jail term BIRD; LIFE; TIME
jailbird CON; LAG
jailed INSIDE
jalopy BANGER; CROCK; HEAP
jam BLOCK; CORNER; CRAM; LOCK; PICKLE; SCRAPE; SPOT; STICK; WEDGE
jammy CUSHY
Jane GREY
Japan can indicate something to do with wood-finishing
Japanese commander SHOGUN
Japanese drama NO
jape CAPER; PRANK
jar GLASS; GRATE; POT; ROCK
jargon BULL; CANT; PATTER; LINGO; SLANG
jaundiced SALLOW; YELLOW
jaunty PERT
jazz RAG; RIFF; SWING; TRAD
jazz dance BOP; JIVE; STOMP
jazz enthusiast (fan, type) CAT
jazz music, piece *see* JAZZ
jazz piece INTRO
jazz style *see* JAZZ
jazzy anagram indicator
jealous GREEN
jeer BOO; FLOUT; HISS; HOOT; SCOFF
jelly BRAWN
Jenny ASS; DONKEY
jeopardy, in anagram indicator
jerk CURE; HITCH; TIC; *see* FOOL
jerry POT
Jersey POTATO; SPUD
Jerusalem SION
jest COD; JOKE; SALLY

jester FOOL; WAG; WIT
Jesuits (etc) ORDER
jet BLACK; FIGHTER; FLY; PLANE; SHOOT; STREAM; SPOUT
Jethro TULL
jetty MOLE; PIER
jewel AMBER; GEM; OPAL; PEARL; ROCK; RUBY; STONE
jewellery *see* JEWEL, JEWELLERY, ITEM OF
jewellery, item of BANGLE; CLIP; RING; ROPE; STUD; *see* JEWEL
jibe DIG; JEER
jiffy MO; SEC
jingle RHYME; VERSE
job BILLET; CAREER; LINE; POSITION; POST; ROLE; STATION; TASK; WORK
Job can indicate something to do with patience
job centre O
jog NUDGE
John CAN; HEAD; HEADS; LAV; LOO
join ADD; BRAID; BRIDGE; ENTER; KNIT; LINK; FUSE; MERGE; SCARF; SEAM; SEW; SOLDER; STAPLE; SPLICE; UNITE; WELD; YOKE; can indicate something to do with marriage
joiner AND
joining can indicate the use of AND
joint ANKLE; BEAM; BRAWN; COLLAR; CUT; DIVE; HAUNCH; HINGE; HIP; KNEE; LEVEL; LINK; LOIN; MITRE; NECK; PLACE; RACK; REEFER; RIB; SCARF; SPLICE; TALUS; TENON; WRIST; can indicate that AND is to be used as a component
joist BEAM
joke CRACK; GAG; JEST; PUN; QUIP
joker CARD; FOOL; FUNSTER; PUNSTER; WIT
jokes, old, trite CORN
jolly FESTIVE; GAY; HAPPY; MERRY; RM (ie. Royal Marine); VERY; can indicate something to do with sailors; *see* DRUNK
Jolson AL
jolt JAR; SHOCK
Jones INIGO
Josephine JO
jostle BUFFET
jostled anagram indicator

jot BIT; NOTE; WHIT
journal DIARY; LOG; MAG
journalism PRESS; WRITING
journalist CUB; ED; HACK; SUB
journalist, routine HACK
journalists PRESS
journey JAUNT; RIDE; SPIN; TOUR; TRIP
jovial MERRY
joy BLISS; DELIGHT; GLEE
Jude rem: he is the patron saint of lost causes
judge ASSESS; DEEM; HEAR; J; LUD; MEASURE; RATE; REF; TRIER; TRY; UMP
judgment DOOM; SENSE
judo expert DAN
jug EWER; POT; URN; rem: this can also mean prison, eg. CAN; *see* PRISON
juice SAP
jumble anagram indicator
Jumbo BIG; LARGE; OS; can indicate a plane or an elephant
jump BOUND; BUCK; CLEAR; HOOP; LEAP; POUNCE; SKIP; SPRING; START
jump, kind of HIGH; LONG
jump over CLEAR
jumper ROO
jumping, jumpy anagram indicator
junction T
junior COLT; LOW; SON; UNDER; YOUNG
junk BIN; BOAT; DROP; DRUG; DUMP; LUMBER; MEAT; SMACK; SPURN; TRASH; TRIPE; *see* RUBBISH.
junked anagram indicator
junket FEAST; TRIP
jury PANEL
just BUT; DUE; EVEN; FAIR; LICIT; MERE; METE; ONLY; RIGHT
just over fifty LI
just over a hundred CI
just over a thousand MI
justice RIGHT; can indicate something to do with NEMESIS

Kk

Katherine SHREW
kebab, type of SHISH
keck RETCH
keen ACUTE; ARDENT; AVID; COLD; CRY; GREET; INTO; LAMENT; LOW (eg. price); MAD; SHARP; can indicate something to do with mourning
keen on INTO
keen on, be DIG
keen, very AVID; MAD
keenness EDGE
keep GUARD; HOLD; MIND; OBSERVE; PRESERVE; REMAIN; RETAIN; STOCK; STORE; TOWER
keep an eye on GAZE; OBSERVE; WATCH
keep in GATE; PEN
keep out BAN; BAR
keep pushing PLY
keep quiet SH; WHIST
keep score TALLY
keeper RING
keepsake TOKEN
ken KNOW; RANGE
Kent area SE
Kent, in SE
Kent town DEAL
Kentish SE
kept HELD; HAD; PENT
Ketch JACK
kettle DIXIE; DRUM
key A; B; C; CAY; D; B; E; G; LEVER; MAJOR; MINOR; PIN; REEF; TONE; TYPE (ie. as on a keyboard); can indicate something to do with an island
keyboard, at the TYPING
kick BLOW; BOOST; BOOT; BUZZ; CROSS; PASS; THRILL
kid BILLY; CHILD; COD; CON; DUPE; FOOL; GOAT; JOSH; LEATHER; RIB; SUEDE; TEASE; TOT; TWIT

kid, American BUB
kids ISSUE
kill BAG; DOIN (ie. do in); END; HANG; ICE; PREY; RUIN; SLAY; STOP; SWAT
kill without legal sanction LYNCH
killed SLAIN; SLEW
killed, be DIE
killed, was FELL
kiln OAST; OVEN; STOVE
killing MINT; PILE; POT; STACK
kin OWN; STOCK
kind CLASS; CLEMENT; GOOD; NICE; RACE; SORT; TYPE
kind-hearted TENDER
kind person ANGEL; BRICK; LAMB
kindred OWN
king CARD; COLE; ER; GEORGE; GR; K; LEAR; MAN; OFFA; PIECE; R; REX; RULER; SAUL; VIP
King Arthur's seneschal KAY
King Edward SPUD
king, old OFFA
King, Old COLE
king's REGAL; ROYAL
king's son HECTOR; PRINCE
kings, one of six GR
kingdom NEPAL; REALM; STATE; UK
kinky anagram indicator
Kipling novel KIM
Kipling verse IF
kiss BUSS; NECK; PECK; TOUCH; X
kisses, give NECK
kit GEAR; RIG; STRIP; can indicate something to do with clothing
kitchen GALLEY
kitty FUND; POOL
Klemperer OTTO
knack ART; CARD; HONOUR (ie. card); SKILL; TRICK; WAY
knave BOUNDER; CAD; JACK
knees-up DO
knew long ago WIST
knife BLADE; CUT; LANCET; STAB
knight KT; MAN; N; PIECE; SIR

knighthood K
knit BOND
knitted anagram indicator
knob BOSS; STUD
knock BASH; BAT; HIT; INNINGS; PAT; PINK; RAP; TAP
knock back DOWN; DRINK; EAT
knock down DECK; FLOOR
knock-out KO
knock up LOB
knocked back ATE; DRUNK
knock out *see* KNOCK UNCONSCIOUS
knocked out of shape anagram indicator
knocked over reversal indicator
knock unconscious KO; STUN
knot BEND (naut.); BIRD; GRANNY; REEF; SLIP; TIE
knotted anagram indicator
know KEN
know, get to LEARN
know(n) once WIST
knowing ARCH; AWARE; FLY; SLY
knowledge KEN; LORE; can indicate something to do with a cab-driver (a requirement of the job being to have "the knowledge")
knowledge, impart INFORM; TEACH
KO'd OUT
Koran, part of SURA

label TAG
labour GRAFT; TOIL; WORK; can indicate something to do with birth, baby etc.
Labour LAB; PARTY

labour organization GUILD; TU

laboured ORNATE

labourer HAND; PEON

labourer, unskilled COOLIE

lace SPIKE; TIE

lace, make TAT

lack NEED; WANT

lack of NO

lacking LESS; SHORT; SINE (legal); omission indicator as “lacking skill” requires ART to be omitted

lad BOY; SON; *see* BOY

ladder RUN; STEPS

ladies LOO

ladles’ man ROUE

ladies’ organisation WI

lady DAME; HER; LASS; SHE; *see* WOMAN

lady, for HER

lady, foreign FRAU

Lady MacBeth can indicate something to do with SPOT

lady, nasty CAT

lady, old GRAN; GRANNY; MUM

lady’s HER

lady, titled DAME

lag CON; WRAP

lager STELLA

Lagos, money in NAIRA

laid SET

laid-back COOL; reverse indicator

laid down SET; PLACED

laid up ILL; reversal indicator; component to be nested within BED (ie. in bed)

lair DEN; HOLE; HOLT

lake COMO; ERIE; L; LOCH; LOUGH; MERE; TARN

Lake District NW

lakes LL

lamb EWE; RAM

Lamb ELIA

Lamb-like ELIAN

Lambeth can indicate something to do with archbishop or palace

lame THIN; WEAK

lament ELEGY; KEEN; MOURN; WAIL; YAMMER
lamp LIGHT
lampoon SQUIB
lance CUT
land ESTATE; FIELD; LIGHT; PARK; PROPERTY; REACH; SOIL; TERRA; TRACT
land mass ASIA; ISLE
land, piece of ACRE; SOD; TRACT
landed LIT; can indicate some form of landowner – *see* LANDOWNER
landholder THANE
landing DOCK; JETTY; QUAY; can indicate something to do with stairs
landlord LETTER; HOST
landowner LAIRD; SQUIRE
lane ALLEY; ROAD; TRACK; WAY
language LANG; LINGO; SLANG; TALK; can indicate a specific language eg. BASQUE, ERSE, FRENCH; NORSE
language class, group NORSE
language, computer JAVA
language, informal SLANG
language, with command of FLUENT
languishing anagram indicator
lanky RANGY; THIN
lapse ERROR; FALL; SIN; SLIP; TRIP
lapse morally SIN
lard FAT
large AMPLE; BIG; GREAT; HUGE; L; MEGA; OS; ROOMY; TIDY; WIDE
large amount TON
large company ICI
large, grow WAX
large number C; M; MANY
large quantity LOT
large scale EPIC
large size OS
large sum MINT; POT
large, very OS
large wave ROLLER
lark ANTIC; CAPER; JAPE
larva GRUB
lash CAT; WHIP

lashings LOTS
lass GAL
lasso KNOT; LOOP; ROPE
last BOTTOM; END; ENDURE; FINAL; STAND; TAIL; WEAR; can indicate something to do with cobbler, shoes, etc; by implication can indicate the last of something eg. Z, OMEGA, AMEN
last (as in 'last of a kind') SOLE
last character Z
last minute LATE
last month ULT
last, not quite the last-but-one component to be used
last word AMEN
last of last letter indicator
last, work on COBBLE
latch LOCK
late EX; DEAD; FORMER; OLD; RECENT; TARDY; can indicate something to do with death, eg. funerals, heaven, meeting one's maker
late edition EXTRA
later AFTER; NEXT; THEN
latest NEW; NEWEST; NEWS; last letter indicator
latest odds SP
lather SWEAT
Latin L; LAT; can refer to some Latin word or phrase eg. 'in Latin thus' clues HOC
Latin bird AVIS
Latin, but in SED
Latin country RUS
Latin name NOMEN
Latin, this HIC
latitude PLAY; SCOPE
latitude, warm TROPIC
laugh HA; HOOT; SCREAM; TITTER
laughable RICH
laughter MIRTH
laughter-maker COMIC; HYENA; JESTER
launch OPEN; PITCH; START
laundry CLEANERS
lavished anagram indicator
lavatory CAN; HEAD; HEADS; JOHN; LAV; LOO; WC

law DECREE; EDICT; LEX; RULE
law, go to SUE
law group *see* LAWMEN
lawmen POSSE; *see* POLICE
lawful LEGAL; LICIT
Lawrence ROSS
lawsuit CASE
lawyer BL; DA; LLB; SILK
lawyers BAR; INN; INNS
lawyer, US DA
lax LOOSE; SLACK; anagram indicator
lay AIR; BET; PLACE; POSE; PUT; SET; SONG; SPREAD
lay out ARRAY; DECK; FLOOR; KO
layer CRUST; HEN; LEVEL; PLY; ROW; TIER
layer of dirt SCUM
layer of ore VEIN
laze IDLE; LOLL; REST
laziness SLOTH
lazy IDLE; anagram indicator
lead HEAD; OPEN; PILOT; PB; STAR; VAN; can indicate that an adjacent word goes to the front; can indicate the use of UP as "to lead at Wimbledon" can clue SET-UP
lead, in the AHEAD; FIRST; VAN; UP
leader AGA; BOSS; DUCE; HEAD; KING; POPE; STAR; initial letter indicator; can indicate something to do with a newspaper's leading article
leader, political P; PM
leaders initial letters indicator, either the initial letters of several words or the first two letters of one word; can require AND to be inserted between the initial letters as "Leaders of Royal Society" clues RANDS; can indicate something to do with a newspaper's leading article(s)
leadership, change of first letter to be changed
leading BIG; CHIEF; HEAD; PRIME; STAR; TOP; UP; initial letter(s) indicator; in conjunction with lady, men, etc. can indicate a ruler or the office of ruler
leading actor, player, role STAR
leading character A; ALPHA; first letter indicator; *see* LEADING ACTOR
leading group VAN
leading fighters VAN

leading journalist ED
leading monk PRIOR
leading position HEAD; STAR; TOP
leads initial letter indicator
leaf BRACT; F; FOLIO; PAGE
leaflet TRACT
leafy one PALM; *see* TREE
league ALLY; UNION
leak BLEED; ESCAPE; SEEP; DRIP
leaked BLED
Leamington SPA
lean HEEL; LIE; LIST; RELY; REST; SPARE; THIN; TILT; TIP
lean on ABUT
Leander can indicate something to do with HERO
leaning BENT
leap HOP; JETE; JUMP
Lear can refer to Shakespeare's play (and so Regan, Goneril, Cordelia) or Edward Lear, the latter suggesting something to do with nonsense
Lear's daughter REGAN
learn CON; HEAR
learn of HEAR
learner L; TYRO
learning LORE
learning method ROTE
lease HIRE; LET; RENT
leather HIDE; KID; OXHIDE; STROP
leather, type of CALF; *see* LEATHER
leathery HARD
leave DEPART; DROP; DESERT; EXIT; GO; PART; QUIT; SPLIT; STRAND; RETIRE; WILL; *see* ABANDON
leave behind WILL
leave car PARK
leave it be STET
leave out OMIT; SKIP
leaves FF; omission indicator; can indicate something to do with tea, mint, etc. or fall, autumn
leaving omission indicator
lecher GOAT; ROUE
lechery LUST
lecture ADDRESS; CHIDE; LECT; SERMON; TALK

lecturer DON
lee SHELTER
leer OGLE; STARE
left GONE; L; LABOUR; LORN; NEAR (ie. side of car in UK); ODD; PORT; QUIT; RED; WENT; omission indicator; run indicator [SINISTER];
left behind L or PORT to be at end of word
left side VO (ie. paper)
leftie *see* LEFT-WINGER
left-winger RED; TROT
leftover END; DREG; SCRAP
leg ON (ie. cricket); LIMB; PIN; STAGE; SIDE
leg, bit of CALF; SHIN
leg injury LIMP
leg, opposite OFF
leg, say (ie. for example) SIDE
leg, upper THIGH
legal LICIT
legal action CASE; SUIT
legal authority COURT; JUDGE
legal case, proceedings, process ACTION; APPEAL; SUIT
legal document DEED; WILL; WRIT
legal removal OUSTER
legal right LIEN
legal type WIG
legend FABLE; MYTH; YETI
legendary bird ROC
legion MYRIAD
legislation ACT; BILL; LAW
legislative assembly DIET; PARL
legislator MP
legislature DAIL; PARL
legitimate LEGAL; LICIT
legs PINS; STAGES
legwear TIGHTS
Leicester CHEESE
length FOOT; L; MILE; YARD
Lent FAST
lentil PULSE
Leo HOUSE; SIGN

Leonard LEN
Leopold BLOOM
less MINUS; omission indicator
-less as a suffix 'less' can be an omission indicator for the element to which it is attached as, for instance, 'artless' signifies that ART be dropped; can indicate a word ending in FREE
less so SO to be omitted
less than BELOW; UNDER
lessee RENTER
lessened LOWER
lesson CLASS; MORAL; PERIOD; TEACHING
lessons COURSE
let ALLOW; ALLOWED; HIRE; HIRED; LEASE; LEASED
let down DEFLATE; LOWER
let go DROP; FREE
let off anagram of LET
let out FREE; FREED; HIRE; LEASED; VENT; anagram of LET
lethargic type CABBAGE
letter NOTE; RUNE; SCREED; can indicate the use of a character (A, B, C etc., or in full eg. EM, ESS, KAY); rem: 'letter' is also an old standby for referring to something to do with a landlord
letter, old RUNE
letter-writer PAUL
letters MAIL; POST; PRINT; anagram indicator; can indicate a run of letters within the alphabet as "nine letters" clues ATOI (ie. A to I, the first nine letters of the alphabet) which is the device used in 'Nine letters recalled in one' to yield IOTA
letters said BEES; CEASE; EASE; ELLS; PEAS; TEASE; USE
lettuce COS
level AIM; EVEN; FLAT; FLOOR; GRADE; PAR; PLANE; POINT; RASE; RAZE; STOREY; TIE; TIED; TIER; TRAIN
level-headed SENSIBLE
level of water TABLE
lever BAR; PRISE; STICK; TREADLE
levy RAISE; TAX
liability anagram indicator
liability, evidence of LOUS
liable APT
liberal AMPLE; BROAD; FREE; LAVISH
Liberal L; LIB
liberated FREE; anagram indicator

libertine RAKE
liberty, at FREE
library equipment SHELF
licence ALLOW; GRANT; PERMIT; RIGHT
licentious FREE; RIBALD
licit LEGAL
lid CAP; COVER; STOPPER; TOP; *see* HAT
Liechtenstein FL
lie FIB; FICTION; LINE; REST; TALE
lie, big WHOPPER
lie in bed KIP
lien RIGHT
lieutenant L; LT
life GO; SENTENCE; SPAN; VALE; ZIP
life, enjoy BE
life, have BE
lifetime DAY
lift HEAVE; HITCH; HOICK; HOIST; JACK; NICK; RAISE; RIDE; STEAL; SWIPE; reversal indicator
lift, sort of SNATCH
lifted up PU; reversal indicator
lifting reversal indicator
lift-shaft WELL
light AMBER; BEACON; BEAM; CANDLE; DAY; FAIR; FEEBLE; GIDDY; GLEAM; GREEN; KINDLE; LAMP; LOW; NEON; MATCH; MOON; PALE; RAY; RED; SHINE; SHY; SPOT; STAR; STROBE; SUN; TAPER; TORCH; UV; VESTA; WINDOW
light, bring to EXPOSE
light, colour ECRU
light meal BITE
light, natural SUN
light period DAY
light, sort of HEAD; SIDE; SPOT
light speed C
lighter BARGE; PALER; SCOW; SPILL
lighting LAMP; *see* LIGHT
lightly cooked RARE
lightning BOLT; FLASH
lights LUNGS
lightweight GR; GRAM; OUNCE; OZ
like AS; DIG; LOVE; TOAST; can indicate some adjective (eg.

ending in -ISH)
like, do not DETEST; HATE; LOATHE; MIND
like this SO; THUS
likely APT; PRONE; SET
likewise AS; SO; TOO
liking CRUSH; FANCY; PENCHANT; TASTE
limb ARM; BRANCH; LEG
limit BORDER; BOUND; BOURN; CAP; EDGE; END; LINE; RATION
limit, beyond OTT
limit, without ALL
limitation nesting indicator
limited abbreviation indicator
limiting nesting indicator
limits first and last letters indicator; nesting indicator; can indicate something which surrounds; *see* LIMIT
limo CAR
Lincoln ABE; GREEN
linden tree LIME
line ANGLE; ARY (ie. a RY); BAND; BARB; CAREER; CORD; DASH; EDGE; EM; EN; FILE; JOB; L; LEY; LIST; NOTE; OCHE; PAD; RANGE; RAY; ROPE; ROW; RY; SCORE; SHEET; STREAK; STRIPE; TACK; TIER; TRACK; TROPIC; VIEW
line, brush STROKE
line, small DASH; EM; EN; L; RY
line up DRESS
line-up FIELD
lineage BREED; STOCK
linen SHEETS
lines BAR; LL; ODE; ODES; POEM; R; RADII; RY; SONNET; TRACK; VERSE [ECLOGUE; RHYME]
lines, part of FEET
lines, some PARA
linger LAG; STAY; TARRY
lining nesting indicator; run indicator
link BOND; BRIDGE; NEXUS; SPAN; THREAD; TIE; YOKE
links CHAIN; MAIL; *see* LINK
lions PRIDE
lip BRASS; CHEEK; EDGE; RIM; SAUCE; VERGE
liquid LOTION; RAIN; WATER
liquid mess SLOSH

liquid, without ARID; DRY
liquor ALE; GIN; RUM; RYE; SAKE; *see* DRINK
list CANT; HEEL; LEAN; ROLL; ROSTER; ROTA; TABLE
listen HARK; HEAR; HIST; homophone indicator
listened HEARD; homophone indicator
listening EAR
listening device BUG
lit IN; ON
lit-up HIGH; *see* DRUNK
literary collection ANA (ie. suffix as in Americana, for example)
literary work VERSE
literature LIT
lithe SPRY; anagram indicator
lithium LI
litter BROOD; REFUSE; STRETCHER; *see* RUBBISH
litter, part of PUP
little BIT; DASH; DROP; MINI; O; PETITE; PUNY; SHORT; SHRED; SPOT; TAD; TRACE; WEE; WHIT; abbreviation indicator
little, a BIT; OUNCE
little brother BRO; SIB
little boy diminutive of male name (eg. AL, ED, TED); *see* MAN
little chap TOM; *see* LITTLE BOY; can indicate something to do with midget etc.
little drink DRAM; HALF; SHORT; TOT
little girl SIS; diminutive of woman's name (eg. DI, MO); *see* WOMAN
little house COT; H
little man PAWN
little money CENT; L; P
little room CELL; DEN
little, saying QUIET
little sister SIB; SIS
little time HR; MO; SEC; T; YR
little woman diminutive of woman's name (eg. JO, MO); *see* WOMAN
liturgy RITE
live ABIDE; ARE; BE; DWELL; QUICK; RESIDE
lived WERE
liveliness BRIO; ESPRIT; GO
lively AGILE; GAMY; PACY; SPRY; anagram indicator
Liverpudlian SCOUSE

lives IS
Lizzie BETH
load CHARGE; FILL; FREIGHT; LADE; LOT; ONUS; PILE; STACK
loaded FULL; LADEN; nesting indicator; *see* DRUNK
loaf BEAN; BREAD; HEAD; IDLE; LAZE; NOODLE
loafer BUM; DRONE; SHOE
loan LENDING
loan, extend RENEW
loaned LENT
lobby HALL; FACTION
local NUMBER (ie. anaesthetic); PUB
local area PATCH
local authority COUNCIL
locate PLACE; SITE; TRACE
located in nesting indicator
location PLACE; SITE; SPOT
loch NESS
lock LATCH; *see* HAIR
lock, end of GATE; K
locks QUIFF, TRESS; *see* HAIR
lode ORE; REEF
lodge DWELL; HOUSE; PLACE; STAY
lodgings DIGS; PLACE
loft ATTIC
lofty HIGH; TALL
log ENTER
logarithm LOG
logic REASON
loiter MOOCH
loll LAZE
London CAPITAL; SMOKE; WEN; note, a fair knowledge of London landmarks, stations and suburbs is assumed, eg. ACTON, POPLAR, SOHO
London area POPLAR; SE
London attraction EYE
London borough EALING
London college LSE
London coppers, police MET; YARD
London, from DOWN

London, heading for UP
London hospital BARTS; UCH
London, part of ACTON; C; E; N; NE; NW; POPLAR; S; SE; SOHO; SW
London, to UP
lone SOLO
long ACHE; DIE; HANKER; ITCH; L; PANT; PINE; SIGH; TALL; WANT; YEARN
long ago ERST
long-ago PAST
long ago, knew WIST
long, before ANON
long-delayed SLOW
long-established OLD
long for COVET
long, not BRIEF; SHORT
long period, time AEON; AGE; CENTURY; EON; EPOCH; ERA
long-suffering PATIENT
long way AFAR; FAR
long while *see* LONG PERIOD
longer MORE
longer, no ONCE; EX
longing DYING; ITCH; PAIN; URGE; WISH; YEN
longs DIES; *see* LONG; can refer to trousers eg. TREWS
loo GENTS
look AIR; APPEAR; EYE; GANDER; GAPE; GAZE; GLANCE; LEER; LO; MIEN; OGLE; PEEK; PEER; SCAN; STARE; WATCH
look after MIND; TEND
look curiously PEER; PRY
look, dirty LOUR
look forward to LIKE
look hard STARE
look inquisitively PEEK; PEER; PRY
look, oppressive LOUR
look out CAVE; WARE
look, sly PEEK
look worried FROWN
look up CALL; VISIT
lookalike DOUBLE; RINGER
looked EYED

looker EYE
looks for gold PANS
looks, sly PEEK
looming NIGH
loop BIGHT; NOOSE; RING
loose FREE; LAX; SLACK; UNTIE; VAGUE; anagram indicator
loose stones SCREE
loosely anagram indicator
loosen FREE; UNTIE
loot ROB; SACK; SWAG
lop CUT
lope RUN
lopped omission indicator
lord BARON; EARL; LD; PEER
Lorraine CROSS
lorry ARTIC; TANKER; TIPPER; TRUCK; WAGON
lose MISS
lose colour FADE
lose force DIE; can indicate omission of F (force), G (gravity)
lose vital forces DIE
loses anagram indicator
loses heart middle letter(s) to be omitted
losing DOWN; omission indicator; anagram indicator
loss DEATH; TOLL; omission indicator
loss, without FREE
lost omission indicator; anagram indicator
lost blood BLED
lot ALL; CO (for company); CROWD; DEAL; DOOM; FATE; GANG; GROUP; MANY; MUCH; PILE; PLIGHT; SET; SIGHT; SITE; STACK; in its meaning of 'fate' can lead to associated words such as FATALIST; can indicate something to do with AUCTION, SALE
lot, a BAGS
lot of can indicate that one is to use most of the letters in what follows to provide either a component, or the complete answer
lot of birds FLOCK
lot of money BOMB; GRAND
lot of paper (writing) REAM
lot of sheep FLOCK
lots of people CROWD; *see* CROWD, GANG
lots HATFUL; OODLES; SIGHT; STACKS; TON; can indicate

something to do with AUCTION, SALE
lots of can indicate that most of a word is to be used
lots of dollars G
lottery DRAW
lotto BINGO
loud BRASH; BRASSY; BRIGHT; F
loud, very FF
loudly F
loudly, not softly F to replace P
loudspeaker TWEETER
lough ERNE; LAKE
Louis JOE
lounge IDLE
lousy CRUMMY; anagram indicator
lout OAF; YOB
love ADORE; DEAR; EROS; FANCY; LIKE; NIL; NOUGHT; O; PET; SEX; ZERO; *see* DARLING, DEAR; [POINTLESS]
love affair AMOUR
love, classic AMOR
loveless indicates the omission of O from associated word
lovely ANGELIC; FAIR; SWEET
lovely girl DISH; PEACH
lover AMOUR; BEAU; BUFF; FAN; FLAME; ROMEO; SWAIN
lover, classical HERO
lover, tragic LEANDER
lovesick anagram of LOVE
low BASE; DOWN; LIGHT; MOO; POOR; UNDER; SAD
low alcohol LITE
low tone MOO
lower ABASE; BELOW; COW; CUT; DIM; DOWN; DROP; LUFF; NETHER; UNDER; can indicate something to do with cattle
lower class NON-U
lower classes DE
lowest part BASE; BED (ie. of river); FOOT
loyal TRUE
loyal person BRICK
loyalty TROTH
LSD ACID; CASH; DOPE; DRUG; MONEY; specifically it can refer to some aspect of pre-decimal currency
lubricate OIL

lucid CLEAR; PLAIN
lucifer MATCH
luck BREAK; CESS (Irish); CHANCE; HAP; LADY
lug DRAG; EAR; HAUL; PULL; SAIL
luggage BAG; CASE
luggage carrier PORTER; RACK
luggage compartment BOOT
lump CHUNK; CLOD; MASS
lump (of butter) PAT
lunar excursion module LEM
lunatic NUT
lunch, out to MAD; NUTS
lunchtime, around I; ONE
lunge PASS; RUSH
lungs (as food) LIGHTS
lure DRAW; TEMPT
lurk behind DOG
lush DRUNK; GREEN; RICH; SOT; TOPER
lust SIN
lusty EARTHY
luxuriant LUSH; PLUSH
luxury car LIMO; ROLLS; RR
lying ABED; FLAT; PRONE
lyric AIR; EPODE; VERSE; WORDS

Mm

macabre SICK
MacBeth THANE
MacBeth character WITCH
MacBeth, part of ROSS
machine LOOM
machine tool LATHE

macho MALE
mad BARMY; BATS; FRANTIC; GAGA; NUTS; RABID; TOUCHED; anagram indicator
mad party member HATTER
Madagascar MR
maddened, maddening anagram indicator
made GOT; anagram indicator
made badly TRASHY
made up LIED
madman NUT
madness RAGE
Mafia chief CAPO
magazine COMIC; GLOSSY; ISSUE; MAG; ORGAN; specific titles eg. HELLO, LIFE, PUNCH, NATURE, TIME, WHICH
magazine, U.S. LIFE; TIME
magic ART
magic formula SPELL
magical feat TRICK
magistrate BEAK; CONSUL; DOGE; JP; REEVE
magistrate, before, facing UP
magistrate's assistant LICTOR
magistrates BENCH
magnificent REGAL
maid MISS
maid, old PRUDE
maiden M; can indicate something to do with OVER
mail ARMOUR; POST
maim WOUND
main CHIEF; HEAD; SEA; STAPLE; WATER; usually has some sea connotation
main point CRUX; GIST; HUB; NUB
Maine ME
maintain AFFIRM; AVER; KEEP; PLEAD; FIX
maintain firmly FIX
maintaining nesting indicator
maintenance CARE
major BIG
majority MASS; MOST
make BRAND; CAUSE; CREATE; DELIVER (ie. as with speech); DO; EARN; FORCE; FORM; GET; MARQUE; TYPE; anagram indicator; run indicator

make an impression ETCH
make arrangements ORDER
make beastly noise GROWL; LOW; MOO
make coins MINT
make corrections AMEND; EDIT; EMEND
make, could anagram indicator
make for HEAD
make fun of RIB
make good MEND
make haste RUSH; TEAR
make hay TED
make heavy demands TAX
make money EARN; MINT
make notes SING
make out SEE
make progress ROLL
make progress socially CLIMB
make recording TAPE
make slow progress PLOD
make smaller REDUCE
make tea MASH
make-up LINER; ROUGE; anagram indicator
make use of TAP
makes anagram indicator; run indicator
makeshift anagram indicator
making anagram indicator; run indicator
Malay dagger KRIS
Malaysian capital KL; M
male BUCK; BULL; HE; M; MACHO; MAN; RAM; STAG; TOM; TUP
male, a French UN
malediction CURSE
malefactor FELON
malfunction BUG; FAULT; FLAW; GLITCH
malfunctioning anagram indicator
malicious BAD; EVIL; SNIDE
malign EVIL
mammal ANIMAL; can call for the name of a specific mammal
mammal, aquatic OTTER
man AL; ALEX; ART; B; BEN; BERT; BISHOP; BLOKE; BOD;

CHAP; DAN; DAVE; DES; ED; ERIC; FELLOW; GENT; GREG; GUS; GUY; HAND; HANDLE; HE; HECTOR; HIM; HOMBRE; IAN; K; KAY; KING; KNIGHT; KT (knight in chess); LAD; LEN; LES; MALE; MIKE; MILES; N (knight in chess); NAT; NICK; NED; NEIL; P; PAT; PAWN; PETER; PHIL; PIECE; Q; QUEEN; R; RAY; REG; ROGER; RON; ROOK; SID; STAFF; TED; TIM; VALET; *see* FELLOW

Man I; IOM; IS; ISLE a favourite with compilers, referring to the island usually with 'Man' at the beginning of the clue so the solver may not realise the underlying significance of the capital letter [FRIDAY]

man, admired HERO

man, classical VIR

man, first ADAM

man, good ST

man in BATTER (ie. cricket)

man in charge KING

man, little PAWN; can call for the short form of man's name eg. LES, TIM; *see* MAN

man of cloth CURATE; DRAPER; REV; *see* VICAR, PRIEST, ETC.

man of fashion RAKE

man of muscle HUNK

man of note often calls for a composer's name

man's HES (ie. he's); HIS

man's address MR; SIR

Man's device LEGS (ie. Manx emblem)

man, strong TITAN

man, the HIM

man, typical JACK

man, young LAD; MASTER

manage BOSS; COPE; HANDLE; RUN; SHIFT; TEND; TREAT

manage to retain SALVE; SAVE

managed RAN; anagram indicator

management ADMIN; BOARD; RUNNING; anagram indicator

management graduate MBA

management group BOARD; TRUST

manager BOSS; CHIEF; COPER; EXEC; HEAD; RUNNER

managers BOARD

mandarin DRAKE

mane HAIR; SHOCK

mangle HACK; PRESS

mangled RENT; TORN; anagram indicator
manifesto LINE
manipulate FIX; RIG; USE; anagram indicator
manipulated USED; anagram indicator
manipulation anagram indicator
mannequin MODEL
manner AIR; MODE; STYLE; WAY
manner of ALA (ie. A LA)
manoeuvrable NIPPY
manoeuvre FEINT; GAMBIT; PLOY; TACTIC; anagram indicator
manoeuvring anagram indicator
manor HALL
manservant VALET
mansion PALACE
mansion, country SEAT
mantra ON
manufactured MADE; anagram indicator
manure HUMUS
manuscript MS
many BAGS; LOT; LOTS; MASS; MASSES; MULTI; OODLES; POTS; can be used to signal a Roman numeral for a large number, such as L, C, D, K etc; *see* GREAT MANY
many, great SLEW; *see* MANY
many people HOST
map CHART; GUIDE; PLAN
map-making department OS
maple ACER
marble AGATE; ALLEY; ALLY
march BORDER; DEMO; FILE; STEP; STRIDE; STRUT
Marco Polo rem: this is also an airport as well as a famous explorer
Marge's rival BUTTER
margin EDGE
marijuana GRASS
marine RN
mariner *see* SAILOR
Marines RN
maritime environment SHORE
mark BADGE; BLAZE; DENT; DOT; EMBLEM; M; LISTEN; NOTCH; NOTE; SCAR; SCUFF; SIGN; SPOT; STAIN; STAR; TALLY; TEE; TICK; can indicate something to do with money (ie. German currency)

Mark can indicate something to do with GOSPEL
mark of distinction STAR
mark, top A; STAR
mark of rank PIP
marker SIGN
market AGORA; EXCHANGE; FAIR; MART; SELL; TRADE
marketing TRADE
marmalade SQUISH
maroon STRAND
marque BRAND; MAKE
Marquis SADE
marred anagram indicator
marriage ALLIANCE; BOND; MATCH; TIE; UNION; WEDDING
marriage settlement DOWER
married M; MATED; SPLICED; WED
married, get MATE; WED
marrow GIST
marry UNITE; WED
Mars ARES
marsh BOG; PEN; MIRE; SWAMP
marshy PLASHY
marsupial ROO
martyr ST
marvel WONDER
Marxist RED
mask COVER
Masons LODGE
mass BODY; BULK; CROWD; GRAM; HEAP; LUMP; M; PILE; RUCK; SERVICE; STACK; TON; TONNE; can signify a specific mountain or mountain range; can signify the general population as "Mass in Greek" clues HOI POLLOI
mass, part of CREDO
Massachusetts MA; MASS
massaged anagram indicator
masseur RUBBER
master ACE; BEAT; BETTER; LEARN; LORD; M; MA; SIR; SKIPPER
master of ceremonies EMCEE
masterful ACE
mastery ART ; CRAFT; SKILL
masts, arrangement of RIG

mat RUG
match AGREE; BOUT; FUSE; GAME; GO; LIGHT; PAIR; SET; SO; SUIT; TALLY; TEAM; TEST; TIE; VESTA; can indicate something to do with wedding, marriage
match, boxing BOUT
match, football TIE
match in series LEG
matched MET
matches CUP; RUBBER
matching TWIN
mate BRIDE; CHINA; COCK; CHUM; COBBER; GROOM; HEN; MUCKER; PAL; TOSH; can indicate something to do with chess
mate, Australian SPORT
mate down under COBBER
material CLOTH; CREPE; DENIM; LACE; REP; SERGE; TICKING; TOILE; TWILL; WOOL; *see* FABRIC
material, roofing SLATE; THATCH
mates PAIR
mathematical quantity LOG
mathematician ADDER; GAUSS
mathematician's power LOG
mathematics, bit of GRAPH
Matilda can signal something to do with lies, lying
matter PUS; TOPIC
Matthew and the rest NT
mature ADULT; AGE; AGED; RIPE; RIPEN
mauled anagram indicator
maverick anagram indicator
maxim SAW; TRUISM
maximum BEST; HEIGHT; TOP
maximum speed C
may MIGHT
May French MAI
maybe anagram indicator
Mayfair WI
mayonnaise DRESSING
mayor's insignia CHAIN
maze WARREN
MC HOST
me, for MY
me, you and US

meadow LEA; LEY
meagre LEAN; SLENDER; SLIM; THIN
meal BRUNCH; COURSE; CURRY; DINNER; DISH; FARE; FEED; FLOUR; GRAIN; LUNCH; PULSE; SNACK; SPREAD; SUPPER; TEA
meal, gave FED
meal, had ATE
meal, hot CHILLI; CURRY
meal ticket LV
meal, take EAT; FEED
meal, took ATE; FED
meals EATS; BOARD
mean AIM; BASE; IMPLY; INTEND; NEAR; PAR; PLAN; STINGY; TIGHT
meaning DRIFT; GIST; IMPORT; INTENT; SENSE
means AGENCY; MEDIA; WAY
means of, by VIA
measure ACT; AMP; BOLT; CARAT; CC; CL; DANCE; DOSE; ELL; EM; EN; ERG; FOOT; FT; GILL; HAND; INCH; JUDGE; LEAGUE; METE; METER; MILE; OPTIC; PACE; PECK; PINT; QUART; ROOD; STEP; TUN; UNIT; WATT; YARD; can also refer to a particular dance
measure, medicinal DOSE
measure of cloth BOLT; ELL
measure of grain PECK
measure of horse HAND
measure of insulation TOG
measure of speed MPH
measure of viscosity STOKE
measure, small DASH; SNORT; SPLASH; can indicate abbreviation of standard measures; *see* MEASURE
measurement see measure
measurement of about 45" ELL
measures FEET; *see* MEASURE
meat BARON; BEEF; FLESH; HAM; LAMB; LOIN; MINCE; MUTTON; OFFAL; PORK; RIB; RUMP; SPAM; STEAK; VEAL
meat, joint of BRAWN, COLLAR; *see* MEAT
meat, piece of CHOP; *see* MEAT
mechanic FITTER
medal AWARD; BRONZE; DSO; GC; GOLD; GONG; MM; SILVER; VC

meddle NOSE
media PRESS
medic DR; *see* DOCTOR
medic, famous GALEN
medical speciality ENT
medical treatment PILL
medication PILL
medicine MED; PILL
medicine bottle PHIAL
medicinal measure DOSE
medico DOC; DR; *see* DOCTOR
meditate BROOD; MUSE
Mediterranean MED
Mediterranean area LEVANT
medium AGENT; ETHER; OIL; TEMPERA
medley anagram indicator
medley-race anagram of RACE
meet APT; COUNTER; FACE; FIT; GATHER; PAY
meeting AGM; CONTACT; DATE; MATCH; RALLY; SEANCE; SESSION; TRYST
meeting for work BEE
meeting place VENUE
mega ACE; SUPER
melody AIR; STRAIN; TUNE
melt THAW
melting snow SLUSH
melt down RENDER
member ARM; BRANCH; JOIST; LEG; LIMB; MP; PART
member, crew HAND; *see* SAILOR
member, younger SCION
members of run indicator
membership fee SUB
memento TOKEN
memo NOTE
memorial tablet PLAQUE
memory RAM; ROM; ROTE
men STAFF; this can require the names of two men to be used together to form a new component or word eg. PATRON; *see* MAN, SOLDIER
menacing look LOUR

mend DARN; REPAIR; anagram indicator
mendacious LYING
Mendelssohn can indicate something to do with ITALIAN (one of his symphonies)
menial BASE; SERF
menswear TIE
mention CITE
mentioned homophone indicator
merchandise GOODS
merchant MONGER
merciless IRON
mercury HG
mercy QUARTER; RUTH
mere BARE; JUST; LAKE; SMALL
merge FUSE; JOIN
merger FUSION
merit EARN; RATE
merriment GLEE
merry GAY; HAPPY; anagram indicator
mesh GRID; NET
mess BOTCH; HASH; SLOSH; anagram indicator
message CABLE; LETTER; LINE; MEMO; NOTE; SIGN; SIGNAL
message received ROGER
message, urgent SOS
messed up/messing about/messy anagram indicator
messenger PAGE
messy situation STY
Met YARD
metal AU; BA; CU; FE; HG; IRON; ORE; PLATE; SN
metal, lump of PIG
metallic TINNY
metalworker BEATER; SMITH
metamorphosis anagram indicator
mete DOLE; SHARE
method HOW; LINE; MANNER; ORDER; SYSTEM; WAY
meticulousness CARE
metre M
metric can indicate something to do with verse
metropolis CITY
Mexican food TACO

microphone MIC; MIKE
mid- as a prefix (eg. mid-July) usually signifies that the middle letter(s) should be taken from the associated word eg. 'mid-July' indicates UL, 'mid-afternoon' indicates R, 'mid-off' indicates F
mid-day A; NOON
mid-life IF
mid-morning N; TEN
middle CORE; *see* MIDDLE OF
Middle East ME; AS
Middle Eastern ME; T
Middle Easterner ARAB
middle of can signify that the middle letter(s) should be taken from the associated word
middle point MEDIAN
middling SOSO
Midlands city STOKE
midnight G
midnight, hour after IAM
midshipman EASY
MIG JET
might BEEF; CLOUT; POWER
Mike can indicate something to do with a microphone; depending on context (eg. "as heard by Mike") can be a homophone indicator
mild LIGHT; LOW; SLIGHT; WEAK
milder LESS
mile M
mile or so KNOT
miles MM
miles away M to be omitted
military ARMY; MIL
military alliance NATO
military commander AGA
military man *see* OFFICER, SOLDIER
military operation MISSION
military prisoner POW
military quarters CAMP
military status RANK; SITREP
military training group OTC
military unit TA
military vehicle JEEP; TANK
military zone SECTOR

milk EXTRACT; PINT; SQUEEZE
milk pudding SAGO
millennium building DOME
miller GLENN
million M
mince CHOP; CUT; GRIND; anagram indicator
mince-tart anagram of TART
minced CUT; GROUND; anagram indicator
mind BRAIN; CARE; NOUS; RESENT; TEND
mine DIG; PIT
Minehead M
miner DIGGER
mineral SPAR
mineral aggregate ORE
Ming POT
mini CAR; SKIRT; SMALL
miniature MINI; SMALL; TOY
minimal LIGHT; SMALL; can indicate use of only one letter from an indicated word
minimal sum IF
minimally, minimum can indicate use of only one letter from an indicated word
minion TOOL
minister CARE; ENVOY; MIN; PARSON; PASTOR; PRIEST; REV; SERVE; TEND
minister, former foreign GREY
ministers CLOTH
ministry MIN; MOD
minister's house MANSE
minor LESS; LIGHT; SLIGHT; SMALL; WARD; can call for an abbreviation as 'minor street' clues ST
minor illness COLD
mint COIN; NEW; POT; TOP
minus LESS; SIGN
minute MIN; NOTE (ie. as in take minutes); WEE
marvel WONDER
mire MARSH; MUD
mirror GLASS; can indicate something to do with reflection, face or Snow White
mirth GLEE
misanthrope TIMON

misbehave, misbehaving, misbehaviour anagram indicator
mischief HARM
mischief-maker ATE (Greek goddess); ELF; IMP; SCAMP
mischievous child ELF; IMP; SCAMP
misconduct anagram indicator
misconstrued anagram indicator
misdemeanour SIN
miser SNUDGE
miserable DOWN; GLUM; SAD
miserably anagram indicator
misery GLOOM; WOE
misfortune ILL
misguided anagram indicator
mishandle BLOW; MUFF
mishandled anagram indicator
misinterpreted anagram indicator
mislaid LOST
mislead DELUDE; DUPE
misleading anagram indicator
misleading statement LIE
misled LIED
mislocated anagram indicator
misplaced anagram indicator
misread anagram indicator
misrepresent BELIE; anagram indicator
misrepresented anagram indicator
misrepresentation LIBEL; LIE; SLANDER; STORY; TALE; anagram indicator
misrepresents anagram indicator
miss FAIL; LACK; LASS; LOSE; MAID; MUFF; NEED; OMIT; SKIP
miss, modern MS
missed omission indicator
missed, not can signify something to do with a married woman
misshapen anagram indicator
missile ARROW; DART; SAM; SCUD
missile-launcher BOW; EROS
missing LACKING
mission ALAMO; RAID; TASK
mist FOG; FRET; HAZE

mistake BISH; BLUNDER; BOOB; ERR; ERROR; GAFF; GAFFE HOWLER; LAPSE; SLIP; anagram indicator
mistake, make ERR
mistaken, mistakenly anagram indicator
mistakes, without CLEAN; CLEAR
Mr Chips can indicate something to do with school eg. MASTER
mistiness FILM
mistreated anagram indicator
mistress, royal NELL
misused anagram indicator
mix BLEND; GARBLE; anagram indicator
mix up JUMBLE; TANGLE; anagram indicator
mixed anagram indicator
mixed-up type PI; PIE
mixing anagram indicator
mixture BREW; MASH; anagram indicator
moan BEEF; GRIPE; GROUSE; SIGH
mob CROWD; HERD; HORDE
mobile PHONE; can indicate something to do with transport, cars, or moving people eg. nomad, ambler
mobilise MARSHAL
mock JEER; RAG; SCOFF; SCORN; SHAM; TAUNT
mockery CHAFF
model COPY; DOLL; DUMMY; FORM; IDEAL; LAST (ie. cobbler's); POSE; POSER; SIT; SITTER; T (ie. from Ford Model T); TOY; anagram indicator
modeling FORMING; POSING; SITTING; anagram indicator
moderate BLAND; EASE; LOWER; MILD
moderate Conservative WET
modern AD; LATTER; MOD; NEW
modern style HIP
modest COY; SHY
modification, modified anagram indicator
modify TEMPER
modish IN
Mogul capital AGRA
moist DAMP
mole JETTY; PIER
mole's work SPYING
mollusc ORMER; SNAIL; WINKLE
Molly BLOOM

molten anagram indicator
moment INSTANT; JIFFY; MO; SEC; TICK; TRICE
momentous SIGNAL
monarch ANNE; COLE; ER; GR; HM; KING; QUEEN; R; RH
monastic clique, group etc ORDER
monastic singing CHANT
Mondeo FORD
money ANNA; BILL; BOODLE; BRASS; BREAD; CASH; CENT; COIN; DOUGH; DOSH; ECU; FEE; FLOAT; FUND; KITTY; LOLLY; L; LUCRE; LY; NOTE; NOTES; P; READY; RIAL; ROLL; SOU; TAKE; TENDER; TIN; RHINO; *see* CURRENCY
money, American BUCK; CENT; ROLL
money, amount of FUND
money, attempt to make SPEC
money, European DM; FRANC; GUILDER; LIRE; LIRA; MARK
money, extra BONUS; TIP
money from overseas *see* FOREIGN CURRENCY
money, get EARN
money given TIP
money instantly needed FLOAT
money, lacking BROKE
money, large amount of *see* MONEY, LOADS OF
money, little D; L; MITE; P; S
money, load(s), lot(s) of BUNDLE; BOMB; MINT; PILE; WAD
money, make EARN; GROSS; MINT
money-makers MINT
money, more RISE
money, old BOB; CROWN; D; DUCAT; GROAT; JOEY; LSD; S; TANNER
money, one taking CASHIER
money, try to get DUN
moneybag PURSE
mongrel CROSS
monitor SCREEN
monk LAMA; TUCK (ie, Friar Tuck)
monk, leading PRIOR
monkey APE; HOWLER
monks ORDER
monograph PAPER
monsoon RAIN
monotonous SAMEY

monotonous speech DRONE
monster DRAGON; HYDRA; OGRE; TROLL
monster's home NESS
month MO; MOON; abbreviations for months are common: JAN, FEB, MAR, APR, MAY, JUN, JUL, AUG, SEPT, OCT, NOV, DEC
month in France MAI
month, last ULT
month, this INST
monthly MAG
mood AIR; FIT; KEY; STATE; TONE; TEMPER; VEIN
moon LIGHT; LUNA
moon about MOPE
moor DOCK; FELL; HEATH
moorland FELL; HEATH
mop SWAB
mope FRET; PINE
Moral Re-armament MRA
moran BOG
more EXTRA; LONGER; OVER; PIU (ie. mus); PLUS; can suggest the answer is a word ending in ER; with a capital letter can refer to something to do with Sir Thomas More eg. Utopia;
more, fifty changes an L to a C
more, five changes a V to an X
more, five hundred changes a D to an M
more than OVER; run indicator (subtly suggesting that a word or phrase contains more letters than necessary)
more or less ABOUT; C; PRETTY
moribund DYING
morning AM; MORN
Morse CODE
Morse signal, unit DASH; DOT; DIT
mortar GROUT
mortgage LOAN
mortified SICK
Moslem ALI
most can indicate that most letters of a word are to be used, either in a run or as an anagram
most desirable BEST
most successful BEST; TOP
mostly all but one letter (sometimes two letters) of a word to be used
mother DAM; MA; MATER; MUM

Mother NATURE
mother, be BEAR; POUR
mother, beastly DAM
motherland HOME
mother's MAS
motion SIGNAL
motivate FIRE
motivation DRIVE; GO
motive REASON
motor CAR; DRIVER; ENGINE; TURBO; can refer to a particular marque commonly: JAG, FORD, MINI, RR, ROLLER
motorcyclist BIKER
motorist DRIVER
motorists AA; RAC
motorway M; MI
motorway organisation AA; RAC
motto SAW
mould CAST; FORM; FUR; SHAPE
moulded CAST
mouldy OFF
mound BANK; BARROW; HILL; PILE
mount ALP; ASS; CLIMB; HILL; HORSE; MULE; SCALE; STAGE; TOR; can indicate that the name of specific mountain is required eg. RIGI; *see* HORSE
mountain ALP; BEN; BERG; IDA; SION
mountain pass COL; GATE
mountain side FACE
mountains RANGE
mounted UP; reversal indicator
mounting reversal indicator
mourn RUE
mouse MICKEY
mouth MAW; GOB; STOMA; TRAP; can indicate the use of an initial letter as 'mouth of the Nile' clues N
mouth, by ORAL
mouthful BITE
mouthpiece GUM; ORGAN
move BETAKE; BUDGE; CASTLE (as in chess); EDGE; FLIT; GO; HURRY; LUNGE; LURCH; ROLL; ROUSE; SELL; SHIFT; SIDLE; STIR; TOUCH; anagram indicator
move awkwardly LUMBER

move carefully EDGE; INCH
move cautiously EDGE; INCH; NOSE
move, decisive MATE
move fast (quickly, swiftly) FLY; HURRY; RUN; RUSH; SCUD; SPEED; SPRINT; ZOOM
move furtively CREEP; SIDLE
move, on the GOING; anagram indicator
move, opening GAMBIT
move out VACATE
move painfully LIMP
move slowly EDGE; INCH
move suddenly DART; LUNGE; NIP
move to side SHUNT
move unsteadily LURCH; REEL
moved SENT; anagram indicator
movement BOBBLE; MOTION; STEP; TIC; TWITCH; anagram indicator
movement, slow LARGO
movement, sudden LUNGE; LURCH
movement, uncontrolled TIC
movements TROTS
movie EPIC; ET; FILM; PIC
moving anagram indicator
mow CUT
Mozart, catalogue of K
MP, is SITS
MP, was SAT
much FAR; LOT
much, too OVER
muck GUNGE
mucked up anagram indicator
mud LUTE; MIRE; OOZE; SLIGHT; SLIME; SLUR
muddle HASH; MESS
muddled anagram indicator
muffled anagram indicator
mug ASS; DUPE; FACE; NOODLE; PAN; SAP; STEIN; *see* FOOL
mule SLIPPER
mullet, type of RED
multinational ICI
multiply BREED; DOUBLE; TRIPLE

multitude HOST; MASS
mum MA; MOTHER; SH
munch CHAMP; CHEW
municipality TOWN
murder KILL; SLAY
murderer CAIN
murderer, become STRANGLE
Murdoch publication (THE) BELL
murmur COO; HUM
murmuring HUM
Murphy can have something to do with potatoes
muscle BRAWN; CLOUT; MIGHT; PEC; POWER
muscle-man HUNK
muscular BEEFY
muse THINK
muses NINE
mushroom CEP (an edible variety)
mushy anagram indicator
music AIR; M; MUS; PIECE; POP; RAP; REGGAE; ROCK; STRAIN; SWING; TUNE
music, black RAP
music, church MASS
music, perform PLAY; SING
music, piece of SNATCH
music, pop MOTOWN; RAP; ROCK
music producer BAND; DJ; *see* COMPOSER
music, slow LARGO
music, some PIECE
musical CATS; EVITA; HAIR; OLIVER
musical family TRAPP
musical instrument BASS; CELLO; DRUM; FIDDLE; FIFE; FLUTE; GONG; HARP; HORN; LUTE; LYRE; ORGAN; PIPE; RECORDER; REED; SAX; SITAR; SPINET; TUBA; UKE; VIOL
musical piece LIED; TUNE
musical prince IGOR
musical show OPERA; *see* MUSICAL
musical, very ASSAI (It.); MOLTO
musically Italian musical terms (and their abbreviations are used commonly as components, and are frequently signaled by the word musically, the most popular being those shown below
broad and slow LARGO

musically loud F
musically quiet P
musically rapid, rapidly MOSSO
musically slowly LENTO
musically, very loud FF
musically, very quiet PP
musicians BAND
musicians' union MU
musketeer ATHOS; SAM (from an old song)
Muslim SUNNI
Muslim judge CADI (Arabic)
Muslim leader IMAM; N
mutineer REBEL; SILVER [CHRISTIAN]
mutt CUR; GOOSE
muzzled MUTE; SILENT
my (my!) can indicate some exclamation eg. COR, CRUMBS, GOSH, HA; *see* EXPRESSION OF SURPRISE etc.
myself ME
mysterious DARK
myth FABLE; SAGA; TALE

Nn

nag HORSE; PESTER; SCOLD; *see* HORSE
nagging anagram indicator
nail CATCH; CLAW; PIN; SPIKE; TACK
nail-biting TENSE
naive GREEN; RAW
naked BARE; BUFF; NUDE; RAW
name CALL; CITE; DUB; HANDLE; N; QUOTE; STAR; TAG; TERM; TITLE; first name *see* MAN, WOMAN, BOY, GIRL
name, add SIGN
name, bad MUD

name-dropping N to be omitted
name, Latin NOMEN
name, unpopular MUD
named alternatively AKA
nameless omission of N as “nameless individual” gives OE (ie. ‘n’ from ‘one’)
namely SC
nanny GOAT; NURSE
nap DOZE; DOWN; KIP; SLEEP; TIP
Napoleon PIG
narcotic DRUG
nark ANGER; GRASS; TELLER
narrative ACCOUNT; STORY; TALE; TELLING
narrow TAPER
narrow escape SQUEAK
narrow part NECK
nasty BAD; ICKY; ROTTEN; SEPTIC; anagram indicator
nasty lady CAT
nasty waste CRUD
nation STATE; or, of course, can mean any country
national NAT
national emblem EAGLE; LEEK
national organisation NT
national representative BULL (ie. John Bull)
native SON; can indicate something to do with oysters
natural PURE; RAW
natural light SUN
natural, not FLAT
nature SORT; TYPE
naturist NUDE
naughty BLUE; OFF; RACY; anagram indicator
naughty child IMP
nauseous QUEASY
naval officer HOOD; MATE; PO; *see* ADMIRAL, CAPTAIN
navigable OPEN
navigate SAIL; STEER
navigational aid, equipment COMPASS; HELM; LORAN; RADAR; RUDDER; SEXTANT; SONAR
navy FLEET; N; RN
Nazi HESS

NCO CORP; CORPORAL; SM
near CLOSE; LOOMING; MEAN
near, come LOOM
nearby CLOSE; HANDY; NIGH
nearly ABOUT; omission indicator, specifically for an associated word to be reduced, usually by one letter, as "nearly correct" clues AMEN (ie. last letter omitted from AMEND); or for a number to be reduced as "nearly all soccer team" clues TEN
nearly all MOST
neat COW; DEFT; OX; TIDY; TRIM
Nebraska NE
necessary MONEY; READY; run indicator
neck BRASS; CHEEK; COL
neck, adornment RUFF
neck, back of NAPE
neck, pain in CRICK
necklace RUFF
need LACK; MISS; WANT
needed DUE
needle IRK; LEAF; NETTLE; PIQUE; SEW; *see* ANNOY
ne'er-do-well IDLER; WASTER
negative ADVERSE; NEG; NO; NOPE; NOT
negative indicator NO
neglect FORGET; OMIT
negligent REMISS
negligible TINY
negotiate DEAL
negotiated anagram indicator
neigh NICKER
Nell GWYN; can indicate something to do with oranges
nerd SAP; TWIT; WIMP
Nero can indicate something to do with fiddle, emperor, Rome, lyre
Nero's capital N; ROME
nerve BOTTLE; CHEEK; DARING; FACE; LIP; NECK; SAUCE; STEEL
nerves STRESS
nervous EDGY; JUMPY; TENSE; anagram indicator
nervous reaction TIC
nervous state JITTERS
nested nesting indicator
net CATCH; ENTRAP; LACE; MESH; TRAP; TRAWL; WEB

Net WEB
nether LOWER
Netherlands NL
nettle IRK; NEEDLE; RILE; STING; *see* ANNOY
network GRID; MAZE; RETE (anat.); TISSUE
network, complex GRID
never NARY; NEER
nevertheless YET
new MINT; MODERN; N; NOVA; RECENT; anagram indicator; can indicate that RE is to be placed before a word as a prefix
new arrival BIRTH
new driver L
New England state CT; MASS; ME; NH, RI; VT
new growth SHOOT
New Hampshire NH
new layout anagram indicator
new, no longer USED
New Year's Day JANI
New York NY
New York area BRONX; QUEENS
Newcastle area NE
newly-wed BRIDE; GROOM
news DOPE; GRIFF; WORD
news agency TASS
news channels MEDIA
newsmen PRESS
newspaper DAILY; FT; RAG; SHEET; SUN; SUNDAY; TIMES
newspaper item CUTTING; REPORT
newspaper, send to FILE
newspapers PRESS
next THEN
next day MORROW
next in line SUCCESSOR
nexus LINK
nice PLEASING
Nice can indicate something to do with the French resort or its locality eg. Cote D' Azur; or can indicate a French word is required
nicely WELL
niche BAY
nick CELL; COLLAR; CUT; NAB; NOTCH; PINCH; PRISON;

ROB; STATION; STEAL; SWIPE; *see* PRISON

nickel NI

nicker NEIGH

nigh CLOSE; NEAR

night DARK; EVE

night, at LATE

night before EVE

night flier BAT

night jar POE

night spot CLUB

nightclub DIVE

nimble AGILE; LITHE; SPRY

nincompoop NINNY

nine IX

Nineteen-eighty-four (1984), character from SMITH

nip BITE; DASH; SPLASH; TOT

nippy COLD; FAST; SHARP

no NAY; O (ie. zero); with an initial capital can indicate PLAY, DRAMA, etc (ie. Japanese theatre); can indicate a word ending in -LESS

no backtracking ON; YAN

no doubt SURE

no end of last letter of following word to be omitted

no good NG; G to be eliminated from indicated word; anagram indicator

no-good CAD; HEEL; ROGUE; ROTTER

no-hoper JERK; LOSER

no leader first letter to be dropped from indicated word

no leaders either first two or three letters to be dropped from indicated word or first letter to be dropped from two or three words

no longer EX; FORMER; ONCE; PAST

no longer fresh AGED; OFF; OLD

no longer young AGED; OLD

no matter which ANY

no points NOSE (ie. no SE)

no, say DENY

No.10 *see* NUMBER 10

no topping on first letter of target word to be omitted

no way can indicate that a component meaning ‘way’ (eg. AVE, RD, ST) is to be omitted

Noah’s vessel ARK

nob SWELL; TOFF
noble BARON; COUNT; DUC; DUKE; EARL; LOFTY; LORD; PEER
nobleman *see* NOBLE
nobody NONE; NOONE (ie. no-one)
nocturnal mammal BAT
noise BOOM; CACKLE; CLINK; COO; DIN; RACKET; RATTLE; REPORT; ROAR; ROW; SOUND
noise, animal BARK; BLEAT; MEW; PURR; ROAR; WHINNY
noise, metallic CLANG
noise, noisy homophone indicator
noiseless DUMB; MUTE
noises, horrible DIN; RACKET
noisily homophone indicator
noisy F; FF; LOUD; VOCAL
non-British omission of B or BR
non-cleric LAIC
non-clerical LAY
non-European omission of E
non-professional LAY
non-ruling OUT
non-specialist GENERAL
none LOVE; NIL; NOUGHT; O; ZERO
none the less omit O from indicated word
nonsense BILGE; BOSH; BULL; BUNK; FUDGE; GUFF; ROT; COD; STUFF; TOSH; TRIPE; TUSH; *see* RUBBISH, JUNK
noodle IDLE; LOAF; MUG
noon N
noose LOOP
Norfolk can signify something to do with The Broads
Norfolk town DISS
norm NORM; PAR; STANDARD
normal PAR; STANDARD
Norman can refer to something to do with the Conquest eg. WILLIAM
North N; initial letter indicator (as “the northern” clues T); reversal indicator
North African MOOR; RIFF
North, Northern N; initial letter indicator; reversal indicator
North of Paris NORD
North Sea, part of WASH

Northern *see* NORTH
Northern holiday WAKE
northerner SCOT
Northumberland area NE
northwards UP
Norwich can signify something to do with The Broads
nose BEAK; HOOTER; MEDDLE; SNOUT
nosegay SPRAY
nosey NASAL
nostalgic for, be MISS
nosy, be PRY
not NOR; NT; omission indicator (usually the following word or its synonym); when followed by a gerund (eg. skating) can signal OFF; can indicate solution ends in -LESS; can indicate a word beginning with UN as "not encountered" clues UNMET
not a lot BIT
not all SOME; run indicator
not allow BAN; BAR
not allowed BANNED; OUT
not, and NOR
not at all NEVER
not at work AWAY; OFF
not available OFF
not bad DECENT; GOOD
not begun first letter to be omitted
not certain MAY
not charged FREE
not concerned omission of RE
not deep PALE; SHALLOW
not done RAW
not empty NT
not enough UNDER
not entirely omission indicator, particularly indicating that an incomplete word is to be used; run indicator
not even ODD; ROUGH
not exactly anagram indicator
not exalted BASE; LOW
not far CLOSE; NEAR; NIGH
not fat LEAN; THIN
not following omission indicator, usually in conjunction with some other indicator pinpointing what element is to be omitted

not good BAD; ILL
not gross NET
not half EASY; SIMPLE; word to be halved
not hard can signal the omission of H from indicated word
not hard-hearted can signal the omission of H from the centre of a word
not healthy AILING; ILL; PEAKY
not in OUT; IN to be omitted
not in favour ANTI; OUT
not known NK
not listened to KNOT
not missed can refer to a woman and her marital status
not much LITTLE; SLIGHT
not new OLD
not on OFF; ON to be omitted
not opening can indicate the omission of first letter
not outstanding LOW
not preserving anagram indicator; omission indicator
not quite letter sequence not to be finished
not recorded LIVE
not required OVER; SPARE
not right anagram indicator; to omit R from associated word; to omit right half of associated word
not so much LESS
not to begin indicates omission of first letter
not up to BELOW; UNDER
not very V to be omitted
not vulgar PURE
not working OFF
not yet LATER
notable STAR
notation SIGN
notch MARK; NICK; SCORE
note A; B; BREVE; C; D; DO; DOH; E; F; FAH; FIVER; FLAT; G; LAH; LINE; ME; MEMO; MI; N; NATURAL; PS; RAY; RE; SEE; SHARP; SO; SOH; TE; TENNER; TI; can indicate something to do with music; can indicate something to do with money
note free omission of a synonym for note (usually A-G or N); *see* NOTE
noted SAW; can indicate something to do with music, song etc.
notedly can indicate something to do with music, song etc

notepad JOTTER
notepaper can indicate something to do with musical score or scoring
notes ROLL; WAD; some combination of components listed under note (ME + RE to give MERE for instance); this is also common shorthand for a piece of music so can indicate anything from air and tune through march up to symphony (or can require a specific example of them); *see* SONG, TUNE
notes from bird TRILL
notes, make SING
notes, supply SING
noteworthy SIGNAL
nothing LOVE; NIL; NIX; NOUGHT; NOUT; NULL; O; ZERO
nothing, for FREE
nothing, having EMPTY
nothing in French RIEN
nothing on OON; *see* NUDE
nothing, say SH
notice AD; MARK; POSTER; REMARK; REVIEW; SEE; SPOT; SPY
noticed SAW
notorious ARRANT
notwithstanding STILL; THOUGH
nourish FEED; FOSTER
nova anagram indicator
novel NEW; anagram indicator; some short titled novel commonly EMMA, KIM, SCOOP, SHE
novel, French ROMAN
novelist BATES; COOPER; HOPE; MANNE; READE; STERNE; WAUGH; WELLS; WOOLF
novelty CHANGE
novice L; TIRO
now AD; HERE; PRESENT
now, before ALREADY
now (then) NONCE
nowadays AD
nub GIST; POINT
nude BARE; NAKED
nudge PUSH
nuisance BIND; BORE; IMP; ORDEAL; PEST; TRIAL
numb DEAD
number AIR; C; D; EDITION; I; K; L; M; N; NO; PI; PIECE;

PRIME; RANGE; SONG; SUM; TUNE; V; X; *see* SONG; can of course indicate the use of any arithmetic number but the following are commonly used as components: ONE, SEVEN, EIGHT, TEN; plus this is an old crossword warhorse, based on the fact that the unwary solver will overlook the secondary meaning of the word with a silent 'b', indicating a specific painkiller eg. ETHER

number, large C; D; K; M; MANY

number of Germans LIED

number of varieties RANGE

number shot BAG

Number 10 can denote something to do with prime minister; can denote something to do with a bus

number, unknown X; Y; Z

number, unspecified SOME

numbers NOS

nun SISTER

nuns ORDER

nun, short SIS

nurse HARBOUR; NANNY; SEN; SISTER; SRN; TEND

nursemaid ALICE

nursing CARE; nesting indicator

nursing home SAN

nut ASS; BEAN; BUFF; HEAD; SNAP

nutcracker anagram of NUT

nuts BARMY; CRACKERS; CUCKOO; MAD; POTTY; ZANY

nymph ECHO; OREAD

Oo

oaf LOUT
Oaks CLASSIC
oar BLADE; ROW
oarsman ROWER; STROKE
oast OVEN
oath CURSE; PLEDGE; VOW; WORD
oath, ancient ODS
obeisance, make KNEEL
obese FAT
obesity FAT
object AIM; DEMUR; END; IT; MIND; MOTIVE; THING
object to MIND
objection BUT; DEMUR
objective AIM; CASE; END; GOAL
objector ANTI; CON
obligation TIE
obligation to pay IOU; OWING
obligation, had an MUST; OWED
oblige FORCE
obliged, is MUST
obliged, was HAD
obliging person, type ANGEL
oblique, obliquely ASKEW; anagram indicator
obliquely, move SKEW
obscene BLUE
obscene matter, publication PORN; SMUT
obscenities SMUT
obscure BLEAR; BLUR; CLOUD; DIM; HIDE; MIST; ODD; anagram indicator; also can indicate that one element in the clue is to replace another
obscuring omission indicator as "obscuring what's above" calls for the omission of a first letter
obscurity anagram indicator
observant SHARP
observation SIGHT; SIGHTING

observe BEHOLD; HEED; KEEP; LOOK; NOTE; SEE; SPOT
observed SAW; SEEN
observer EYE; SEER
obsession MANIA
obstacle BAR; BARRIER; BLOCK; LET; SNAG; WALL
obstinate DOUR
obstinate fellow MULE
obstruct BAR; BLOCK; STOP
obstruction BAR; LET; STOP
obtain EXIST; GET; LAND; STAND
obtained GOT
obtuse can indicate something to do with an angle
obvious CLEAR; OVERT; PLAIN
occasion CHANCE; DATE; DAY; DO; ENTAIL; PARTY; REASON; TIME
occasion, have NEED
occasion, on one ONCE
occasional ODD
occupant INMATE
occupation LINE
occupational therapist, therapy OT
occupied, be WORK
occupied with AT
occupies, one who TENANT
occupy nesting indicator
occupy, illegally SQUAT
occupying nesting indicator
occur ARE
occurence EVENT
occurring in nesting indicator; run indicator
occurs IS
ocean DEEP; MAIN; SEA; *see* SEA
octet from Germany ACHT
odd DROLL; LEFT; QUEER; RUM; STRANGE; anagram indicator
odd bits *see* ODD CHARACTERS
odd characters can signal that only the odd-numbered letters in an indicated sequence are be used eg. "odd bits of iron traps" clues IOTAS
odd type of *see* ODD CHARACTERS
oddball CRANK; anagram indicator

oddly anagram indicator; indicator for odd numbered letters to be used as "croft oddly" clues COT
oddly reduced *see* ODD CHARACTERS
odds EVENS; SP
odds and ends TRUCK (Sc. and U.S.)
of course NATCH
of French DE; DU
of us OUR
off AWAY; BAD; GONE; HIGH; START; SOUR; anagram indicator; omission indicator
off course, to be ERR; STRAY
off-form anagram indicator
off-key FLAT
off, opposite LEG
off target anagram indicator
offal LIVER
offence CRIME; SIN; SLIGHT
offence, give MIFF; SLIGHT
offend INSULT; SIN
offensive PUSH; RANK; RUDE; can indicate something to do with military attack
offer BID; EXTEND; PRESENT; TENDER
office DUTY; ROOM; SEXT
office, bishop's SEE
office building BLOCK
office worker TEMP
officer BOSN; BOSUN; BRIG; CAPT; CO; COL; COP; DI; ENSIGN; GEN; JAILER; LT; MAJOR; MATE; NCO; OC; PO; PURSER; SUPER; SM
officer commanding OC
official CLERK; ELDER; OFF; REF; USHER
offpeak can indicate something to do with activity on mountain eg. yodelling
offshoot BRANCH
offspring BROOD; ISSUE; LITTER; SEED; SON
oh dear ALAS; MY; WELL
oik *see* LOUT, YOB
oil CASTOR; CRUDE; DERV; EASE; can signal something to do with painting
oil mess SLICK
oil reservoir SUMP

oilman RIGGER
ointment BALM; SALVE
OK, okay FAIR; FINE; GOOD; KOSHER; RIGHT; SWELL; WELL
Oklahoma OK
ointment BALM; SALVE
old AGED; ARCH; AGED; EX; FORMER; GREY; LATE; O; PAST; RUSTY; YORE
old article YE
old boat ARK
old bird DODO
old boy OB
old chap COVE
old city TROY; UR
old copper D
old counsel REDE
old craft ARGO
old days PAST
Old English OE
old-fashioned DATED; OUT; PASSE; TRAD; SQUARE; STEAM; anagram using the letters OLD
old-fashioned denial NAY
Old Father usually refers to the Thames
old fighter VET
old flame EX
old, grow AGE
Old Harry DEVIL; NICK
old hat SQUARE; *see* OLD-FASHIONED
old Iranian MEDE
old jokes CORN
Old King COLE
old lady GRAN; MUM
old letter RUNE
old lover EX
old man PA; POP; *see* FATHER
old maid PRUDE
old money D; LSD; S
old people AGED
old Scottish AULD
old soldier VET
old sovereign GR

Old Testament OT
Old Testament character LOT
old, the YE
old times BC
old vehicle CRATE
old wife EX
old woman HAG; MA; *see* MOTHER
old, you THEE; THOU; YE
older SENIOR
oldest, the YE
Olympian can indicate a Greek god eg. HERA
omen SIGN
ominous BAD; DIRE; EVIL
omit CUT; DROP; SCRATCH; SKIP; omission indicator
on AT; LEG; OVER; RE; ordering indicator (the component preceding ON to be directly followed by the next component, as "sent on course" clues HIGHWAY); also rem: although innocently placed in the clue ON itself can be part of the answer
on behalf of FOR
on board an element to be nested between S and S (ie. Steamship); can refer to chess
on hand CLOSE; NEAR
on holiday OFF
on reflection reversal indicator
on the move anagram indicator
on the side WITH
on top of OVER; preceding indicator
once EX; FORMER; can signal the use of an archaism; *see* ONCE KNOWN for an example
once known WIST
once more AGAIN
one A; ACE; AN; ANE (Scots); I; SINGLE; SOLE; UNIT
one and all EACH
one aspiring HOPER
one, every PER
one of the Scots ANE
one flying can indicate a bird
one hears homophone indicator
one in France UN; UNE
one in Germany EIN
one in Scotland ANE; YIN

one-night stand GIG
one on the way out GONER
one's IS
one short of century, hundred OO
one time ONCE
one upset ANTI
onion BULB; *see* HEAD
only BUT; JUST; LONE; MERE; SINGLE; SOLE
onset (of) initial indicator
oomph ZING
ooze SEEP
open AIRY; BROACH; FREE; LEAD; OUT; OVERT; RAISE; START; UNDO; UNLOCK; first letter indicator
open country PLAIN
open, in the OUT
Open University OU
opener BAT
opening ADIT; CLEFT; ENTRY; GAP; HOLE; MOUTH; ONSET; PORT; PORTAL; START; VENT; initial letter indicator; preceding indicator
opening move GAMBIT
openly gay OUT
opera AIDA; NORMA; OP
opera house (US) MET
operate USE; WORK
operated anagram indicator
operatic part AIDA; LULU; NORMA
operating ON
operation OP; PLAY; USE; anagram indicator
operation, in ON
operator DRIVER
opinion ANGLE; NOTION; POINT; SAY; SLANT; TAKE; THOUGHT; VIEW; VOICE
opponent ANTI; FOE
opponents ANTIS; EN (from bridge); NE; SW, WS
opponents, our THEM; THEY
opponents' ground AWAY
opportunity BREAK; CHANCE; ROOM
oppose BUCK; FACE; RESIST
opposed (to) AGIN, ANTI; V
opposer NOE

opposing ANTI; CON
opposite REVERSE
opposition opposing sides in bridge eg. EN
opposition, being in V
opt CHOOSE
optic in conjunction with another word eg. 'optics expert' can signal something to do with bars or drinking
option CHOICE; HEADS; TAILS
options MENU
optimism HOPE
optimistic ROSY; UPBEAT
opulent RICH
or rem: although innocently placed in the clue OR itself can be part of the answer
or, France OU
oral SAID; homophone indicator
oral contraceptive PILL
orally homophone indicator
orange AMBER; FLAME
orator's homophone indicator
orbit PATH; can indicate something to do with EYE
orchestra LSO
orchestra, part of BRASS; FIDDLES; STRINGS; WIND
orchestrated anagram indicator
ordain RULE; STATE
ordeal TEST; TRIAL; STRAIN
order BID; BIDDING; CH; DECREE; DEMAND; DO; EDICT; ENJOIN; FIAT; FILE; GARTER; LAW; OBE; OM; PO (ie. postal order); RANGE; RULE; SET; SORT; TRIM; anagram indicator; an architectural order eg. IONIC, DORIC
Order of the British Empire OBE
order, out of LAY; anagram indicator
ordered BADE; BID; anagram indicator
orderly NEAT; SISTER; TIDY
orders anagram indicator
ordinary language PROSE
ore ROCK
organ EAR; EYE; GLAND; HEART; LIVER; LUNG; NOSE; SKIN
organisation BODY; CIA; UN
organisation, national NT
organise RUN

organised RAN; anagram indicator
organised workers TU
organiser, party WHIP
Oriel can indicate something to do with Oxford
orient E; EAST; PEARL
oriental E; EMAN (ie. E-man, eastern man)
oriental criminals TONG
oriental dress SARI
oriental vessel JUNK; WOK
origin BUD; ROOT; SOURCE; START
origin of initial letter indicator
original CARD; EARLY; EX; FIRST; MASTER; NEW; OLD; initial letter indicator; anagram indicator
original American *see* AMERICAN INDIAN
originally initial letter indicator; in conjunction with a homophone indicator can indicate a word with the sound of a word's initial letter as "originally thinking aloud" can clue TEA
originating BORN
originator of first letter indicator
ornament ADORN; BANGLE; DECOR; TRIM
ornamental anagram indicator
ornate BAROQUE
orphan ANNIE; OLIVER; TWIST; WARD
'orrible can indicate that the associated word has initial H omitted
oscillate SWING
osier WILLOW; WITHY
ostentation POMP; SHOW
ostler GROOM
OT book NUMB
Othello MOOR
other anagram indicator
other people REST
other things ETAL (ie. et al)
other things, and ETAL
other-worldly FEY
others ETAL; REST
others, and ETAL
otherwise ELSE; OR; anagram indicator
Otis can indicate something to do with regret (from Cole Porter song)
Ottoman TURK

OU course PPE
our country UK
our ground HOME
our group US; WE
our part of the world WEST
our side US
our time AD
ourselves US
oust EJECT
out ABSENT; GONE; OVER (ie. no longer available); anagram indicator (as 'let out' cues an anagram of LET); nesting indicator; omission indicator; can refer to being absent, insensible, being asleep eg. DREAM
out for can indicate some kind of hunting activity as "out for a duck" clues FOWLING
out in Amsterdam UIT
out, is BLOOM; BLOOMING
out more INLESS
out of anagram indicator; nesting indicator; run indicator
out of bed UP
out of date OLD
out-of-form anagram indicator
out of one's mind STONED; *see* DRUNK
out of order US (ie. useless); anagram indicator
out of water DRY
out to lunch MAD; NUTS
outbreak anagram indicator
outbuilding SHED
outburst anagram indicator; run indicator
outcome, level DRAW; TIE
outdo TOP
outdoes anagram of DOES
outfit BUNCH; FIRM; GANG; GARB; GEAR; LOT; RIG
outhouse BARN; SHED
outing TRIP; anagram indicator
outlaw BAN; HOOD
outlet HOLE; SHOP; STORE; VENT
outline BORDER; DRAFT; ETCH; SKETCH; TRACE
outlying part RIM; *see* BORDER
outmoded DATED
outpost PICKET

outrage AFFRONT; FURY
outrageous GROSS; OTT; anagram indicator
outrageously anagram indicator
outset, of, from the initial letter indicator
outside nesting indicator
outside broadcast OB
outside, on the external letters of word(s) to be used
outsiders first and last letters to be used
outskirts of first and last letters to be used
outspoken BOLD; FRANK; PLAIN
outstanding ACE; DUE; HIGH; OWING; TALL; TODO (ie. to do); can refer to some kind of relief work eg. rilievo
outstanding, not LOW
outwit TRUMP
ovation HAND
oven OAST; STOVE
oven, just out of HOT
over ACROSS; ALONG; ATOP; DONE; DOWN; GONE; ON; OUT; PAST; RE; UP; anagram indicator; reversal indicator; preceding indicator; can indicate something to do with cricket eg. balls, maiden
over-amorous RANDY
over, go CROSS; FORD
over-hasty RASH
over the limit, top OTT
over there YON; YONDER
overact HAM
overacted HAMMED; HAMMY
overall SMOCK; SUPREME; reverse or anagram of ALL; *see* CHIEF, HEAD, MAIN
overcast CLOUDY; DULL
overcome WORST; anagram indicator; nesting indicator
overcook BURN; CHAR
overdose OD
overdrawn OD
overdue LATE; reverse or anagram of DUE
overeat GORGE; reverse or anagram of EAT
overexcited GIDDY
overflow BRIM; SLOP; WOLF
overgrown REEDY; WEEDY
overhead ABOVE; HIGH; UP

overhead railway EL (ie. in U.S.)
overindulge PIG
overseer BOSS
overt CLEAR; OPEN; OUT; PLAIN
overtake CATCH; PASS
overthrow EVERT; USURP; anagram indicator; reversal indicator
overthrown *see* OVERTHROW
overtime OT; reverse indicator for time (EMIT) or for synonyms for time, hence ARE, eg.A, etc
overtips OR (ie. the end letters of 'over'); OS (ie. the end letters of 'overtips')
overture START; initial letter(s) to be used
overweight TON; reversal indicator for measures of weight, hence MARG, NOT, ZO, etc
overwhelm SMOTHER
owing DUE
owl HOOTER
owned HAD; LETON (ie. let on)
ox YAK
Oxbridge distinction BLUE
oxen, two YOKE
Oxford OU; SHOE (hence can indicate something to do with shoe)
Oxford, at UP
Oxford course GREATS; PPE
oxygen O; OZONE

Pp

pace AMBLE; SPEED; STEP; TROT
Pacific state TONGA
pack BAG; CRAM; DECK; KIT; LOAD; STOW; TAMP; TIN; STUFF
pack animal BURRO; MULE
pack, one PROP
package PACKET; PARCEL
packaging WRAPPING
packet PARCEL; SHIP; STEAMER
pad FLAT
Paddington BEAR; STATION
paddle OAR; ROW
paddy IRE
page BOY; CALL; LEAF; P
page, edge of MARGIN
page-boy BUTTONS
paid MET; PD; STOOD
paid, be EARN
paid for MET
paid worker PRO
paid, yet to be OWING
pain ACHE; COLIC; GYP; STING; STITCH
pain, exclamation of, indication of OW
pain, feel SMART
pain in the neck CRICK; DRIP
painful ACHY; SORE
painfully anagram indicator
paint OIL; TEMPERA
paint ingredient RESIN
painter ARA; BACON; HALS; INGRES; LELY; MASTER; RA; ROPE; SARGENT; TITIAN; TURNER
painting ART; ICON; MURAL; OIL
painting, abstract OPART (ie, op art)
paintings ART

pair BRACE; COUPLE; DUO; PR; TWIN; TWO; repetition indicator; can indicate two components to be used with AND as "Pair of initials between Lowry's" clues LANDS (ie. L-AND-S)
pal ALLY; BUD; CHUM; MATE; OPPO; PARD
pale ASHY; DRAWN; DOUGHY; FADED; FAIR; FENCE; LIGHT; PASTY; POST; SALLOW; WAN; WHITE
pale ale LIGHT
Palestine group PLO
Palestrina can refer to one of his works eg. MASS
palindrome can indicate that a word or the answer reads the same both ways eg. NOT ON
palm HAND; HIDE
paltry CHEAP; TIN
pampas PLAIN
pamphlet TRACT
pan KNOCK; MUG; ROAST
panel BOARD; JURY
pang TWINGE
panic ALARM; FLAP; SCARE; TERROR; rem: this is also a plant
panic, in anagram indicator
pant LONG
pantry LARDER
paparazzi can indicate something to do with the press
paper DAILY; ESSAY; FT; LEAF; MS; ORGAN; QUIRE; RAG; REAM; ROLL; SHEET; STANDARD; SUN; TIMES; TISSUE
paper worth money BILL; CHEQUE; NOTE
papers FILE; PRESS; QUIRE; REAM
papers, many REAM
par EQUAL; LEVEL; NORMAL
par, be on a MATCH
par, below EAGLE
parade AIR; MARCH; SHOW
paradise EDEN; HEAVEN
paralyze NUMB; STUN
parasite DRONE; LOUSE; MITE; PEST
parasites LICE
parcel (out) ALLOT
pare CUT; TRIM
parent DAD; DAM; FATHER; MA; MOTHER; MUM; PA; POP; PAR; SIRE
Paris apart from the French capital can also refer to Paris, the

Classical figure, and in this context can indicate something to do with the Trojan War, death of Achilles, heel, Helen etc
Paris and ET
Paris correspondent can indicate the French equivalent of an English word; *see* FRENCH
Paris, description of GAY
Paris, first person in JE
Paris, in can indicate the use of a French word, *see* FRENCH for the common ones
Paris paper FIGARO; LE MONDE
Paris suburb ORLY
parish CURE
Parisian, a UN; UNE
Parisian, of the DE; DES; DU
Parisian who QUI
park HYDE
park-keeper RANGER
parked, parking P
parking area LOT
parlance DICTION
Parliament DIET; P; PARL; RUMP
Parliamentarian MP
parrot KEA; LORY
part BIT; PT; MEMBER; ROLE; SEVER; SOME; SPLIT; UNIT; run indicator
part for actor ROLE; SCRIPT; WORDS
part of run indicator
part of Bible NT; OT; VERSE; or a book from the Bible eg. JOB, MARK
part of body ORGAN etc
part of circle ARC
part of foot ANKLE; HEEL; SOLE
part of orchestra BRASS; WIND; *see* ORCHESTRA, PART OF
part of speech VERB
part of theatre APRON; STAGE
part-time soldiers TA
participant, willing SPORT
participate SHARE
participated in anagram indicator
particle ATOM; BOSON (physics)
particular ASPECT; CERTAIN; DETAIL; FOG; PET; POINT;

RESPECT

partner ALLY; BUD; CONSORT; DATE; E (from bridge); LOVER; N; MATE; OPPO; PARD; S; W; can also refer to one of the partners in a specific partnership eg. DUCK/DRAKE, STALLION/MARE, EMPEROR/EMPRESS; *see* ALLY, FRIEND, PAL

partner, with a PAIRED

partners, partnership EW; NS; SN, WE (from bridge)

parts (of, in) anagram indicator

party ANC; BALL; BASH; BINGE; CAMP; CON; DANCE; DISCO; DO; FACTION; FETE; FLING; GANG; GREEN; LAB; LIB; RAVE; SET; SIDE; SNP; SOCIAL; SPREE; STAG

party, African ANC

party, Aussie DING

party-giver HOST

party man HATTER

party member GREEN

party of revelers ROUT

party official WHIP

party organiser WHIP

partygoer RAVER

pass ALLOW; COL; CROSS; DIE; ELAPSE; GATE; HAND; LUNGE; PERMIT; SPEND; TICKET

pass, mountain COL; GATE

pass on HAND

pass out METE

pass over FORD; SKIP

pass up SHUN

passage AISLE (or, with homophone indicator, ISLE); ALLEY; HALL; LANE; ROAD; TUNNEL; VENT; WAY

passage, slow LARGO

passe OVER

passenger FARE; rem: this is also a breed of pigeon

passing DEATH; GOING; anagram indicator

passing of time indicates the omission of T in associated word

passion ANGER; DESIRE; HEAT; IRE; LOVE; LUST; RAGE; WRATH

passion, with less PALER

passionate HOT

passionately anagram indicator

passport endorsement VISA

past AFTER; AGO; EX; FORMER; GONE; LATE; OVER; PT
pasta DOUGH; NOODLES
pasta, some NOODLE
paste GLUE; GUM; STICK
pastime HOBBY
pastry CAKE; CRUST; FILO (Gk.); FLAN; PUFF; TART
pasty PALE; PIE
patch BED; DARN; ORBIT; PLACE; REPAIR; SPOT; TRACT
patent OVERT
path TRACK; TRAIL; WAY
pathetic anagram indicator
pathological anagram indicator
patience, patient can indicate something to do with JOB
patient CASE
patio YARD
patriarch JOB; JACOB; LEVI
patriotic LOYAL
patrol PROWL
patron ANGEL; CLIENT
patronising, be DEIGN
patter SPIEL
pattern CHECK; FORMAT; MODEL
paucity DEARTH; LACK
paunch BELLY; POT; TUM
pause BREAK; DELAY; STOP; WAIT
paving SETT
paving slab FLAG
paw FOOT
pawn GAGE; HOCK; P; PIECE; POP
pawnbroker UNCLE
pay BONUS; DO; EARNINGS; FEE; FOOT; GIVE; MEET; RATE; REMIT; SETTLE; STAND; WAGE; *see* PAYMENT
pay attention HEED; LIST; LISTEN
pay heed RECK
pay increase RAISE; RISE
payment ANTE; BONUS; CHARGE; COST; FEE; GIRO; PRICE; RENT; SALARY; TITHE; *see* PAY
payment, advance ANTE
payment, demand DUN
payment, extra BONUS

PC facility MOUSE
pea PULSE; SEED
pea container POD
peace PAX
peace agreement TRUCE
peacemakers UN
peach CLING; DISH; GRASS; SNITCH
peak ACME; BEN; CAP; TIP; TOP; TOR
peaky DOWN
peal RING; TOLL
pear TUNA (ie. prickly pear)
pearler DIVER
pearls ROPE
peasant, Arab FELLAH
pebble STONE
pecked BIT; BITTEN
peculiar ODD; RUM; anagram indicator
peddle TOUT
pedestrian BANAL; DULL; TRITE
pedestrianised the letters CAR to be omitted from word
pediment GABLE
peel RIND
peer EARL; EQUAL; LOOK; LORD; NOBLE; PRY
peerless BEST
peeved CROSS
peevish CROSS
peg CLIP; NOG; PIN; TEE; THOLE
peg-leg STUMP
Pegasus HORSE
pelt FUR; STONE; *see* SKIN
pen COOP; DOCK; FOLD; NIB; POUND; STY; WRITE; can call for the name of an author; can indicate something to do with SWAN
penance, do ATONE
penalty COST; FINE; PRICE
penchant LIKE
pennant FLAG; STREAMER
penned in nesting indicator
penniless BROKE
penning nesting indicator
Pennsylvania PA

penny D; P
penny-pinching MEAN; STINGY
pens nesting indicator
pensioner OAP
penultimate N; indicator for last but one letter
people CHAPS; CLAN; FOLK; KIN; MEN; NATION; ONES; RACE; SOME; TRIBE
people, leading LIGHTS
people, many HOST
people, other REST
people, those THEM; THEY
pep GO; LIFE
pepper SEASON; SEASONING
per BY
per item EACH
perception ANGLE; SENSE; VIEW
perch BASS; POLE; ROD; ROOST; SETTLE; SIT
perennial HARDY
perfect HONE; IDEAL; MINT; UTTER; can indicate something to do with verb tense
perform ACT; DO; PLAY; SING
perform again REDO
performance ACT; DEED; GIG; SHOW; TURN
performance, great BLINDER
performance, in ON
performed DID; SANG; anagram indicator
performed, being ON
performer ACTOR; ARTISTE; TURN
performing ON; anagram indicator
perfume SCENT
perhaps can indicate that we have been given an example and we should look for a general category eg. "mother perhaps" calls for PARENT, "perhaps Siamese" can call for CAT; can act as an accessory to a homophone indicator; can act as an acknowledgement that the compiler is stretching a point; anagram indicator
peril DANGER; RISK
period AGE; CLASS; DATE; DAY; ERA; POINT; SHIFT; SPACE; SPAN; SPELL; STAGE; STOP; TERM; TIME; WHILE; *see* TIME
period, dark NIGHT
period, historical AGE; DATE; ERA

period of abstinence LENT
period of calm REST
period of expansion, growth BOOM; UP
period of prosperity BOOM
period of study CLASS; TERM
period of work STINT
period, prosperous BOOM
periodical MAG; RAG; *see* MAGAZINE
perish DIE
perk BONUS
permanent way RAIL; RY
permed SET
permission, get, obtain CLEAR
permit ALLOW; LET; PASS
permitted LET; OK
permission OK
perpendicular ERECT; PLUMB
perplex BAFFLE
Persian CAT
persistence PLUCK
persistent CHRONIC; HARD
persisting CHRONIC
person ONE; BEING; BOD; MAN; PARTY
person, extraordinary ONER
person, ferocious TARTAR
person, first I
person, ineffectual DRIP; WIMP
person, kind, generous, loyal ANGEL; BRICK; GEM
person, inexperienced TYRO
person, nasty GIT; *see* PERSON, NASTY
person, presiding CHAIR
person, sad NERD
person, second YOU
person, silly, stupid ASS; DUNCE; PRAT; PUDDING; TWERP; TWIT; *see* FOOL
person, treacherous CUR; RAT; WEASEL
person unpleasant CREEP
personal OWN
personal assistant PA
personal domestic activity DIY

personal problem ED
person, wonderful *see* PERSON, KIND
personality SELF
perspiration BO
persuade URGE
pert SAUCY
perturbed anagram indicator
perverse anagram indicator
perversion WARP
perverted WARPED; anagram indicator
pet BATE; CARESS; CAT; DOG; RAGE; TIFF
pet, Darling NANA
Peter PAN; SAFE; can indicate something to do with diminishing
Peter Pan, like AGELESS
petition BEG; SUE
petrol GAS; FUEL; JUICE
perversely anagram indicator
pet CAT; DOG; TIFF
peter out DIE (usually Peter has a capital initial to confuse)
petty complaints, make CARP
phase STAGE
philosopher AYER; HEGEL; KANT; LOCKE; MILL; OCCAM; PLATO; SAGE; STOIC
philosophy VIEW
phobia FEAR; THING
phone CALL; DIAL; LINE; MOBILE; RING; TEL
phoned RANG
phosphorus P
photo, photograph PIC; SHOT; SNAP; STILL
photography can indicate something to do with lighting
photogenic PRETTY
physical education. instruction, training PE; PT
physician DOG; GALEN; LUKE; *see* DOCTOR
physicist CURIE; MACH; PAUL
physics establishment CERN
physique BODY
piano GRAND; P; QUIET; UPRIGHT
piano part KEY
pick BEST; CREAM; ELITE; FLOWER; OPT; PRIME; SELECT; TOOL; TOP

pick-me-up TONIC
pick up RESUME; SPOT
picket FENCE
pickle BIND; CORNER; CURE; JAM; MESS; SPOT; STEW
pickle, in a CURRIED
picnic can indicate something being easy, piece of cake, etc.
picture FILM; IMAGE; MURAL; OIL; PIC; PRINT; SKETCH; SNAP
pictures ART
picturesque anagram indicator
pie DISH; PASTY; TART
pie-eyed see drunk
pie top CRUST
piece BIT; CHIP; CHUNK; FLAKE; ITEM; LUMP; MAN; MORSEL; PART; PATCH; PORTION; SHARD; SLAB; TAG; TUNE; *see* CHESSMAN, CUT
piece of run indicator
piece of advice TIP
piece of cake EASY
piece of film CLIP
piece of ground, land LOT; PARCEL; PATCH
piece of news ITEM
piece of paper SHEET; TICKET
piece of wood BOARD; PALE; PLANK
pieces, in anagram indicator
pier JETTY
pierce ENTER; SPEAR; STAB
pierced CUT
piercing tool AWL
pierhead P
Piersporter VIEN; WINE
pig BOAR; HOG; RUNT; SOW [POKE; STY]
pig food SWILL
pig-pen STY
pig, smallest RUNT
pigeon CARRIER; HOMER [PASSENGER]
pigment UMBER
pike LUCE; STAFF
pile HEAP; HILL; MINT; NAP; POT; STACK; TOWER
pile, combustible PYRE

pile of sheaves STOOK
pilfer RIFLE; STEAL
pilgrimage EU
pill TABLET
pill-box INRO
pillage REAVE; SACK
pillar POST; STELE
pilot FLYER; TEST; TRIAL
piloted LED
pin CASK; CLIP; PEG; RIVET; SPIKE; THOLE
pin-up NIP
Pinafore can indicate something to do with Gilbert and Sullivan, Doyly Carte
pinch BIT
pinched DRAWN
pinching nesting indicator
pine LONG
pink CORAL; KNOCK; ROSE; ROSY
pins LEGS
pint BEER; JAR; PT
pints, two QUART
pipe CHANTER; FLUE; REED; TUBE
piping HOT; REEDY
piquant TANGY
piquancy TANG
pique PET
pirate FLINT; HOOK; KIDD; MORGAN; PEW; ROVER; SILVER
pit ABYSS; BED; MINE
pitch FIELD; HURL; KEY; SHY; SPIEL; TAR; THROW; TOSS; can indicate something to do with music or sound
pitch, on the BATTING; IN; PLAYING
pith CORE; HEART
pithy TERSE
pity SHAME; RUTH
place AREA; BED; FLAT; HOME; LAY; LIEU; LOCATE; LOCATION; LOCUS; LODGE; NICHE; PAD; PL; POINT; POSE; POST; PUT; ROOM; SET; SITE; SPOT; STEAD
place, all over the anagram indicator
place, cleric's BRAY
place, cosy NEST
place for entertainment CLUB; FAIR

place for fighting RING
place for reading AMBO
place, high EYRIE; PEAK
place, in ON; anagram indicator
place in opposition PIT
place, in this HERE
place, iniquitous DEN
place of birth NATAL
place of convalescence SPA
place of debauchery STY
place of entertainment CLUB; FAIR
place of seclusion LAIR
place of vice DEN
place of worship CH; TEMPLE
place, out of anagram indicator
place, perfect NICHE
place, relaxing HAVEN
place, safe ARK
place, that THERE
place, this HERE
place to confine PEN
place to hide LAIR
place to live, stay *see* ACCOMMODATION
place to play PITCH
place to stop BERTH; PORT
place, uncomfortable HOLE
placed LAID; PUT; SET
plagiarise STEAL
plagiarism THEFT
plagiarist PIRATE
plague SCOURGE
plague-carrier RAT
plaid TARTAN
plain BALD; BLUNT; OVERT; SIMPLE; SOBER; STEPPE
plait BRAID
plan AIM; CHART; DESIGN; DRAFT; FRAME; IDEA; MAP; PLOT; THOUGHT; anagram indicator
plan, prepare DRAFT
plan to steal CASE
plane BUS; DRESS; EVEN; FIGHTER; FLAT; JET; KITE; LEVEL;

MIG; SHAVER; TREE; TOOL
planet EARTH; MARS
plank BOARD
planned anagram indicator
planning DESIGN
plant ARUM; ASTER; BROOM; BURY; BUSH; CHIVE; CRESS; DILL; DOCK; FACTORY; FERN; FLAG; GORSE; GRASS; HEATH; HEATHER; HERB; HOP; INTER; IVY; LAY; LOVAGE; MALLOW; MINT; MOSS; NETTLE; ORRIS; PEA; PLUNGE; PUT; REED; RAPE; ROOT; RUE; SEDGE; SENNA; SOW; TARO; THRIFT; WEED; WORKS; YARROW; *see* FLOWER, SHRUB
plant, North American SEGO
plant, part of ANTHER; STALK; STEM
planted SOWN
planter SEEDER; SOWER
plaster RENDER
plastic anagram indicator
plate COAT; COVER; DISH; LAMINA; METAL; can indicate baseball plate calling up PITCHER etc.
plate, metal FISH
plateau FLAT; TABLE
platform CAGE; DAIS; DECK; PLANK; PODIUM; STAGE
platform, mobile DOLLY; LIFT
platform, part of PLANK
play ACT; BAT; BET; BRAND; CAST; FRISK; FUN; GAME; ROOM; SKETCH; SHOW; SPORT; STRUM; VENT; WORK; anagram indicator; can signal a famous play, often by Shakespeare, and often abbreviated eg. MND
play, area REC
play, be in ACT; APPEAR
play for time STALL
play, present STAGE
play school RADA
play, section of ACT
play with words PUN
playboy RAKE
played anagram indicator
player ACTOR; BLACK; BLUE; PIPER; WHITE; can signify an orchestra member, usually a musical instrument; *see* FOOTBALLER
player, best CHAMP

player, bit EXTRA
player, extra RESERVE
player, top ACE; SEED; STAR
player, unskilful HAM
player's warning FORE
players BAND; CAST; GROUP; LSO; SIDE; SQUAD; TEAM; can indicate something to do with orchestra, music
playground REC
playing ON; anagram indicator
playing area PITCH
plaything DOLL; TOY
playwright BEHAN; BOLT; PINTER; SHAW
plead BEG; CLAIM
pleasant GOOD; NICE; SWEET; TREAT
please CONTENT; DELIGHT
pleased CONTENT; GLAD; HAPPY
pleasure DELIGHT; FUN
pleasure, gain ENJOY
pleasure, give TICKLE; TREAT
pleat FOLD; TUCK
plebeian RED
pledge GAGE; OATH; TROTH; WORD; can signal something to do with pawnshops
plentiful AMPLE
plenty ALOT (ie. A LOT); AMPLE; LOT
plight LOT
plinth BLOCK; SOCLE
plonk DUMP; WINE
plot BED; GARDEN; PLAN; TRACT
ploy CABAL; DODGE; GAMBIT; RUSE; TRICK
ploy, deceptive SELL
ploy, winning MATE
plucky GAME; can indicate something to do with player of string instrument
plug AD; BUNG; PUSH; SHOOT; STOP; STOPPER; TAMP
plum CREAM; GAGE; TOP
plumb SOUND; WEIGHT
plump FAT; ROUND; ROUNDED; STOUT
plunder LOOT; PREY; ROB; SACK
plunge DIP; DIVE

plus CROSS; SIGN
plush RICH
Pluto DIS
plutonium PU
ply BEND; STRAND
Plymouth, feature of HOE
PM can indicate something to do with the afternoon; *see* PRIME MINISTER
pocket POUCH; can indicate something to do with snooker
pocket, in UP
pod CASE
poem CANTO; EPIC; IF; LL; ODE; SONNET; VERSE
poet AUDEN; BARD; BRIDGES; BROOKE; BURNS; CLARE; DANTE; DONNE; ELIOT; HEINE; HOMER; HOOD; KEATS; LEAR; MARTIAL; MARVEL; OVID; OWEN; POPE; POUND; RILKE; SHELLEY; VIRGIL; YEATS
poet's work ODE; POEM; VERSE; *see* POEM
poetry *see* POEM
poetry, of ODIC
poetry, short FOOT
point AIM; CAPE; E; END; GIST; HEAD; ISSUE; N; NESS; NODE; NUB; PEAK; PIN; PRONG; S; SPIKE; TINE; TIP; TRAIN; W
point, main CRUX; GIST; HUB
point of view ANGLE; TAKE
pointed ACUTE; SHARP
pointed remark BARB
pointer ARROW; DOG ; NEEDLE
pointless INANE; *see* POINTLESSLY
pointlessly can indicate that N, E, W, and/or S should be omitted
points some combination of N, E, W and S
points, with no NOSE; *see* POINTLESSLY
poison BANE; anagram indicator
poisoner ASP
poke BAG; eg.G; GOAD; PROD; ROOT; URGE
poker hand FLUSH; STRAIGHT
Poland PL
pole N; NORTH; PERCH; POST; ROD; S; SOUTH; SPRIT; STAFF; STAKE
police BILL; COPS; GARDA; GUARD; LAW; MET; YARD
Police Department PD
police force MET; MP; RUC; YARD

police officer DI; DS; PC; SUPER
police post BOMA
police, secret KGB
police station NICK
policeman COP; COPPER; GARDA; MOUNTIE; MP; PC; PLOD; SPECIAL [LOT, PATCH]
policeman, plain-clothes DI; DS
policy LINE; PLANK
polish BUFF; FINISH; GLOSS; RUB; SAND
polished SLICK
polite CIVIL; SUAVE
politer NICER
political PARTY
political group CELL; PARTY
political leader P; PM; *see* PRIME MINISTER
political organisation PARTY
political power STATE
political spokesman's words SPIN
politician CON; LAB; LIB; MP; TORY
politician, American DEM
politicians PARTY
poll COUNT; HEAD
polluted anagram indicator
Polo CAR
polo mallet STICK
Polonius can indicate something to do with lending (character in Hamlet)
pompous STUFFY
pond MERE; POOL
pooch DOG
Pooh BEAR
Pooh's friend ROO
pool BATH; KITTY
pool, heated SPA
poor BAD; DISMAL; ILL; LAME; LOW; NEEDY; OFF; ROPEY; SHODDY; THIN; anagram indicator
poor actor HAM
poor grade D; E
poor grades DD; DE; ED; EE
poorly AILING; ILL; anagram indicator

poor relief ALMS
Pooter signals something to do with the book 'The Diary of a Nobody'
pop DAD; FATHER; HOCK; PA; PAWN
pop-group BAND
pop star STING
Pope LEO; URBAN
poppycock ROT; *see* RUBBISH
popular IN; HOT; LAY; LIKED; MASS
popular music MOTOWN; POP; RAP; ROCK
popular person, thing HIT
popular success HIT
porcelain, Chinese MING
pork-pie HAT; LIE; UNTRUTH
porridge BIRD; GRUEL; OATS
port HOLE; L; LEFT; PT; sea port, commonly RIO; also ACRE, ADEN, DEAL, DOVER, HULL, ORAN
port, Scottish OBAN
portent OMEN; SIGN
porter ALE; CARRIER; STOUT
porter's house LODGE
portion BIT; DOLE; LOT; PART; PIECE; RATION; SHARE; SLICE
portly STOUT
pose ACT; PUT; SIT
posed SAT
posh SMART; U
posh car LIMO; ROLLS; RR
position LAY; LIE; PLACE; POSE; POST; PUT; SITE; SLOT; SPOT; STANCE; STAND
position, awkward CORNER; SPOT
position, commanding TOP
position, in advantageous UP
position of authority CHAIR
positioned SAT
positive PLUS; POS; SURE
positive reaction AY; AYE; JA; OK; OUI; YES
positive result GAIN; WIN
possess HAVE; KEEP; OWN
possessed HAD; OWNED
possessed of nesting indicator

possession, was in HAD
possessions, enjoy HAVE; OWN
possessive sort OWNER
possessor OWNER
possibility CHANCE; MIGHT
possible ON; anagram indicator
possibly anagram indicator; also can indicate that the general category of the example given is called for
post CHAIR; JAMB; JOB; MAIL; NEWEL; PILLAR; PLACE; POLE; RAIL; SEND
postal order PO
postal service RM
posted SENT
poster AD; BILL; STICKER
postman PAT
postpone DEFER
postulate POSIT
posture POSE; SET; STANCE; STAND
pot BELLY; CROCK; DIXIE; GRASS; KITTY; MING; PAUNCH; PRIZE; SHOOT; TUB; TUM; URN; WOK
potassium K
potato EDWARD; MURPHY; SPUD
potato, battered CHIP; FRITTER
potential anagram indicator
potential growth BUD; SEED
potential, having ABLE
potentially anagram indicator
pottery CHINA; CRAFT; DELFT; MING
pottery centre STOKE
pottery material CLAY
pottery, piece of SHARD
potting can indicate something to do with snooker, etc.
pouch POCKET
poultry GOOSE; HEN
poultry disease ROUP
pounced STRUCK
pound BEAT; HIT; L; LB; LAM; NICKER; ONER; ONCER; PEN; QUID; RAM
pound coin, note ONCER; ONER; QUID
pour LASH; RAIN; STREAM
pour away DRAIN

pout BIB; MOUE
powder FLOUR; MEAL; TALC
powdered GROUND
power AC; DC; ARM; CLOUT; LIVE (ie. as in live cable); MIGHT; P; STEAM; SWAY; TEETH
power cut OUTAGE
power supply AC; COAL; DC; STEAM
power symbol MACE
power unit WATT
powerful MIGHTY; STRONG
powerful man TITAN [SAMSON]
PR *see* PUBLIC RELATIONS
practicable, practical ON
practice DRILL; HABIT; PE; PT; USE; can indicate something to do with law or medicine
practice, out of, without RUSTY
practise USE; DRILL
praise EXTOL; GLORY; LAUD
prank DIDO (ie. U.S.); JAPE; TRICK
prattle BABBLE
pray ASK; BEG; ENTREAT
prayer AVE; COLLECT; GRACE; ORISON
prayer, finish to AMEN
prayer, hour of SEXT
pre-Christian BC
pre-prepared envelope SAE
precariously anagram indicator
precinct MALL
precious metal AG; AU; GOLD; OR; SILVER
precipitate RAIN
precipitation RAIN
precipitous SHEER; STEEP
precise EXACT; NICE; PRIM
precisely DEAD
precocious child BRAT; IMP
predicament FIX; HOLE; SCRAPE; SPOT
preen GROOM
prefer FAVOUR; LIKE
preference LIKING
preference, express OPT

pregnant GREAT
prejudice BIAS
prejudice, without OPEN
prejudiced SEXIST
premier FIRST
prepare DRESS; PLAN; anagram indicator
prepare bread KNEAD
prepare for exam CRAM; REVISE; SWOT
prepare for war ARM
prepare to drive TEE
prepare to fire COCK
prepare to fight ARM
prepared PAT; READY; SET; anagram indicator
prepared to fight ARMED
prepared to fire COCKED
prepared to row OARED
presbyter ELDER
prescription anagram indicator
present AD; GIFT; GIVE; HERE; NOW; OFFER; STAGE
present, at NOW
present left LEGACY
present play STAGE
presentation anagram indicator
presented GAVE
presently SOON
preservative TAR
preserve CAN; CURE; JAM; KEEP; PICKLE; POT; SMOKE; TIN
preserved nesting indicator, specifically that an element is to be nested within CAN or TIN
preside CHAIR
president CHAIR; P; *see* U.S. PRESIDENT
President, U.S. ABE; BUSH; FORD; GRANT; POLK; TAFT
presidential office OVAL
press CROWD; IRON; MANGLE; MEDIA; SURGE; URGE; can indicate something to do with key (ie. which is pressed)
press down TAMP
press release PR
pressing SORE
pressman *see* JOURNALIST
pressure F; STRESS; can signify something to do with weather maps

eg. BAR

pressure, apply EXERT; LEAN

prestige CACHET; KUDOS

pretence ACTING; POSE; SHAM

pretend AFFECT; FAKE; FEIGN; PLAY; POSE; SHAM

pretension SIDE

pretentious ARTY; PHONY

pretentious person, type PSEUD; SNOB

prettified TWEE

pretty BONNIE; FAIR; TWEE

pretty woman DISH

prevalent RIFE

prevent AVERT; BAR; BAR; CHECK; DETER; FOIL; STEM; STOP

previous BACK; EX; OLD; FORMER; LATE

previous night EVE

previously cooked COLD

prey KILL

price COST; FEE; FIGURE; PR; RATE

price-fixers RING

price-fixing group RING

price, low IP (ie. one p)

prick STING; TINGLE

prickly SPINY

pricy DEAR; STEEP

pride can indicate something to do with lions

priest ABBE; CURE; ELI; LAMA; LEVI; P; PASTOR; PR; PRIOR

prima donna DIVA

primarily initial letter indicator

primary BASIC; CHIEF; MAIN

primate APE; MONKEY

prime minister BLAIR; DERBY; EDEN; HEATH; MAJOR; NORTH; PM; PEEL

prime LOAD; PLY; *see* FIRST RATE

primed SET

primp PREEN

prince HAL; IGOR; P; PR

prince's friend HORATIO

princess AIDA; ANNA; ANNE; BEGUM; RANA

principal ARCH; CHIEF; HEAD; LEAD; MAIN; STAR; TOP

principal role LEAD; STAR

principle CAUSE; IDEAL; PLANK
print COPY; DAB; ETCHING; TYPE
printed RAN
printing unit EM; EN
prior PAST; preceding indicator; can signpost a word beginning with ANTE
prison BIRD; BRIG; CAN; CAGE; CLINK; GAOL; JAIL; JUG; SLAMMER; STIR
prison, in CANNED; JUGGED
prison officer SCREW
prison, old QUAD; QUOD
prisoner CON; LAG; LIFER; POW
private GI; HIDDEN; INNER; OWN; RANKER; TOMMY
private investigator PI
prize CUP; NOBEL; PALM; PEARL; PLATE; PLUM; POT; PURSE
prizegiver NOBEL
probing nesting indicator
problem FAULT; HOLE; KNOT; NIGGLE; POSER; SNAG; SPOT; STEW; STRAIN; SUM; TANGLE; TEASER; anagram indicator
problem, personal BO
problematic anagram indicator
problems HASSLE; anagram indicator
problems, with anagram indicator
proceed GO; HEAD; LEAD
proceeds GAIN; RETURN; TAKE; YIELD
procedure ORDER; SYSTEM; WAY
process TREAT; anagram indicator
process of, in the WHILE
process, part of STAGE
processed, processing anagram indicator
procession FILE; LINE; MARCH
proclaim STATE
Procrustes can indicate something to do with legs, eg. stretching one's legs
procure EARN; GET
prod EGG; GOAD; POKE; PUSH; URGE
produce BEAR; CREATE; CROP; DO; FORM; ISSUE; MAKE; STAGE; YIELD; anagram indicator; manipulation indicator
produce form SHAPE
produce newspaper PRINT
produce young BEAR; CALVE

produced BORE; DID; MADE
product SON; YIELD
product of mine ORE
production anagram indicator
productive RICH
professional EXPERT; PRO
professional(ly), not LAY
professional post CHAIR
professor PROF
professorship CHAIR
profit BOOT; GAIN; INTEREST; NET
profit, in UP
profitable ROARING
programme COURSE; PLAN; anagram indicator
programmer CODER
progress WAY
progress, in ON; ONGOING
progress, make slow CRAWL; INCH; PLOD
progress, slow CRAWL
progress, rate of MPH; PACE; SPEED
progressive LEFT; NEW
project CAST; HURL; IDEA; PITCH; PLAN; PUT; THROW
projectile BALL
projectiles AMMO
prohibit BAN; BAR
prohibited TABU
prohibition BAN; BAR; TABU
prolific LAVISH; RICH
prom FRONT; PIER
promenade WALK; *see* PROM
prominence HILL
prominent BIG
promise IOU; OATH; SWEAR; VOW; WORD
promising BRIGHT; RIPE
promissory note IOU
promontory CAPE
promontory in Scotland MULL
promote FOSTER; HYPE; MARKET; PEDDLE; RAISE; STAGE
promoted, was ROSE
promotion AD; BOOST; HYPE; SALE; reversal indicator

promotional material AD; PUFF; *see* ADVERTISEMENT
prompt CUE; eg.G; GOAD; PUSH; REMIND
promptly PAT
prone LYING
prone, is LIES
pronounce SOUND
pronounced ORAL; SAID; homophone indicator
pronouncement homophone indicator
pronouncements DICTA
prong TINE
prop LEG; SHORE
propaganda SELL
propel DRIVE; PUSH; ROW; SEND
proper APT; DUE; FIT; PRIM; PUCKA; REAL; RIGHT; U
proper English U
proper in China TAO
property ASSET; ESTATE; FLAT; HOUSE; LAND; REALTY
property, U.S. REALTY
property right LIEN
prophet AMOS; ELI; MOSES; SEER
proponent of war HAWK
proportion RATIO
proposal MOTION; OFFER
propose OFFER; PLAN; TENDER
proposition IDEA; OFFER; POINT
proprietor OWNER
prosaic DULL; FLAT; *see* DULL
prosecutor, American, U.S. DA
prospect HOPE
prosper GROW
prosperous period BOOM
prospector can indicate something to do with gold prospecting eg. PAN
prostrate PRONE
protected species BAT
protecting nesting indicator
protection GLOVE; JACKET; MAC; SHELL
protective cloth APRON; BIB
protective clothing APRON; BIB; MAIL
protector APRON; BIB; GLOVE; MAC; VISOR

protest DEMO; MARCH; OBJECT; SITIN (is sit-in)
Protestant LUTHER; ORANGE
protester, hunt SAB
protesting ANTI
protuberance BUMP; KNOB; LUMP
proverb SAW
provide BRING; CATER; GIVE; LAYON (ie. lay on); anagram indicator
provide information SHOP
provide money FUND
provided, providing IF
province BAG; BC; FIELD; NATAL; NI; ULSTER
province, European TYROL
provision RIDER
provoke ANGER; NEEDLE; TEASE
provoked anagram indicator
proximate NEAR
prudent SAGE; WISE
prudish PRIM
prune DOCK; PARE; TRIM
pry NOSE; PEER; SNOOP
prying NOSY
PSV BUS
psyche MIND
psychiatrist SHRINK
psychic sense, skill etc ESP
psychologist JUNG
pub BAR; INN; LOCAL; PH
pub, City Road EAGLE
public OPEN; OUT; OVERT; can refer to a public house, or something to do with a public house, *see* PUB
public admission OUT
public relations PR; can indicate something to do with SPIN
public transport BUS; TRAM
publication BOOK; EDITION; ISSUE; MAG; ORGAN; PAPER; RAG; TRACT
publications PRESS
publicise AIR
publicist PRO
publicity AD; ADVERT; HYPE; PLUG; FOSTER; PR; PUFF

publicity, wild HYPE
publish AIR; ISSUE; RUN
published RAN; OUT
publisher OUP
publishing house OUP
pudding DUFF; DUMPLING; RICE; SWEET; TART
puff BLOW; BLURB; DRAG; WIND
puffed up VAIN
pull CLOUT; DRAG; DRAW; HAUL; LUG; TOW; TUG; YANK
pull out EXTRACT; LEAVE; QUIT
pulled to bits anagram indicator
pullover JERSEY
pulp MUSH; PAP
pulpit AMBO
pulse BEAN; BEAT; DAL (another spelling of dhal); LENTIL; PEA; SEEDS; THROB
pump HEART; TICKER
pumpkin GOURD
punch BIFF; CHOP; CROSS; DIE; FIST; HOOK; JAB; LEFT; RIGHT; SLUG; SOCK
punctuation mark COLON; COMMA; DASH; STOP
pundit SAGE
pungency TANG
punish BEAT; CANE; FINE; TAN
punished BEAT; anagram indicator
punishment CANE; FINE; LINES
punt BET; GAMBLE
punter BETTER
pupil L; can indicate something to do with the eye
pupil, former, once OB
pupils CLASS; FORM; STREAM
puppies LITTER
purchase BUY; GRIP
purchaser can indicate a form of money as "Japanese purchaser" clues Y or YEN
pure CLEAN; SIMPLE; WHITE
puritan, smug PRIG
purple PLUM; PUCE
purplish-brown PUCE
purpose AIM; END; GOAL

pursue CHASE; DOG; HUNT; *see* PURSUING
pursuing indicator that one component should follow another
pursuit CHASE; HOBBY; HUNT; INTEREST
push HEAVE; JAM; NUDGE; PLUG; PLY; SHOVE; TOUT; URGE
puss CAT; TOM
pussy, French CHAT
put ADD; LAY; PLACE; PLANT; SET; SLIP (ie. as in slip clothing on),
put an end to SCOTCH
put away EAT; DINE; DRINK; HIDE
put back reversal indicator
put down LAID; LAY; REST; SNUB
put extra ADD
put forward TABLE
put in nesting indicator
put money on BET; WAGER
put off DEFER; DETER; STALL
put on APPLY; DON; SHAM; STAGE
put out CROSS; DOUSE; EJECT; anagram indicator
put right CURE; MEND; REDO; anagram indicator
put to flight ROUT
put to sea LAUNCH
put together PIECE
put up BOARD; reversal indicator
put up with BEAR; STAND
put years on AGE
putrid OFF
putter CLUB
puzzle MAZE; POSER; REBUS; RIDDLE
puzzle writer SETTER
puzzle's first part ACROSS
puzzle's second part DOWN
puzzled anagram indicator
Pylos, king of NESTOR
Pyrenean city PAU

Qq

quack SHAM
quaff DRINK; SUP
quail BEVY; FLINCH
quaint CUTE; TWEE; anagram indicator
quake ROCK
Quaker FRIEND
qualification *see* DEGREE
qualification, without LAY; UTTER
qualified ABLE; FIT
qualified, not LAY; UTTER
qualified teacher BED
quality AIR; TONE; TRAIT
quality, delightful CHARM
quantity AMOUNT; BATCH; GRAM; LOT; SIZE; TON; *see* MEASURE, WEIGHT
quantity of drink CASK; CUP; DRAM; GLASS; SHOT; TUN
quarrel ARROW; BOLT; BRAWL; CLASH; DISPUTE; DUEL; ROW; RUNIN (ie. run-in); SPAT; TIFF; can refer to something to do with archer
quarry BAG; CHASE; DIG; GLASS; PREY; STONE
quarter AREA; BILLET; E; EAST; FOURTH; MERCY; N; NORTH; S; SOUTH; W; WEST
quarterdeck SUIT (ie. one of four in the pack!)
quarters BERTH; some combination of N, E, W or S
quartet FOUR
quartet heard FOR; FORE
quash ANNUL
quaver TRILL; WARBLE
quay CAY
queen ANNE; BESS; CARD; CAT; DIDO; E; ER; KITTY; MARY; PIECE; PUSS; Q; QU; R; TITANIA; VIP
Queen ELLERY; *see* QUEEN
queen, beauty MISS
Queen Elizabeth BESS; ER; rem: can also refer to the liner as well as the monarch

Queen's English RP
queer ODD; RUM; anagram indicator
query ASK; WHY
quest HUNT; SEARCH
question ASK; GRILL; HOW; ISSUE; MATTER; POSER; PRY; PUMP; Q; QU
question mark can imply that an example is being given; or can imply some humour in the clue construction; or that the compiler is stretching a point
questionable IFFY; SHADY
questioning ASKING; POSING
queue FILE; LINE; WAIT
quick ALIVE; DEFT; FAST; FLEET; LIVE; LIVING; NIPPY; PRESTO; SHARP; SMART
quick, was RACED; RAN; SHOT; SPED
quickly APACE; FAST; PRESTO
quid L; POUND; can signal something to do with tobacco, pipe etc
quiet DEAD; MUM; P; PEACE; SH; WHIST
quietly P; SH
quintet FIVE; TROUT (ie. by Schubert)
quip JOKE; *see* JOKE
quirk TRAIT
quirky anagram indicator
quit CEASE; LEAVE; RESIGN; STOP; omission indicator
quitch GRASS
quite ALL; CLEAN; FULLY
quits EVEN; LEVEL; SQUARE
quite SOME; VERY
Quixote *see* DON QUIXOTE
quiz GRILL; PUMP; TEST
quod *see* PRISON
quota SHARE
quotation TAG
quotation marks bear in mind that quotation marks are commonly used to confuse, so they can be placed around a single word to disguise its function in the clue, such as an indicator; or they can be used to break the connection between adjacent words, thereby putting you off the track; or to make you think about a book or play when the solution is nothing of the sort!
quotation, trite TAG
quote CITE; COPY; NAME; PRICE

Rr

R RIGHT
rabbit BUCK; CHAT; CONY; DOE; RATTLE; TALK; WAFFLE
race BELT; BLOOD; BREED; DART; DASH; DERBY; EVENT; FLAT; HEAT; MILE; NATION; OAKS; RELAY; RUN; RUSH; SCUD; SPEED; SPRINT; STOCK; TT
race, had a RAN
race meeting TT
racecourse ASCOT; EPSOM; REDCAR
racehorse ARKLE; CHASER; STAYER
races TT; anagram indicator
racket BAT; CON; DIN; DODGE; FIDDLE; NOISE; SCAM
racy PAST
radical RAD; RED; ROOT; can refer to a radical chemical eg. AMYL, METHYL
radio SET
radio entertainer DJ
radio operator, receiver HAM
radioactive HOT
radioactive element U
radius BONE; R
RAF man ERK
raffle DRAW
rafter BEAM
rag PAPER; PRANK; RIB; SCRAP
rage BATE; PAD; FASHION; FURY; IRE; PET; RANT; RAGE; STORM; TEMPER; WRATH
ragged anagram indicator; also rem: it has two separate pronunciations and meanings (so it is likely to be used one way, say as a verb, when you should really see it as an adjective)
raid BUST; MISSION
raid, carefully planned STING
rail BAR; BIRD; BLAST; LINE; RAGE; RY; TRACK
rail formerly BR
railing FENCE
raillery BANTER

railroad COERCE
rails, go off the ERR; SIN
railway RLY; RY
railway company, old LMS
railwaymen NUR
rain POUR; R; SPIT; TEEM
rain, fine MIST
rain, sounds like REIGN; REIN
rainbow TROUT
rainstorm can indicate an anagram of RAIN
rainwear MAC
raise GROW; LIFT; LUFF; REAR; UP
raise spirits ELATE; LACE
raised BRED; HOVE; UP; reversal indicator
raising reversal indicator
raising agent YEAST
rake GATHER; ROUE; SCRAPE
rake-off CUT; SHARE; TAKE
rally EVENT; MEND; RISE
ram BEAK; FORCE; TUP
ramble HIKE
rambler ROSE
rambling anagram indicator
ramp SLOPE
rampage, on anagram indicator
rampant anagram indicator
ramshackle anagram indicator
ran FLOWED; SPED; *see* RUN
ranch SPREAD
random anagram indicator
range AMBIT; BAND; CHAIN; KEN; LINE; SCOPE; SWEEP; can call for a specific mountain range eg. URAL
range, entire AZ (ie. A to Z)
rangy LANKY
rank ROW; TIER; anagram indicator
rankle CHAFE; FESTER; GALL
ransack RIFLE
ransacked anagram indicator
rant RAVE
rant and rave THUNDER

rap BLAME; HIT
rapacity GREED
rapid eye movement REM
rapidity SPEED
raptor EAGLE
rapturous SENT
rare anagram indicator
rascal IMP; LIMB (old word); SCAMP
rash HASTY; HIVES; IMPRUDENT
rasp FILE
rat STINKER
rate BAT; DEEM; LICK; PRICE; SCOLD; SPEED; TEMPO
rate, first A
rate of progress MPH; PACE; SPEED
rate, set PACE
rating HAND
ration SHARE
rational LOGICAL
rationed anagram indicator
rations FARE; SHARE; anagram indicator
rattle SHAKE; anagram indicator
rattled SHOOK; anagram indicator
ratty SHIRTY
Ratty can indicate something to do with 'Wind in the Willows' or Graham, its author
rave RANT
ravel TANGLE; TWIST
ravine GORGE
raving RANT
raw GREEN; HARD
raw material ORE
ray BEAM; LIGHT; RE (alt. spelling of the 2nd note of the scale); SKATE (ie. fish)
reach HIT; LAND; MAKE
reached MADE
reacting anagram indicator
reaction, automatic, nervous TIC
read CON
read, aloud homophone indicator
read carefully CON

read, out homophone indicator
read rapidly SCAN; SKIM
reader LECTOR
readily PAT; SOON
reading VERSION
reading-desk AMBO
readjusted anagram indicator
ready BRASS; CASH; COCKED; DUE; FIT; GAME; MONEY; PAT; RIPE; SET; TENDER; *see* FOREIGN CURRENCY
ready, get EARN; RIPEN
ready to fight ARMED
ready to fire, shoot ARMED; COCKED
real ACTUAL; RIGHT; TRUE
real, not FALSE; PASTE; PSEUDO; SHAM
realise CASH; NET
reallocated anagram indicator
realm REGION
ream BORE
rear BACK; BUM; END; HIND; STERN; TAIL
rear, at the last letter indicator
rearrange anagram indicator
reason CAUSE; GROUND; MIND; MOTIVE; SANITY; SPUR; WHY
reasonable CHEAP; FAIR; OK
reassessed, reassessment anagram indicator
rebel CADE (insurgent during time of Henry VII); RISE
rebelled ROSE
rebound, on the reversal indicator
rebuild, rebuilding, rebuilt anagram indicator
rebuke BERATE; CHIDE; RATE; SCOLD
rebuked CHID; CHIDDEN
recalled, recalling reversal indicator
recast anagram indicator
recede EBB; FALL; WANE
receipts TAKE
receive COLLECT; GET; TAKE
received HAD; GOT
receiver CATCHER; FENCE; SET (eg. radio)
recent LATE; MOD; NEW
recent, comparatively, more LATER

recently LATE
receptacle BAG; BIN; BOWL; DRAWER; HOPPER; TRAY; *see* CONTAINER
recess APSE; BAY; BREAK; CLOSET; NICHE
recession DIP; SLUMP; TROUGH; reversal indicator
recipe PLAN; anagram indicator
recited anagram indicator; homophone indicator
reckless RASH
recklessly anagram indicator
reckon FANCY; THINK [TELLER]
reclassified anagram indicator
reclining reversal indicator
reclusive type LONER
recognise KNOW; OWN; SEE
recollected anagram indicator; reversal indicator
recommend URGE
recommendation PLUG
reconciliation DETENTE
reconstructed, reconstruction anagram indicator
reconvened anagram indicator
record ALBUM; ANNAL; BOOK; CAN; CARD; CD; DIARY; DISC; ENTER; ENTRY; EP; FILE; FORM; LIST; LP; LOG; MONO; NOTE; PLATTER; REC; ROLL; SINGLE; STAMP; TABLE; TALLY; TAPE; TRACE; TRACK
record, betting BOOK
record company INDIE
record illegally BUG
record, part of TRACK
record player DJ
record presenter DJ
recorded, not LIVE
recording TAPE; *see* RECORD
recount RETAIL; TELL
recover RALLY
recovering OVER
recovery RALLY
recreated anagram indicator
recreation area COMMON
recruit, raw ROOKIE
recruitment DRAFT
Rector R

recurrent reversal indicator
recycled anagram indicator
red CHERRY; LEFT; ROUGE
red, in the DEBT; OWING
red-light NOGO (ie. no-go)
red, see RAGE
redcoat can indicate something to do with Santa Claus
redden BLUSH; FLUSH
reddish RUSTY
redefined anagram indicator
redesign CHANGE; anagram indicator
redesigned anagram indicator
redirected anagram indicator
reduce CUT; DAMP; DOCK; LESS; LESSEN; LOP; LOWER; PARE; REMIT; abbreviation indicator
reduce in rank DEMOTE
reduce risk HEDGE
reduced CUT; DOWN; LOW; LOWER; LESS; THIN; abbreviation indicator
reduction CUT; DROP; PALL; abbreviation indicator; can call for a word ending in -LESS
reed GRASS
reef BANK; CAY
reefer GRASS; JOINT
reel SPOOL; TURN; WIND
re-established anagram indicator
refashion, refashioned anagram indicator
refer RELATE; SEE
refer to QUOTE
reference NAME
reference book, work DICT; OED
referring to ON; RE
refined anagram indicator
refined man GENT
reflect MUSE; PONDER; THINK
reflection from, in combined reversal and run indicator
reflection, on reversal indicator
reform ALTER; CHANGE; anagram indicator
reformed anagram indicator
refrain ABSTAIN; AVOID; *see* SONG

refresher DRINK; FEE
refuge HID
refuge, place of ARK
refurbished anagram indicator
refusal NAY; NO; SHANT
refusal, French NON
refuse DENY; DROSS; GARBAGE; LEAVINGS; SLAG; TRASH; WASTE; *see* RUBBISH
refuse to believe DISCOUNT
refuse to deal with BLACK
refuse to recognize CUT; SNUB
regain RECOVER
regard EYE; RESPECT
regarding ASTO (ie. as to); RE
regardless of omission indicator
regiment RA; RE
region AREA; CLIME; REALM; ZONE
register LIST; LOG; R; ROLL; SIGN
register points SCORE
regressed reversal indicator
regret MOURN; RUE; SORROW
regretful SORRY
regrettably ALAS
regroup anagram indicator
regular EVEN; FLAT; OFTEN; SET; USUAL
regular intervals can indicate the use of even letters in a sequence
regulated anagram indicator
regulation LAW; RULE; anagram indicator
regulations CODE; *see* RULES
regurgitated reversal indicator
reign RULE; SWAY
rein STRAP
reinforce BRACE; LINE; PROP
reinforced nesting indicator
reinforcement BRACE; PROP; STRUT
reiterating reversal indicator; repeat indicator
reject SCORN; SPURN
rejected LORN; OUT; reversal indicator
rejig anagram indicator
rejoin anagram indicator

rejuvenated anagram indicator
relate REFER; REPORT; RETAIL; TELL
related AGNATE; AKIN
related to OF
relation ACCOUNT; AUNT; BROTHER; FATHER; GRAN; KIN; MA; MUM; NAN; NIECE; PA; RATIO; SIB; SIS; SISTER; TALE; *see* FATHER, MOTHER; can indicate something to do with STORY
relations KIN; TIES
relationship RATIO; TIE
relative REL; *see* RELATION
relax EASE; LOLL; LOUNGE; PATIENCE (ie. exhortation) REST; SIT
relaxed COOL; EASED; EASY; LOOSE; anagram indicator
relaxed, more LOOSER
relaxing anagram indicator
release ACQUIT; DROP; FREE; ISSUE; SPARE; UNLOCK; anagram indicator
released FREE; OUT; anagram indicator
releasing omission indicator
relentless STERN
relevant GERMANE
reliable SOUND; TRUSTY
reliable type BRICK; TYPE
relief AID; BAS; EASE
relief, that's a PHEW
relief work CAMEO
relieve EASE
religion ZEN
religious PI
religious authority POPE; ROME
religious belief ZEN
religious ceremony MASS; RITE
religious experience VISION
religious fraternity ESSENE; SECT
religious group CHURCH; ORDER; SECT
religious instruction, knowledge RE; RI
religious leader LAMA; R; RABBI
religious person MONK; NUN
religious statement CREED
religious symbol CROSS
religious texts AV; NT; OT

religious work AV; TRACT
relinquish FORGO
relish GUSTO; SAUCE; SPICE
reluctant AVERSE; LOATH; LOTH
rely BANK; COUNT; LEAN
remain ABIDE; BIDE; LIE; STAY; STICK; TARRY
remainder REST; OTHERS
remained LAY
remaining LEFT; ODD; OVER
remains ASH; DUST; LEES; STUB
remark CRACK; NOTE; QUIP; SALLY; SAY
remark, cutting BARB
remarkable anagram indicator
remarkable person ONER
remarkably anagram indicator
remedy BALM; CURE; SALVE
remember RETAIN
remembered anagram indicator (ie. re-membered!)
remind NUDGE; PROMPT
reminder CUE; NUDGE; PROMPT
remixing anagram indicator
remnant RUMP
remote BACK; FAR
removal OUSTING
removal, legal OUSTER
remove CUT; DELETE; DOFF; FIRE; PEEL; SACK; STRIP; TAKE; can indicate a verb to be preceded by DE, as "remove name from plan" clues DESIGN (ie. de-sign); anagram indicator
removed FAR; omission indicator; anagram indicator
rend RIP; TEAR
render GIVE; YIELD; anagram indicator
rendered anagram indicator
rendez-vous MEET; VENUE
renegotiated anagram indicator
renounce QUIT
renovated anagram indicator
rent GASH; HIRE; SLIT; RIP; TEAR; TORE; TORN
rep AGENT
repartee, engage in FENCE
repast MEAL

repair MEND; PATCH; SEW; anagram indicator
repaired, repairing anagram indicator
repatriate DEPORT
repeat APE; COPY; ITERATE; PARROT; REDO
repeatedly AGAIN; repeat indicator
re-penning anagram indicator
repetition ROTE; repeat indicator
replaced CHANGED; anagram indicator
replacement SPARE; anagram indicator
replayed serve LET
report BANG; CRACK; PAPER; NOISE; POP; SAY; RELATE; STORY; homophone indicator
reported, it's homophone indicator
reportedly homophone indicator
reporter, young CUB
repose REST
repository BANK; TILL
represent MEAN; SHOW
representation anagram indicator (ie. re-presentation)
representative AGENT; ENVOY; MP; REP
represented anagram indicator
reprimand CARPET; RAP; RATE; RATING; ROCKET
reproach TWIT
reprobate RIP
reproduce APE; COPY; anagram indicator
reproduced, anagram indicator
reproduction COPY; FAKE; anagram indicator
reproof, gave CHID
reptile CROC; EFT; SNAKE; *see* SNAKE
republic EIRE
Republican troops IRA
reputation FAME; NAME
repute ODOUR
request ASK; BEG; ORDER; PLEA; PRAY; PRAYER
require NEED; MAKE
required MADE
required, not OVER; SPARE
required, what is SPEC; *see* REQUIREMENT
requirement MUST; NEED; WAIT
research DIG

research centre, facility, place LAB
research scientist BOFFIN
researcher BOFFIN
rescue SAVE
rescuer SAVER; SAVIOUR
resent MIND
resentment ENVY
resentment, show BRIDLE
reservation BOOKING; BUT; RES; can indicate something to do with American Indians
reserve BAG; BOOK; STORE; STOCK; TA
reserve, in BY
reserved BOOKED; SHY
reserved person OYSTER
reserves BOOKS; STOCK; STORE; TA
reservoir LAKE; SUMP; TANK
reset anagram indicator
reshuffle anagram indicator
reside DWELL; LIVE; LODGE
residence ABODE; CASTLE; DWELLING; FLAT; GAFF; HOME; HOUSE; PAD
residence, take up SETTLE
resident INMATE; NATIVE
residential street CLOSE
residual piece STUB
residue ASH
resign QUIT
resin LAC
resist OPPOSE
resistance R
resolution anagram indicator
resolve AIM; PLAN; anagram indicator
resolved, resolving anagram indicator
resort SPA; anagram indicator; can refer to a specific popular resort eg. in Britain: HOVE, abroad: FARO, NICE, RIO; SPLIT
resorted anagram indicator
resound RING
resounded RANG
respect REVERE; WAY
respect, show BOW

respectable DECENT; FAIR
respond PLEAD; REACT; YIELD
response TIC
response, disgusted UGH
responsible for OVER
responsibility CHARGE; RAP
rest COST; BREAK; EASE; FF (ie. following pages); LEAN; LIE; NAP; REPOSE; SIT; SPIDER
rest, place of BED; COT
rest, take a KIP; NAP; SIT
restaurant DINER; CAFE; CAFF
restaurant car DINER
restaurant, commonly, popularly CAFF
rested SAT
restful SERENE
resting place BED; COT; GRAVE
restoration anagram indicator
restore CURE; MEND; STET
restrain CURB; DAM; FETTER; REIN; REPRESS; SMOTHER; STAY; STEM
restrained anagram indicator
restrained, not FREE; LOOSE
restraint BRIDLE; CURB; DAM; FETTER; REIN
restraint, without FREE; LOOSE
restrict BIND; CHAIN; CRAM; PEN; TIE
restrict movements GATE; HOBBLE; PEN
restricted anagram indicator; run indicator
restricting nesting indicator
restriction LET; TIE
restructured anagram indicator
result DRAW; END; ENSUE; EVENT; FOLLOW; GAIN; SCORE; TIE; WIN
resurgence RALLY
retail RECOUNT; SELL; TELL
retail outlet DELI; SHOP; STORE
retailer MONGER; SELLER; SHOP; STORE
retain HOLD; KEEP; SAVE; STET
retain, manage to SAVE; SALVE
retained KEPT
retaliation can indicate a word ending in BACK

retch KECK
reticent COY
retinue SUITE; TRAIN
retired ABED; EX; RET; can indicate a component is to be nested within the letters BED (ie. in bed)
retired person can indicate something to do with being in bed
retirement BED; reversal indicator
retiring SHY; reversal indicator
retort SALLY
retouch EDIT
retreat BACK; DEN; EBB; FLEE; FLIGHT; LAIR; NEST; NOOK; RECEDE; SHELTER; STUDY
retrograde reversal indicator
retrospective, retrospectively reversal indicator
return BACK; GAIN; PROFIT; NET; RET; YIELD; reversal indicator
returned BACK; GAVE; reversal indicator
returning reversal indicator
revamped anagram indicator
reveal BARE; SHOW; UNFOLD; VENT
revealed OUT
reuse, reusing anagram indicator
reveals run indicator
revelry RIOT
revels anagram indicator
reverberating reversal indicator
reverse BACK; TURN; reversal indicator
reverts reversal indicator
review CRIT; PARADE; anagram indicator
review, enthusiastic RAVE
reviewed anagram indicator
revised anagram indicator
revision anagram indicator
revival RALLY; anagram indicator
revive RALLY
revolt RISING; UPRISING
revolting UP; anagram indicator
revolution SPIN; TURN; anagram indicator; reversal indicator
revolutionary CHE; MAO; MARAT; RED; TROT; reversal indicator; anagram indicator
revolve SPIN; TURN; TWIST; WHIRL

revolver ARM; COLT; GUN; ROTOR; SPINNER; WHEEL
reward PURSE; TIP
rewritten anagram indicator
rhetoric CANT; IRONY
rhyme JINGLE; VERSE
rhythm BEAT; LILT
rib BAIT; BONE; CHAFF; GUY; KID; SCOFF; STITCH; TEASE; TWIT
rib enclosure CASE
ribbing TEASE
ribbon BAND; BOW; TAPE
rich CREAMY; FAT; HIGH; PLUSH; LUSH; ROLLING
Richard DICK; RICK
rick STACK
rickety anagram indicator
riddle POSER; STRAIN
ride on horseback CANTER
ridge CREST; CHINE; FRET; FURROW; REEF
ridicule DERIDE; GUY; ROCK; SCOFF
ridicule, object of BUTT
ridiculous anagram indicator
riding UP
riding equipment TACK
rifle ARM; GUN; SACK
rig EQUIP; GEAR; KIT
rigged anagram indicator
right CLAIM; DUE; EXACT; JUST; LIEN; MEND; MORAL; OK; PROPER; R; RT; SO; TRUE; anagram indicator (in the sense of make right); can indicate that what precedes it provides either the clue's definition or an example of same
right away NOW; can indicate that R is to be omitted
right, exactly PAT
right in China TAO
right, just FINE; PAT
right, legal LIEN
right, property LIEN
right of way LANE
right, say RITE
right-wing DRY; TORY
right-winger TORY
rigid FIRM; LOCKED; STERN

rile GALL; IRK; NAG
rim EDGE; LIP
rim, wheel FELLOE
rind PEEL
ring BELL; BUZZ; CALL; CHIME; CIRCLE; COIL; CYCLE; DIAL; DING; GANG; HALO; HOOP; INNER; KEEPER; LUTE; O; OUTER; PEAL; PHONE; ROUND; SET; TOLL; WASHER
Ring can indicate something to do with Wagner's Ring Cycle
ring-leader word to begin with O
ring-tailed O to be added to end
ringer BELL; DOUBLE
ringing sound PING; *see* SOUND
ringlet LOCK; TRESS
rinse SWILL; WASH
riot, rioting, riotous anagram indicator
rip REND; RENT; TEAR
rip off ROB; STEAL; anagram of RIP
ripe, not GREEN
riposte SALLY
rippling anagram indicator
rise ASCENT; HILL; KNOLL; MOUNT; RALLY; REBEL; SLOPE; STIR; SURGE; TOR; reversal indicator
risen UP
rising UP; reversal indicator
risk BET; CHANCE; DANGER; DARE; PERIL
risk, reduce HEDGE
risk, take BET; CHANCE; DARE; GAME; WAGER
risque BLUE; RACY
rival VIE
river FLOW; R; a specific river name – common British examples: AIRE, AXE, CAM, DEE, EXE, FAL, FORTH, OUSE, SEVERN, SPEY, STOUR, TAFF, TAMAR, TAY, TEE, TEES, TEST, TRENT, WEAR, YARE; common foreign examples: DON, INDUS, NILE, ODER, PLATE, PO, RHINE, RHONE, URAL, VOLTA
river barrier DAM
river bottom BED
river mammal OTTER
river, stretch of REACH
rivet PIN; STUD
road AI; AVE; DRIVE; LANE; M; MI; RD; ST; WAY
road back DR

road junction T
road, Roman VIA
roam RAMBLE; WANDER; anagram indicator
roan BAY
roar BELLOW; BOOM
roast BASTE; BEEF; PAN; SLATE (ie. criticise)
roasting anagram indicator
rob NICK; PINCH; STEAL
robber MUGGER
robbery HEIST; THEFT
robe GOWN
Robert BOB
Robin HOOD
robust HARDY; RUGGED
rock CRAG; GEM; GIB; ICE; JAR; ORE; SHAKE; STAGGER; WAVER; anagram indicator
rocked, rocking anagram indicator
rocket RETRO; VI
rocket organisation NASA
rocks ICE
rocks, on the can indicate a word ending in ICE
rocky anagram indicator
rod BAR; CUE; GAT; PERCH; POLE; STAFF; SWITCH
rodent CONY; MOUSE; RAT
rodents MICE
Roderick ROD
Rodin rem: he is the sculptor famous for "The Kiss" and "The Thinker"
roe DEER
rogue CAD; CUR; FIDDLER; SCAMP
roguish ARCH
role PART
role, principal LEAD; STAR
role, small CAMEO
role, to be in ACT
roll BAP; BUN; CARPET; LIST; SPOOL; SURGE; TURN; TWIST; WAD; WIND
roll up FURL
rolled RAN; WOUND; anagram indicator; reversal indicator
roller BREAKER; SWELL; WAVE

rolling RICH; anagram indicator; reversal indicator
rolls anagram indicator; reversal indicator
Roman RC; can indicate a Latin term, or Roman numeral(s)
Roman chap VIR
Roman coin AS
Roman couple II
Roman emperor NERO
Roman road VIA
Roman, severe CATO
Roman, you TU
romancer LIAR
Rome, from, in etc can indicate that Latin is to be used such as NUN (Latin for now)
Romeo LOVER; WOLF
romp ORGY; SPREE
Romulus and Remus can indicate something to do with Rome, twins, common age
roof THATCH; TOP
roof, parts of EAVES
roof, sort of THATCH
roofer TILER
rook CHEAT; CON; MAN; PIECE; R; SKIN
room ATTIC; CELL; DEN; HALL; LOUNGE; SALON; SCOPE; SPACE; STUDIO; STUDY
room for concerts HALL
room, little CELL; RM
root BELIEF; CAUSE; POKE
rope CORD; PAINTER; SASH; SHEET; SISAL; STAY; TETHER
rope fibre ISTLE
rope maker ISTLE
ropey POOR
rose BRIAR; PINK; TUDOR; reversal indicator
roster LIST; TABLE
rosy PINK
rot BULL; BUNK; ERODE; *see* RUBBISH
rota LIST; TABLE
rotate SPIN; TURN; WIND
rotten BAD; OFF; anagram indicator
rotter CAD; HEEL
roue RAKE

rouge RED
rough CRUDE; RAW; RUDE; RUGGED; VAGUE; anagram indicator
roughed up anagram indicator
roughly ABOUT; anagram indicator
rough water stretch RIP
roulette WHEEL
round ABOUT; BALL; BOUT; BULLET; C; CANON; HEAT; LAP; O; PLUMP; RING; SHOT; TURN; anagram indicator; nesting indicator; reversal indicator; can indicate something to do with drink or drinking places
round, go ROLL; TURN
round of drinks SHOUT
rounds BEAT; OO; OS
rouse STIR
route ROAD; WAY
route, less frequented BROAD (ie. B-road!)
route, part of STAGE
route, trade CANAL
routine ACT; DRILL; HABIT; ROUND; RUT
routine, dull RUT
routine journalist HACK
routine task CHORE
rove ROAM; WANDER
rover RANGER
Rover DOG
row BANK; BOTHER; DIN; FILE; LINE; NOISE; OAR; POTHER; RANK; SCRAP; SCULL; SHINDY; SPAT; TIER; TIFF
rowan ASH
rowing club LEANDER
rowdy BULLY; TED; anagram indicator
rowers CREW; BIGHT
rowing position BOW
royal R; REGIUS; can refer to a specific monarch, in full or abbreviated; *see* KING, QUEEN, MONARCH, RULER
royal address SIRE
royal characters ER; *see* KING, QUEEN, MONARCH, RULER
royal family HOUSE; ORANGE; TUDOR
royalty ER
rub CHAFF; PRESS
rubbish BIN; BOSH; BULL; BUNK; CHAFF; COBBLERS;

DRECK; DROSS; GARBAGE; GASH; JUNK; LITTER; PIFFLE; PULP; ROT; TAT; TOSH; TRASH; TRIPE; TWADDLE; *see* NONSENSE

rubbish, place for BIN; HEAP

rubbishing anagram indicator

ruddy FLAMING; RED; ROSY

rude BRASH; *see* CHEEKY.

ruff FRILL; TRUMP (at cards)

ruffian LOUT; TOUGH

rug MAT; WIG

rugby RU; with capital initial letter can refer to the SCHOOL

rugby crowd RUCK

rugby player CENTRE; FLANKER; HOOK; HOOKER; PROP; WASP

rugby players PACK

rugby team BATH; WASPS

ruin BREAK; DISH; MAR; ROT; SMASH; SPOIL; UNDO; WRECK; anagram indicator

ruined BROKE; anagram indicator; *see* RUIN

ruining anagram indicator

rule GOVERN; LAW; REIGN

Rule Britannia can indicate use of ARNE, its composer

rules CODE; SYSTEM

ruled by UNDER

ruler ER; GR; KHAN; KING; LORD; QUEEN; RAJA; REGENT; SULTAN; TSAR

ruling IN

rum GROG; ODD; OFF; STRANGE; anagram indicator

rummaged, rummaging anagram indicator

rumour CRY; NOISE; TALK; *see* GOSSIP

rumour, according to homophone indicator

rump END

rumpus FUSS; RIOT

run BELT; BOLT; CHAIR; CHASE; COOP; COURSE; DASH; ESCAPE; EXTRA; FLEE; FLOW; FLY; GO; HARE; HIE; LADDER; LOPE; PELT; R; RACE; RUSH; SHOOT; SINGLE; SNAG; SPEED; SPRINT; STREAK; TEAR; TROT; ZIP; can indicate something to do with smuggling

run away BOLT; ELOPE

run fast DART; DASH; PELT; ZIP; *see* RUN

run in COLLAR; NICK

run into MEET
run off BOLT; ELOPE; SCATTER
run out RO; anagram of RUN
run over RECAP; REVIEW; SPILL
run quickly RIP
runabout anagram of RUN
rung STEP
runner BEAN; MILER; SKI; VINE; an old standby to indicate a river *see* RIVER
runners FIELD
running HARING; ON; can indicate something to do with smuggling; anagram indicator
running around nesting indicator; anagram indicator
running away FLIGHT
runs R; RR; anagram indicator; run indicator
runs away can indicate that R or RR to be omitted
rupees R
rupture BREACH; BREAK
ruse SCAM
rush CHARGE; DART; FLY; HARE; LUNGE; RACE; REED; RUN; TEAR; ZOOM; *see* RUN
rushed HASTY; RAN; SPED; TORE
Russian IVAN
Russian lady RIASA
Russian plane MIG
rust can indicate something to do with fungus
rustic HICK; PEASANT; YOKEL
rusty OLD
rut FURROW
ruth PITY
Ruth BABE

Ss

sabotaged anagram indicator
sac BAG; CYST
sachet BAG
sack AXE; BAG; DRESS; FIRE; WINE
sacrificing omission indicator
sacrosanct HOLY
sad BLUE; DOWN; GRAVE; LOW
saddle COL; LAND; LUMBER; SEAT
saddle, in the RIDING; UP
sadly ALAS; anagram indicator
safe PETER
safe conduct PASS
safe place ARK
safe-breaker anagram of SAFE
safety device FUSE; NET
sag DIP; DROOP; FLAG; SINK
saga EDDA; EPIC; MYTH; STORY; TALE
sage SOLON
said ORAL; homophone indicator
sail LUG; ROYAL
sail, set RIG
sailor AB; HEARTY; JACK; OS; RATING; REEFER; SALT; SEAMAN; TAR; can indicate a famous sailor eg. DRAKE, NELSON, ROSS
sailor, doomed BUDD
sailors RN
saint S; ST; rem: many towns are prefaced by ST, eg. St Albans, so the reference might be pointing towards a geographical area eg. county; with names like St Joseph or St Paul, a US state might be the target
St Peters, part of DOME
salad SLAW
salary CUT; SCREW
sale AUCTION; DEAL
sale, for GOING

sale, have for STOCK
sale item LOT
salesman LOMAN (ie. in Miller's play); REP
salesman, work as TRAVEL
salesperson REP
sales talk PATTER; PITCH; SPIEL
sally JEST; QUIP; SORTIE
Sally SAL
salmon CHAR; COHO; PARR
saloon BAR; INN; PUB; also can indicate something to do with a car
salt AB; LICK; NACL; SEASON; *see* SAILOR
salt in France SEL
salt-water BRINE; SEA; SWEAT; TEAR
salute GREET; TOAST
same DITTO; DO; ID; IDEM; repetition indicator; when associated with a reversal indicator can signal a palindrome
same again DITTO; DO; repetition indicator
sample SIP; TASTE; TASTER; TEST; run indicator
sampled run indicator
sanctimonious PI
sanction ALLOW; FINE
sanctuary DEN
sand BEACH; BUNKER; SHORE
sand, bit of GRAIN
sand bank BAR
sandhill DUNE
Sandhurst RMA
sandpiper KNOT
sandwich filling HAM
sandy GRITTY
sandy ground LINKS
sane SOUND
Santa CLAUS
sap DOPE; MINE; NERD
sappers RE
Sarah SAL
sarcastic BITING
sarcastic, somewhat DRY
sash CORD; ROPE
sash, Japanese OBI

seated SAT
satellite IO; MOON
satirise SQUIB
satisfaction, give PLEASE; SATE
satisfactory FINE; OK
satisfied FULL; MET; SMUG
satisfy DO; MEET; PLEASE
satisfying MEETING; PLEASING; SATING
satyr GOAT
sauce CHEEK; GALL; LIP; NERVE; PESTO; TOPPING
saucy LIPPY; PERT
sausage BANGER
savaged anagram indicator
save AMASS; BAR; BUT; STORE
save from wreck SALVE
saving BAR; BUT
savings account ISA
savings plan PEP
savoury PASTY
savoury spread PATE
saw ADAGE; CAUGHT; EYED; MAXIM; SAYING; SPOTTED; can indicate something to do with a proverb, saying, motto, etc. which often, in their full form, can be the required answer, especially in the larger crosswords
say AS; AVER; eg. (for example); EXPRESS; MOUTH; OPINE; REMARK; SPEAK; STATE; TELL; UTTER; homophone indicator; or can indicate that the reference word is an example of the required word for instance "left, say" can clue SIDE (note: for simplicity in the glossary we miss out 'say' where synonyms are examples; for example LIMB is listed under 'wing' alone whereas to make this connection valid the clue will normally read something like "wing, say")
say no DENY
say nothing SH
say, they homophone indicator
say, you might homophone indicator
saying *see* SAW
saying little QUIET
saying nothing MUTE
scald BURN
scale KEY; can indicate something to do with temperature scale, for

example C, F

scam CON; FIDDLE; JAPE; PRANK; RACKET; STING; SWINDLE; TRICK

scamp IMP; ROGUE

scandal DIRT

Scandinavian monster TROLL

Scandinavian saga EDDA

scant SHORT; SLIGHT; STINT

scar SEAM

scare FRIGHT; UNMAN

scarf BOA; STOLE

scarlet RED

scathing BITCHY; SHARP; TART

scatter SOW; SPREAD

scattered SOWN; SPREAD; anagram indicator

scavenger TOTTER

scene PLACE; SETTING; SPOT

scene, disorderly RAG

scene of combat ARENA; LIST; RING

scenery FLAT(S)

scent SMELL; SPOOR; TRAIL

schedule FORM; LIST; ROTA

scheme CABAL; DODGE; PLAN; PLOT; SCAM; THEORY

scheme, unrealistic BUBBLE

schism BREACH; BREAK; RIFT

schnozzle NOSE

scholar BA; MA; PUPIL

school COACH; COED (ie. co-ed); ETON; FISH; HARROW; LYCEE; REPTON; STOVE; SCH; TEACH; TRAIN; TUTOR; can indicate something to do with fish

school group, organisation PTA

school leader HEAD; S

school, play RADA

schoolboys HOUSE

schoolchildren CLASS; FORM

schoolmaster HEAD; SIR

Schubert catalogue D

science SC

science fiction SF

science man BSC

scientist BOFFIN
scoff EAT; MOCK
scoffed ATE
scold NAG; RATE
scoop STORY; TROWEL
scone CAKE
scope AMBIT; EXTENT; LATITUDE; RANGE; ROOM
score CUT; GOAL; LINE; NET (ie. to put in net); NICK; NOTCH; POINT; RUN; TALLY; TRY; can indicate something to do with music, composer
score, golf BIRDIE; BOGIE; EAGLE
score, part of NOTE
score, poor NIL; O
score in darts BULL
scored GOT
scorer an old standby for a composer – so know your tunesmiths!
score, two-under EAGLE
scorn, express JEER
scornful DERISIVE
Scot ANGUS; CELT; GAEL; IAN; KEN; MAC
scotch BLOCK; END; STOP; WEDGE
Scotch DRINK; RYE; *see* SCOTCH
Scotland's extended LANG
Scot's attire KILT; TARTAN
Scots church KIRK
Scot's exclamation, expression OCH
Scot's historic AULD
Scots lawyer WS (Writer to the Signet)
Scotsman *see* SCOT
Scott WALTER
Scottish bank BRAE
Scottish, beautiful BRAW
Scottish bog MOSS
Scottish chap, fellow MON; *see* SCOT
Scottish dance FLING; REEL
Scottish explorer ROSS
Scottish, fine for BRAW
Scottish footballers HIBS
Scottish head RECTOR
Scottish headland MULL

Scottish hillside BRAE
Scottish island ARRAN; IONA; MULL; SKYE; TIREE
Scottish one ANE
Scottish order THISTLE
Scottish peak BEN
Scottish port OBAN
Scottish religious reformer KNOX
Scottish river SPEY
Scottish site, historic SCONE
Scottish tower BROCH
Scottish town AYR; WICK
Scottish youngster BAIRN; WEAN
scoundrel CAD; CUR; HEEL; RAT; ROTTER
scour FLUSH
scourge CAT; KNOUT; WHIP
scout ROVER; SPY
scout leader S; SIXER
scout, young CUB
scowl LOUR; LOWER
scrabble piece TILE
scramble, scrambled, scrambles anagram indicator
scrap BIN; BIT; BOUT; BRAWL; DROP; FIGHT; PIECE; RAG; SHRED; SPAR
scrape GRAZE; RAKE; TROUBLE
scrapped FOUGHT; anagram indicator
scrappy anagram indicator
scratch DITCH; DROP; ERASE; MARK; OMIT; RUB; SCORE; SCRAP; SCRAPE; omission indicator
scrawled anagram indicator
scream CRY; LAUGH; YELL
scream of pain OW
screen CHECK; COVER; HIDE; SHOW; SIFT; VEIL; VET; WINNOW; can indicate something to do with television, eg. TV, show, soap opera
screw FIX; TURN; WAGE; WARDER; anagram indicator
screwed (up) anagram indicator
screwball NUT; ODD
Screwtape Letters can signal something to do with the Devil
scrimmage MAUL
scrimp STINT
scripture, Ancient Hindu VEDA

scriptures AV; NT; OT; *see* BIBLE, BOOK
Scrooge' s partner MARLEY
scripture lessons RI
scrub CLEAN; *see* SCRATCH
scrub land HEATH
scuff BRUSH
sculpted anagram indicator
sculptor MOORE; RODIN
sculpture BUST
scull OAR; ROW
scum DROSS
scurrilous COARSE; RIBALD
scurry BUSTLE
scuttle SINK
scuttled SANK; anagram indicator
scuttling anagram indicator
sea DEAD; DEEP; IRISH; MAIN; MED; OCEAN; RED; S
sea, at anagram indicator
sea-bird DIVER; ERNE; GULL; TERN
sea in France MER
sea mollusc ORMER
sea-pink THRIFT
sea, put to sea LAUNCH
seafood CRAB; ORMER
seal CLOSE; SHUT; STAMP
sealed TIGHT
seals POD
seaman AB; RATING; *see* SAILOR
seaman, sort of ABLE
seamen ABS; CREW; *see* SAILOR
search COMB; FISH; FRISK; RIFLE; LOOK; QUEST; SCOUR
search in water FISH
seaside place BEACH; PIER; PROM; SHORE
season FALL; LENT; SALT; SPRING; SUMMER; TEMPER; TIDE; TIME; WINTER
season for Americans FALL
seasonal growth HOLLY
seasoning CHIVE; SALT; SPICE; THYME
seat BASE; BENCH; BOTTOM; CHAIR; FOOT; FORM; HOME; PEW; REAR; RUMP; SADDLE; SETTLE; SOFA; STALL;

STOOL; THRONE
seat in theatre STALL
seat of Irish kings TARA
seats STALLS; *see* SEAT
seaweed KELP; WRACK
sec INSTANT
second AID; BACK; FLASH; HELP; INSTANT; LATTER; MO; REJECT; S; SEC; TICK; TRICE; WINK; can signal that the second letter of an indicated word is to be used as “second in command” clues O, “second-rate” clues A, etc.; can indicate something to do with a boxer or boxing
second class B
second-hand USED
second person YOU
second person in Paris (France, French) TU
second prize SILVER
second rate B
secondary LESS
secrecy STEALTH
secret society TRIAD
secretarial worker TEMP
secretary PA; TEMP
secrets, divulge RAT
sect CULT
section E (as in E-section); PART; PIECE; UNIT; run indicator
section of tree LOG
sector BELT; ZONE
secure BAG; BIND; FAST; FIX; GET; HOOK; LOCK; MOOR; NAIL; PIE; REEVE; SAFE; SEAL; STITCH; STRAP; SURE; TIE; nesting indicator
secure by rope REEVE; TIE
secure place CASTLE
secured BOUND; TIED; nesting indicator
secures TIES; nesting indicator
securing nesting indicator
security BAIL; GAGE
security device LOCK; NAIL; NUT; PIN; *see* FASTENER
security organization CIA
sediment SILT
seduce PULL
seducer WOLF

seductress VAMP
see BEHOLD; GRASP; LO; LOOK; NOTE; READ; SIGHT; SPOT; TWIG; V; VID; VIDE; can indicate something to do with religious diocese, commonly ELY, others: CHESTER, TRURO
see if CHECK; TEST
see red RAGE
see-through SHEER
seed GERM; GRASS; ISSUE; PEA; PIP; SESAME; SOW; STONE
seed-husks CHAFF
seeds PULSE
seedy ILL; anagram indicator
seedy bar DIVE
seeing that SINCE
seek ASK; COURT; FISH
seek to win COURT
seem APPEAR; LOOK
seemly APT; FIT; RIGHT
seen EYED
seep LEAK
seethe BOIL; BUBBLE
seething anagram indicator
segment CLOVE; PART
seize CLUTCH; GRAB; GRASP; POT; TAKE
seizure FIT
seizure of power COUP
select ELITE; PICK
selected CHOSE; PICKED; NAPPED
selection NAP
self AUTO; eg.O; ID
self-esteem EGO
self image EGO
self-respect PRIDE
self-satisfied SMUG
selfishness GREED
sell FLOG; PUSH; RETAIL
semi HOUSE; as a prefix can indicate half a word or element is to be used
semi-nude use two letters from NUDE
semi-retirement IMES
send EXIT; POST; REMIT

send account BILL
send payment REMIT
send up SQUIB
sender MAILER; POSTER
senescence AGE
senility AGE
senior ELDER; HIGH; OLDER; can indicate one element is to precede another
senior citizen OAP
senior manager EXEC
senior teacher HEAD
senor DON
sensation HIT
sensational LURID
sensational book BLOOD
sense NOSE; NOUS; SIGHT; TASTE; WIT; WITS
sense, common NOUS
sense of exhilaration KICK
sensible SANE; SOUND; WISE
sensitive TENDER
sent HIGH; anagram indicator
sent back reversal indicator
sent off anagram of SENT
sent up reversal indicator
sentence LIFE; TERM; TIME; can indicate something to do with prison, penal code etc.
sentence, long LIFE
sentiment CORN
sentimental CORNY; MUSHY; SOPPY; TWEE
sentimentality GOO
sentimentally pretty TWEE
separate APART; ASUNDER; PART; SUNDER
sepulchre TOMB
sequence CYCLE; RUN; SUITE; TRAIN; TURN
sergeant GO; NCO
sergeant-major SM
sergeant-major, regimental RSM
series CHAIN; LIST; RUN; SER
series of games RUBBER
serious CHRONIC; EARNEST; GRAVE; HEAVY

seriousness EARNEST; WEIGHT
sermon SER
servant AIDE; BUTLER; MAID; MAN; PAGE; VALET
serve ACE; DO; MINISTER; TEND; WAIT; anagram indicator
serve, replayed LET
served DID; anagram indicator
served as WAS
served in nesting indicator
service ACE; FORCE; LET; MASS; NAVY; REFIT; RITE; RN; RAF; can indicate something to do with a church service, or a tea service
service area (trackside) PIT
service, bad FAULT
service, cancellation of LET
servicemen RA; RAF; RE; REME; RI; RM; RN
serving Americans GIS
servitude YOKE
session BOUT; SITTING; TERM; TIME
session, in SITTING
set EMBED; FACTION; GEL; GROUP; LAID; LAY; LOT; PLACE; PUT; TACKY; anagram indicator
set aside SAVE; SAVED
set-back BLOW; COST; SNAG; reversal indicator
set, full BEARD
set in nesting indicator
set in motion TRIGGER
set of figures LIST; TABLE
set off GO; TRIGGER
set out anagram indicator
set sail EMBARK
set up START; reversal indicator
setback reversal indicator
sett BURROW
setter DOG; I; ME
setting MATCH; SCENE; TACKY; runs indicator
setting up reversal indicator
settle FOOT; LAND; LIE; MEET; PAY; PERCH; ROOST; SINK
settled DONE; FIXED; LIT; MET; OVER; PAID; anagram indicator
settlement TOWN
settler ANGLE; INCOMER; PAYER

settlers COLONY
settling anagram indicator
set-up DIAL (ie. LAID reversed)
Seurat can indicate something to do with dots, dotty (ie. characteristic of pointillism, his painting style)
seven-point ball BLACK
sever CUT; HACK; PART
severe DOUR; GRIM; HARD; HARSH; STERN
several SOME
sew TACK
sewer NEEDLE
sex OATS
sex-appeal IT; SA
sex, changing F to be substituted for M or vice versa
sex symbol STUD
sexual gratification OATS
sexual romp ORGY
sexy RANDY
SF author VERNE; WELLS
shabby articles TAT
shack HUT; SHED
shackle FETTER
shade AWNING; BLIND; CAST; HUE; NUANCE; TINT; TONE; *see* COLOUR
shadow DOG; FOLLOW; TAIL; TRACE; TRACK
shady dealer SPIV
shaft ADIT
shake RATTLE; ROCK; WORRY
shaken anagram indicator
shaky WEAK; FEEBLE; anagram indicator
Shakespeare BARD; BILL; WILL
Shakespearean character DULL; NYM; PUCK; LEAR; ROMEO; SNUG; TIMON
Shakespearean fairy MOTH
Shakespearean villain IAGO
shake-up anagram indicator
shallow FLAT
sham COD; FAKE; FRONT
shame ABASH; PITY; STAIN
shameful act CRIME; SIN

shamefully anagram indicator
shape CAST; CUT; FORM; HAMMER
shaped WROUGHT
share CUT; DEAL; LOT; RATION; as a ploughshare can indicate something to do with farming
share out ALLOT
share, take unfair HOG
shares STOCK
shark can indicate something to do with loan, lending etc
sharp ACUTE; BITTER; HARD; NIPPY; SOUR; STAFF; TART
sharpen HONE; STROP
sharper *see* SWINDLER
shatter SMASH
shattered BROKE; anagram indicator
shattering anagram indicator
shaver PLANE; TODD
shaw GROVE; THICKET; WOOD
shawl WRAP
she can indicate the answer is a woman's name or is an occupation ending in -ESS
she (with some reference to France) ELLE
sheathe CASE
shed BYRE; CAST; HOVEL; HUT; anagram indicator; omission indicator
shed tears CRY; WEEP
sheen GLOSS
sheep DOLLY; EWE; FLOCK; RAM; TUP
sheepdog COLLIE
sheepish OVINE
sheer FINE; STEEP; TACK
sheet COVER; PAGE
sheets QUIRE; REAM
sheet of paper LEAF; PAGE
shelf BAR; LEDGE; RACK
shell CONCH
shellfish CLAM
shelter BOWER; COT; COVER; HAVEN; HOME; LEE; REST; RETREAT; SCREEN; SHED; TENT
shelter, temporary TENT
sheltered by run indicator
shepherd TEND

sheriff's men POSSE
sherry CREAM
shield COVER; SCREEN
shift CHANGE; LUG; MOVE; SPELL; WHILE; anagram indicator
shifted, shifting, shifts anagram indicator
shifty anagram indicator
shimmering anagram indicator
shine GLOSS; GLOW; TWINKLE
shining AGLOW
shiny BRIGHT
ship ARGO; BARQUE; BRIG; COASTER; CRAFT; CUTTER; FERRY; FREIGHTER; KEEL; LINER; REEFER; SLOOP; SS; STEAMER
ship, American USS
ship, one jumping RAT
ship's officer MATE; *see* OFFICER
shipman MATE; *see* SAILOR
shipment CARGO; LOAD
ships FLEET
shipwreck anagram of SHIP
shire COUNTY; HORSE
shirk SLACK
shirt T
shivering anagram indicator
shivering fit AGUE
shoal BAR
shock AMAZE; APPAL; DAZE; HAIR; JAR; JOLT; MANE; STAGGER; STUN; anagram indicator
shock, bit of a HAIR; TRESS
shock-absorber BUFFER
shocked anagram indicator
shocked cry OW
shocking anagram indicator; can signal something to do with electricity
shock treatment ECT
shoddy anagram indicator
shoddy clothes, stuff TAT
shoe BROGUE; CLOG; OXFORD
shop DELI; GRASS; INFORM; RAT; RATON (ie. rat on); SQUEAL; STORE
shopping area, facility, precinct MALL

shop assistant can indicate something to do with counter
shoot BAG; BUD; DART; FILM; FIRE; GUN; HUNT; PLUG; POT; SCION; SNAP; SPRIG; SPROUT; STEM; SUCKER; SWITCH; TEAR; anagram indicator
shooter SNIPER; *see* GUN
shooting up reversal indicator
shore BANK; BEACH; BEAM; EDGE; STRAND
short BROKE; CURT; CUT; DRAM; MINI; S; SHY; SCANT; SKINT; UNDER; WEE; omission of first or last letter(s); abbreviation indicator
short cut BOB; CREW
short distance EM; EN; FT; INCH; YD
short film PIC
short of LESS
short of experience GREEN; RAW
short of water DRY
short spells FITS
short stretch YARD; YD
short time HR; MIN; MO; SEC; TICK
short while *see* SHORT TIME
shorten CUT
shortcoming FAULT
shortly omission of first or last letter(s)
shot BULLET; DRAM; DRIVE; GO; HIT; INNER; LEAD; LOB; NIP; OUTER; OVER; PUTT; ROUND; SWIG; TOT; TRY; anagram indicator
shot, high LOB
shots, many RALLY
should AUGHT; OUGHT
shoulder BEAR; CARRY
shout BELLOW; CALL; CHEER; CRY; YELL
shovel SPADE
show CATS; FAIR; HAIR; INDICATE; MUSICAL; PARADE; PLAY; REVEAL
show approval CLAP; CHEER
show concern CARE
show disapproval audibly BOO
show of *see* EXPRESSION OF
show off FLAUNT
show prominently SPLASH
show respect, reverence BOW

show sorrow CRY
show surprise START
show tiredness FLAG
show the way LEAD
showed the way LED
shower RAIN; SPLASH; rem: different pronunciation leads to the notion of exhibitor, projectionist etc.
shower, brief SPAT
showers anagram indicator
showing ON; anagram indicator
showing anger CROSS; MAD
showy FLASHY
shred MINCE; RIP; TEAR
shrewd ARCH; CANNY
shrine ORACLE
shrink FLINCH; can indicate something to do with psychiatrist
shrinking COY; TIMID
shrivelled up anagram indicator
shrouded HID
shrub BOX; BROOM; ELDER; SPURGE
shuffled, shuffles anagram indicator
shufti LOOK
shun AVOID; omission indicator
shut CLOSE; LATCH
shut up CLAM; PENT
shy CAST; COY; LOB; RES; SHORT
shyness RESERVE
sibilant S
sibling BRO; BROTHER; SIS; SISTER
sick AILING; DOWN; ILL; PEAKY; anagram indicator
sicken AIL
sickly DOUGHY; PALE; anagram indicator
sickly-looking SALLOW
side AIR; BANK; CLUB; EDGE; FACET; FLANK; L; LEFT; PART; PORT; R; RIGHT; SPIN; TEAM; VERGE; WING; also sides on a cricket ground: OFF, ON, LEG, etc.; can indicate one of the points of the compass
side of first or last letter of ensuing word to be used
side, on the WITH
sides first and last letters indicator
sides, both RL; LR

sides changing within target word, R to replace L, or vice versa; or first and last letters to be interchanged
siege, old can indicate something to do with the siege of Troy and its participants eg. Achilles, Helen, Nestor, Paris, Priam
sieve RIDDLE; STRAIN
sift SIEVE; RIDDLE; WINNOW
sigh of pleasure AH
sight CATCH; EYE; LOT; SEE; SPOT
sign CROSS; MARK; MARKER; OMEN; SHOW; TRACE; can indicate sign of the zodiac, eg. ARIES, LEO, LIBRA, SCORPIO.
sign, computer SLASH
sign of embarrassment BLUSH; FLUSH
signal BECK; CUE; DASH; DOT; FLAG; NOD; NOTE; PETER; anagram indicator
significance IMPORT; MEANING; POINT
significant, be COUNT
Silas MARNER
silence GAG; MUZZLE; SH
silence, call for SH
silent DUMB; MUM; TACIT
silent comic CHAPLIN
silicon CHIP
silly DAFT; INANE; SOFT; RASH; anagram indicator; with a whimsy indicator can indicate something to do with window (it has a sill!)
silly behaviour ANTIC; PRANK
silly person PRAT; TWIT
silver AG
Silver can indicate something to do with Stevenson's character, eg. cook, Long John, Treasure Island
similar AKIN; ALIKE
similar things SUCH
simmer STEW
simple BARE; EASY; HERB; MERE; PLAIN; PURE
simple-minded person *see* SIMPLETON
Simple Simon *see* SIMPLETON
simpleton GULL; LOON; NOODLE; SAP; *see* FOOL
simplicity EASE
sin ERR; ERROR; FALL; GREED; LAPSE; LUST; PRIDE; SLOTH; VICE
since AS; AGO
sincere EARNEST

sing CHANT; CHIRP; CROON; GRASS; NARK; TALK; TRILL; TROLL
singe BURN; CHAR
singer ALTO; BING; BASS; BASSO; BUFFO; CHER; DIVA; TREBLE; can indicate a bird known for its singing eg. LARK
singing CHORAL
singing, monastic CHANT
single I; ONE; ONLY; RUN; S; UNIT; UNWED
single person ONE
singlet VEST
singular ONE; S
sinister LEFT; PORT
sinister, not, nothing RIGHT
sink DOWN; FOUNDER; SAG
sir KNIGHT; MISTER
siren HORN
sisal ROPE
sister NUN; SIB; SIS; can signal something to do with hospital eg. WARD
sister, little SIS
sister, weird WITCH
sit POSE
sit-in DEMO
site DIG; LOT; PLACE
site of castle MOTTE
sitter DOLLY (ie. easy catch in cricket); MODEL; POSER
sitting SESSION
situation BERTH; LIE; SPOT; STATE; nesting indicator
six VI
six counties NI
six-footer can indicate an insect, commonly ant
sixth sense ESP
66 ft CHAIN
size GLAZE
skate FISH; GLIDE; RAY
skating ONICE (ie. on ice)
skating arena RINK
skating, not, no longer OFFICE (ie. off ice)
sketch DRAFT; DRAW; SKIT
sketched DRAWN; DREW

skewer SPIT
skid SLIDE; SLIP
skilful ABLE; CANNY; DEFT; SLEIGHT
skilfully ABLY
skill ABILITY; ART; CRAFT; MASTERY
skill, basic R
skill, with *see* SKILLED
skilled ABLE; DEFT
skimp STINT
skin FELL; FUR; HIDE; PEEL
skin, feature of PORE
skin, hard CORN
skip DANCE; JUMP; LEAP; MISS; OMIT; anagram indicator; omission indicator
skipper CAPT; can indicate something to do with butterfly
skipping anagram indicator; omission indicator
skirmish BRUSH
skirt MINI
skulk PROWL
sky, canopy of DOME
slab TABLET
slack IDLE; LOOSE
slacken EASE; REMIT
slag WASTE
slander MUD; SLUR
slang, tasteless NAFF
slant ANGLE; SPIN
slap HIT
slash CUT; SIGN (ie, computer)
slat FLAY; ROOF; STAVE
slate PAN; ROAST; TILE
slaver SLOBBER
sledge HAMMER; LUGE
sleek SMOOTH
sleep DOSS; DOZE; KIP; NAP; NOD; ZZ
sleep, part of REM
sleep, somewhere to BED; COT; BUNK
sleeper can indicate something to do with railway track
sleeve ARM
slender SPARE; THIN

slice of run indicator
slide SLIP; SKID
slight CUT; LITTLE; SCANT; SLUR; SMALL; THIN
slim LEAN; SLENDER; THIN
slime MUD
slimmed down can indicate first and last letters to be omitted
sling CAST; DUMP; anagram indicator
slip BLUNDER; DRESS; ERR; ERROR; GLIDE; LAPSE; SAG; SKID; SLIDE
slip into DON
slip up ERR; SIN
slipper MULE
slippery SHADY
slippery surface ICE
slipping LAX; anagram indicator
sliver CHIP
slobber SLAVER
slog CHORE; HIT
slogan CHANT
slop SPILL
slope LEAN; LIST; RAMP; RISE; TILT
sloshed anagram indicator; *see* DRUNK
slot NICHE; GROOVE; RUT
slough SHED
slovenly person SLOB
slow DULL; LATE; LENTO
slow ball LOB
slow, go POTTER
slow movement, music, passage LARGO
slowly LENTO; can indicate something to do with speed, rate
slug BALL; HIT
sluggish SLOW; anagram indicator
slur TIE (mus,)
slurred anagram indicator
sly *see* CUNNING
Sly a character in 'The Taming of the Shrew' so can indicate something to do with the play or its characters eg. tinker
sly look PEEK
smack BLOW; CLIP; CUFF; HIT; SLAP; TANG; TAP; TASTE
small BABY; MINI; SLIGHT; WEE; abbreviation indicator

small amount BIT; CHIP; DAB; DRIB; OZ; PINCH; PINT; TAD
small amounts can indicate that only initial letters of associated words be used
small boy abbreviated form of boy's name eg. ANDY; *see* LITTLE BOY
small business BUS; CO
small car MINI
small distance INCH
small establishment COTTAGE
small group CELL; DUO; TRIO
small island I; IS; ISLE; KEY
small-minded PETTY
small Parisian PETIT(E)
small part BIT
small quantity CL
small room CELL
small thing ATOM
small unit MIL
small, very MINI
smaller LESS
smaller, make CUT; REDUCE
smaller quantity LESS
smallest LEAST
smart CHIC; CLEVER; CUTE; DAPPER; NATTY; NEAT; NIFTY; POSH; QUICK; STING; SWISH
smart guy ALEC
smarten up GROOM
smash, smashed anagram indicator
smasher DISH
smashing SUPER
smear BLUR; DEFAME; LIBEL; SLUR; SPLODGE
smell BO; HUM; PONG; REEK; SCENT; STENCH; STINK; TANG
smell, bad, unpleasant BO; *see* SMELL
smelly OLID; RANK
smelt STANK
smile BEAM; GRIN; LEER
smirk LEER
smithy FORGE
smitten anagram indicator
smoke CIG; CURE; FAG; PIPE

smooch NECK; SPOON
smooth BLAND; DRESS; EVEN; FLAT; IRON; LEVEL; PRESS; SAND; SATIN; SLEEK; SLICK; SLIPPY; SUAVE [GLABROUS]
smoother FILE; IRON; *see* SMOOTH and consider adding -ER to a synonym
smug PI
smuggle RUN
smuggled RAN
smuggling nesting indicator
smut SOOT
snack BITE
snack bar BUFFET
snacks EATS
snaffle BIT; PINCH; STEAL
snag BIND; BUG; CATCH; RUB; TEAR
snake ADDER; ASP; BOA; MEANDER; RATTLER; TWINE; VIPER
snap BARK; BREAK; CRACK; NUT; PHOTO; SHOOT; SPELL (ie. cold spell); TANG
snappy CHIC; TESTY
snare CATCH; NET; TRAP
snarl GROWL; RAVEL
snatch GRAB; REST; WREST
sneak GRASS; SLIP
snip CUT
snitch GRASS; PEACH
snooker can indicate something to do with cue, pot etc
snooker, play at CUE
snooker sequence BREAK
snooker shot PLANT; POT
snooker, success in POT
snoop PRY; SPY
snooze ZZ
snout HOOTER; NOSE
snow CRACK
snow, covered in WHITE
snow, soft SLEET; SLUSH
snub REBUFF
snug COSY; TIGHT
snuggle NESTLE
so ERGO; HENCE; SIC; THUS

so-and-so BLOOMING

so-called homophone indicator; can also indicate a nom-de-plume, one popular among compilers being ELIA (used by essayist Charles Lamb); also SAKI

so long TATA (ie. ta-ta); VALE

so what? WELL

soak RET; SOP; STEEP; WET

soak, soaking BATH

soak, wanting to RET (archaic)

soapbox STUMP

soaring reversal indicator

sob BLUB; CRY

sober TT

soccer authorities, body FA

social division, group, order, position CASTE; CLASS

social error GAFFE

social gathering BALL; BEE; DANCE

social occasion BASH; *see* PARTY

socialist PINK; RED

socially acceptable DONE; IN; U

socially unacceptable NONU (ie. non-U); OUT

society S; TRIAD

society girl DEB

sock HIT; SMITE

soda MIXER

sodium NA

so far AS

soft LIMP; P; PLIANT; S; TENDER

soft-hearted P to be nested in centre of component

soften MELT

softly, not loudly P to replace F

soil EARTH; MARK; SPOT

soil acidity PH

solder FUSE

soldier ANT; GI; GUNNER; MAN; MARINE; MERC; NCO; PARA; PRIVATE; SM

soldier, old VET

soldiers GIS; MEN; OR; RA; RE; REGIMENT; REME; RO; SQUAD; TA; UNIT; can indicate something to do with TOAST

soldiers, group of SQUAD; UNIT; *see* SOLDIERS

soldiers, some RESERVE; TA; *see* SOLDIERS

sole LONE; can indicate something to do with the foot
solemn DEAD; GRAVE
solemn individual OWL
solemn pronouncement OATH
solicit TOUT
solicitor BEGGAR; NP (ie. Notary-Public); TOUT
solid FIRM
solid figure CONE; CUBE
solidarity UNION
solitary LONE; LONER; SOLE
solitary type LONER
solo LONE
solution KEY; LIGHT (ie. crossword solution); WATER; anagram indicator
solve CRACK
some ANY; PART; PIECE; can indicate a word which means something less, eg. NET; run indicator
some cabbage HEART
some days WEEK
some French DES
some music PIECE
some of run indicator
some spirit DRAM; TOT
somebody ONE
somehow anagram indicator
someone PERSON
Somerset town STREET
something, do ACT
something of run indicator
something one can't do without MUST
somewhat ABIT (ie. a bit); run indicator; can indicate the possible stretching of a point by the compiler, where the connection between concepts is slight
some time ago ONCE
son S
song AIR; ANTHEM; ARIA; BALLAD; CHANT; DITTY; GLEE; LAY; LIED; PSALM; ROUND; TUNE;
song and dance FUSS
song, bird's TWEET
song, part of VERSE
song series CYCLE

songwriter BERLIN; LENNON
songs CYCLE
soon ANON
soon, too EARLY
soothe EASE
soothing BALMY
sop BRIBE; BUNG; SOAK
soprano SOP
sorcerer MAGE
sore MAD; RED
sorrow MISERY; REGRET; WOE
sorrow, show CRY; WEEP
sorry POOR; SAD; RUING; anagram indicator
sorry, be RUE
sorry to say, I'm ALAS
sort ALIGN; ARRANGE; CLASS; KIDNEY; KIND; ORDER; TYPE; anagram indicator; can indicate a particular sort of person as "possessive sort" clues OWNER
sorted out anagram indicator
sort of anagram indicator
Soule's advice some implication stemming from "Go West, young man" (from editorial by J.L.B.Soule in 1851 American newspaper)
sound AUDIO; BANG; BLIP; CHORD; CLANG; CLASH; DRONE; FIT; PING; PLUMB; PURR; RING; SANE; STRAIT (ie. stretch of water); TICK; TICKING; TING; TONE; TRILL; WATER; WHINE; WISE; homophone indicator, as in 'by the sound of it'
sound, beastly GROWL; GRUNT
sound happy PURR
sound, hollow BONG
sound horn TOOT
sound of bell DING; PEAL; TING; TOLL
sound of cat MEW; PURR
sound of pain GROAN
sound of pleasure AH
sound of sheep BAA
sound pleased PURR
sound, triumphant HA
sound unhappy CRY
sounding homophone indicator
soundly homophone indicator
soundly disapprove BOO; HISS

sounds like homophone indicator
soup BROTH
soup, kind of LEEK
sour DOUR; OFF; TART
source CAUSE; eg.G; FOUNT; ORE; ROOT; WELL; initial letter indicator; run indicator
source of inspiration MUSE
source of mineral MINE; PIT
source of song can indicate a bird eg. TIT
source of warning ALARM; BLEEPER
South S; last letter indicator
South Africa SA; ZA
South African SA
South African white BLANK
south of France SUD
souvenir RELIC
sovereign ER; GR; *see* KING, QUEEN
sow SEED
SP ODDS
spa HYDRO; SPRING
space EM; EN; GAP; HOLE; ROOM; VOID
space, confined COOP
space creature ET
space station MIR
space, vertical SHAFT
spacecraft LEM
spacer WASHER
spade S; SHOVEL
spades S
Spain E
spaniel COCKER; CLUMBER
Spanish coin, currency (old) REAL
Spanish for POR
Spanish gent DON
Spanish, hero CID
Spanish royal REAL
Spanish. the EL; LAS; LOS
Spanish, what QUE
spar BOON; BOX; SPRIT; YARD
spare LEAN; OVER; SLENDER; THIN

sparkle GLISTEN
Spartan BASIC
spasm FIT
spate FLOOD
spawn SPAT
speak GAS; ORATE; SAY; UTTER; homophone indicator
speak haltingly STAMMER
speak harshly GRATE
speak slowly DRAWL
speak vehemently RANT
speak well of PRAISE
speaker ORATER
speaking DICTION
speaks in French DIT
spear GAFF; IMPALE; STAB
spec BRIEF
special SP; anagram indicator
special edition EXTRA
special force PARAS; SAS
special troops PARAS
specially anagram indicator
specie BREED; KIND; TYPE
species KIND
specify STATE
specimen SAMPLE; TASTE
specimens of run indicator
speckle STIPPLE
spectacle SIGHT
spectacles OO
spectators GATE
speculate BET; GUESS
speculator BETTER; BULL; STAG
spectre GHOST
speech ADDRESS; ARGOT; DICTION; LECTURE; ORAL; ORATION; SAY; TALK; colloquialism indicator; homophone indicator; can refer to a specific language
speech, by ORAL; VOCAL; homophone indicator
speech, make ORATE
speech, part of NOUN; VERB
speeches ORATORY

speechless MUTE
speed BAT; CLIP; DRUG; HASTE; HIE; KNOT; KNOTS; LICK; MPH; NIP; PACE; PAR; RATE; RUSH; TEAR; TEMPO
speed, at APACE; PAST
speed, maximum C
speed of engine, increase REV
speed of light C
spell CHARM; SHIFT; SNAP; TERM; TIME
spell in America usually refers to taking advantage of the different spelling in the U.S. (COLOR, LITER, ESTHETE etc.) to provide a component in building up an answer
spelling SP
spells, short FITS
spend PASS
spent GONE; PAST; anagram indicator
sphere BALL; GLOBE
spherical shape ORB
spice CHILLI; MACE
spicy HOT
spiel PATTER; PITCH
spies CIA
spike BARB; LACE; NAIL; PIN; POINT
spill FALL; LIGHTER
spill the beans GRASS; SING
spilled, spilling, spilt anagram indicator
spilt SHED
spin ROLL; SIDE; SLANT; TURN; anagram indicator
spine BACK; GUTS
spinner TOP
spinning anagram indicator
spire TOWER
spirit ANGEL; BOTTLE; CORE; DASH; DEMON; DEVIL; ELAN; ELF; ETHOS; GHOST; GIN; GO; GUM; HEART; IMP; OUZO; PERI; RUM; SCOTCH; SHADE; SHORT; SOUL; WRAITH
spirit, some DRAM; SHOT; TOT
spirited GAME; RACY
spirits, measure of TOT
spirits, raise ELATE
spit RAIN
spite MALICE
spiteful CATTY

spiteful woman CAT
splash anagram indicator
splendid BRAVE; GRAND; SUPERB
splice GRAFT
split BREAK; CHAP; CLEAVE; CLEFT; CLOVE; CUT; FLED; GO; GONE; GULF; LEAVE; LEFT; PART; QUIT; RAN; REND; RENT; RIP; RIVE; SCHISM; SNAP; SUNDER; TORN
split into two run indicator, where element crosses two words within the clue
split by nesting indicator
splitting anagram indicator; nesting indicator
splodge BLOT; BLOTCH; SMEAR
spoil MAR; RUIN
spoilt anagram indicator
spoke RUNG; SAID
spoken ORAL; SAID; homophone indicator
spoken, having SAID
spokesperson VOICE
sponge CADGE; WIPER
sponsor BACK; BACKER
spool REEL; ROLL
Spooner can indicate the initial letters of two words are to be transposed as in "Spooner's dog, lean for so long" which gives TOODLE-PIP!
sport ANGLING; BRICK; CRICKET; FIVES; FOOTER; FUN; GAME; GOLF; PLAY; RACING; RU; WEAR; anagram indicator
sported WORE; anagram indicator
sporting GAME; anagram indicator
sports gear KIT; STRIP
sports car GT
sportsmen BATTER; DIVER
spot BIND; CORNER; DEFECT; DOT; DRIP; DROP; ESPY; FIX; FLECK; MOTE; PATCH; PLACE; POCK; POINT; SEE; SIGHT; SITE; SPECK; SPLODGE; STAIN; ZIT
spot, nasty WEN
spots RASH
spotted in run indicator
spouse HUBBY; MATE; WIFE
spout GUSH; ORATE
sprawling anagram indicator
spread BUTTER; MARG; MARGE; PASTE; PATE; RANCH; SPAN;

STREW; TED; anagram indicator
spread over nesting indicator
spreading anagram indicator
spree BINGE; FLING; JUNKET; ROMP; anagram indicator
spring BOUND; CAPER; COIL; FOUNT; HOP; JUMP; LEAP; SHOOT; SPA; SPRIG; STEM; VERNAL; WELL
spring from STEM
spring time MAY
springs anagram indicator
sprinkle HOSE; PEPPER; SPLATTER; SPRAY
sprinkling SHOWER
sprint RUN
sprit SPAR
sprite ELF; IMP
spruce NEAT; SMART; TIDY; TRIM
spun anagram indicator
spurious BAD; anagram indicator
spurt RUSH
spy AGENT; BOND; MOLE; PEEK; PLANT; SEE; SPOT
spy organisation CIA
squabble SETTO (ie. set-to); SPAT; WRANGLE; *see* ROW
squad CREW; FLEET; TEAM
squadron WING
squalid SLUMMY
squalid house SLUM
squander BLOW; BLUE; WASTE
squandered BLEW; anagram indicator
square EVEN; FOUR; NINE; PAY; QUAD; SETTLE; S; STRAIGHT; T
squashed anagram indicator
squatting nesting indicator
squeal SHOP
squeeze HUG; PRESS; WRING
squeezing nesting indicator
squint CAST
squire PAGE
squirming anagram indicator
squirrel's home DREY
stab CRACK; GO; JAB; SPEAR; TURN
stabilise PEG

stable FAST; FIRM; STATIC
stable worker GROOM
stableman GROOM
stables MEWS
stack HEAP; PILE; RICK; POT
stadium GROUND
staff BAR; CANE; CROOK; HANDS; MAN; PIKE; POLE; ROD; STICK; SHARP; TEAM; can indicate something to do with bread (ie. the staff of life)
staff officer SO
stage APRON; LEG; LEVEL; MOMENT; MOUNT; PHASE; PRESENT; PUPA; STEP; TIER
stage production PLAY
stage, take the ACT
stagger LURCH; REEL; ROCK; SHOCK
staggering anagram indicator
stain BLOT; MARK; SHAME; SLUR; SPOT
stainer DYER
stairs FLIGHT
stake ANTE; BET; PILE
stakes POOL
staked ON
stale MUSTY; OFF
stale, become DATE
stalk BRANCH; DOG; STEM; TAIL
stall BOOTH; SHY; STOP; TARRY
stammering the first letter of a component to be repeated
stamp DIE; FRANK; SEAL
stance POSE
stand BROOK; EASEL; GANTRY; HACK; LAST (ie. cobbler's); PLACE; POSE; SET; STALL; TEE; TREAT; WEAR
standard ENSIGN; FLAG; JACK; NORM; NORMAL; ONPAR (ie. on par); PAR; STOCK
stand, one-night GIG
standing PLACE; RANK; RATE; REP; UP; reversal indicator
standstill OMPH
stank SMELT
stannic TIN
staple RICE
star LEAD; LEADING; LION; NAME; NOVA; PAPER; PIP; SUN; VEGA

star group LEO; VIRGO
star, Hollywood COOPER; GABLE
star, tennis SEED
starchy FORMAL; STIFF
stare GLOWER; LEER
stark CLEAR
start BEGIN; ENTER; FLINCH; FOUND; JUMP; LAUNCH; OFF; ONSET; OPEN; SHY; TRIGGER; initial letter indicator
start filming ROLL; SHOOT
start of play ACTI (ie. ACT I)
start of puzzle ONE
start operation LAUNCH; ROLL
start to finish first and last letters of a word to be transposed
started SHIED
started, just OFF
starter COURSE; ENTREE; initial letter indicator
starter, without a omission indicator for an initial letter
starters can indicate the initial letters of associated words or the first two or three letters of one word
starts off see start
state AVER; COMA; EXPRESS; FORM; REALM; SAY; a national state in its full form eg. GOA, OMAN; or abbreviation eg. UK, US; an abbreviation for a state within a country, usually American; *see* AMERICAN STATE; rem: an eastern state can refer to one on the eastern side of the U.S. as well as an eastern country
state, Atlantic RI
state, French ETAT
state, German REICH
stated homophone indicator
stately home PILE
statement COMMENT
statement, inaccurate LIE
statement, legal PLAINT
statement of faith CREED
statement of intent WILL
States US
statesman can indicate a man from a specific American state eg. TEXAN
statesman, old Roman CATO
static STABLE
station FORT

statistic FIGURE
statue FIGURE; IDOL
stature HEIGHT
status RANK
status, of BIG
statute LAW
staunch STEM; TRUE
stay ABIDE; BIDE; BRACE; DWELL; LAST; LINGER; LODGE; PROP; REST; ROPE; TARRY; TIE
stead PLACE
steady FIRM; STABLE
steal LIFT; NICK; PALM; PINCH; POACH; POCKET; ROB; RUSTLE; SNAFFLE; SWIPE; WHIP
steal away ELOPE
stealthily, move EDGE; INCH
steam STEW
steamer BOILER; KETTLE; PACKET; SS
steep HIGH; RET; SHEER; SOAK
steeple SPIRE
steer BULL; COW; OX
steerer COX
steering device HELM; RUDDER
stem BOUGH; BOW; CHECK; SHOOT; STALK; STAUNCH; STOP
stem of plant CANE
stench PONG; REEK
step PACE; PAS; STAGE; TREAD; WALK
stepped TROD
steps DANCE; FLIGHT; or can indicate a specific dance
steps, take DANCE
stern AFT; BACK; GRAVE; HARD; HIND; REAR; SEVERE; STRICT
stew JAM; MESS; OLIO; SIMMER; STEAM; anagram indicator
steward REEVE
stick BAT; BATON; CANE; CLEAVE; CLING; CLUB; CUE; GLUE; GUM; JAM; LANCE; LEVER; PASTE; PIERCE; POLE; ROD; STAFF; STRING; TWIG; WAND; WEAR
sticker POSTER
sticky TIGHT
sticky stuff, substance GEL; GUM; LAC; TAR
stiff BODY; HARD; RIGID; can signify something to do with death or a mortuary eg. CORONER

stifle STUNT
still BUT; EVEN; HUSH; YET
stimulate AROUSE; SPUR; URGE ; WHET
stimulus SPUR
sting NETTLE; SCAM; SMART
stingy MEAN; *see* TIGHT-FISTED
stinking HIGH
stinker CAD; RAT
stint SCANT; SCRIMP; SKIMP
stipulation RIDER
stir ADO; BUDGE; BUSTLE; CAN; MOVE; ROUSE; ROUST; SHIFT; WHISK; *see* PRISON; anagram indicator
stirred MOVED; anagram indicator
stirring, stirring up anagram indicator
stoat ERMINE
stock CATTLE; COWS; KEEP; HANDLE; RACE; RESERVE; STORE; USUAL; can indicate something to do with farm animals
stockings HOSE
stockings etc HOSIERY
stock item LINE
stole BOA; FUR
stolen HOT
stomach BEAR; BELLY; FACE; GUT; STAND; TUM
stomach, interior of PIT
stone AGATE; FLINT; GEM; HONE; LOGAN; MARBLE; PIP; PIT; RUBY; SEED
stoned HIGH
stones SCREE
stoop BEND
stop AVAST; BAN; BAR; BLACK; BLOCK; CEASE; COMMA; CURB; DETER; DOT; END; FREEZE; HALT; PAUSE; PERIOD; POINT; PREVENT; QUIT; STALL; STAUNCH; STAY; STEM; WHOA
stop at sea AVAST
stop-cock TAP
stop eating FAST
stop, full PERIOD
stop in U.S. PERIOD
stop moving FREEZE
stoppage BAN; BAR; BLOCK; END
stoppage, current DAM

stopper BUNG; PLUG
storage structure RACK
store BARN; DELI; HOARD; KEEP; RACK; RESERVE; SAVE; SHOP; SILO; STASH; STOCK
stored in run indicator
storehouse DEPOT
storey FLOOR; LEVEL
stories ANA; FICTION; LIES; rem: can refer to the floors of a building
stories, collection of ANA
storm GALE; HAIL; RAGE; RAIN; RANT; RAVE; anagram indicator
stormy anagram indicator
story ACCOUNT; CONTE (Fr.); DOPE; EPIC; FABLE; LIE; PARABLE; PLOT; RELATION; SAGA; SCOOP; TALE; YARN; rem: can also refer to the floor of a building
story-line PLOT
story-teller LIAR
storytelling LIES
stout ALE; AMPLE; FAT; PLUMP; PORTER; PORTLY
stove AGA
stow PACK
straight DIRECT; EVEN; FAIR; JUST; NEAT; SQUARE
straight man FEED
straight, not CURLY
straight up SHEER
straightened out anagram indicator
strain AIR; BREED; DITTY; RICK; RIDDLE; SIEVE; SIFT; SONG; TAX; TUNE
strained TAUT; TENSE
strained food PUREE
strait SOLENT; SOUND; ST
strand LOCK; PLY; THREAD; TRESS; rem: can refer to the shoreline eg. BEACH
strange ODD; RUM; WEIRD; anagram indicator
strangely anagram indicator
stranger ALIEN; anagram indicator
strap BEAT; BIND
stratagem DODGE; RUSE; TRICK
strategy PLAN
stratum LAYER

straw THATCH
straying ROVING; anagram indicator
streak BAND; BAR; FLASH; LINE; RUN; WISP
stream BECK; BROOK; BURN; CREEK; FLOW; POUR; RILL; RIVER; SPOUT; TRICKLE; can indicate some aspect of water; can indicate a small river eg. CAM; also can refer to a class at school
street AVE; CLOSE; CRESCENT; GATE; MEWS; ROAD; ST; WAY
street, French RUE
streetcar DESIRE
streetwise HIP
strength BRAWN; FORCE; MIGHT; POWER
strengthen TEMPER
strenuously anagram indicator
stress ACCENT; TAX
stretch REACH; STRAIN; TENSE
stretch of run indicator
stretch of river REACH
stretch, short YARD; YD
stretch of water RIVER; SEA
stretched TENSE; TAUT; anagram indicator
stretcher BRICK; LITTER
stride MARCH; PACE; STEP
strict HARD; HEAVY; STERN
strike BASH; BEAT; CLOCK; CUFF; DASH; DELETE; HIT; KNAP; KNOCK; LAM; LASH; LUNGE; PLUG; RAID; RAM; RAP; REACH; SPEAR; TAP; WHACK; anagram indicator [GOLD; OIL]
strike out DELETE
striker BAT; FIST; FORWARD; HAMMER
striking OUT; SIGNAL; can indicate something to do with matches
string CORD; ROW; STICK; TWINE; designation of string-note on instrument, B, G etc.; *see* NOTE, KEY
stringy TOUGH
strip BAND; BAR; BARE; LATH; RIDGE; SASH; STAVE; TAPE; THONG
stripe BAND; BLOW
stripling SPEAR
stripped off omission indicator
stripper TURPS
stroke BLOW; CRAWL; HOOK; LASH; LINE; TOLL

stroll AMBLE; TODDLE
strong F; FIRM; MANLY; STR
strong ale PORTER
strong chap, man HEMAN (ie. he-man); TITAN
strong point FORTE
strongbox COFFER; SAFE
stronghold FORT
strongly flavoured RICH
struck anagram indicator
structure anagram indicator
structure, tall TOWER
structured anagram indicator
struggle FIGHT; STRIVE; VIE; WAR
struggle, struggling anagram indicator
struggle for breath GASP; PANT
strut BRACE; MARCH
stud BOSS; RIVET; rem: can refer to a horse
student L; MEDIC; PUPIL; READER
student society, member of FRAT
student, successful BA
students NUS
students' fun RAG
studentship PLACE
studied READ; runs indicator
study CON; CAN (var. of con); CRAM; DEN; DO; EYE; MULL; PERUSE; READ; SCAN; SWOT
study hard BONE; CRAM; SWOT
study period CLASS; LESSON; TERM
study programme COURSE
stumble FALL; TRIP
stuff CRAM; GORGE; MATTER; PACK; RAM; REP
stuff, cheap TAT
stuffiness FUG
stumble TRIP
stumbling anagram indicator
stump WICKET
stumped ST
stun KO; SHOCK
stunner DISH; KO; PEACH
stunt DEFORM; STIFLE

stupid CRASS; DENSE; DIM; DULL; DUMB; SILLY; THICK; LOOPY; anagram indicator [POINTLESS]
stupid person ASS; CLOT; DOLT; DRIP; DUNCE; PRAT; PUDDING; TWIT
stupidly anagram indicator
sturdy FIRM; STABLE
stutter letter to be repeated
sty PEN
style DASH; GRAVER; MANNER; MODE; NAME; TITLE; TON; TONE; WAY; anagram indicator
style, Classical ATTIC; DORIC; IONIC
styled anagram indicator
stylish CHIC; CLASSY; FLASH; HIP; SWISH
stylishness FLAIR
suave SMOOTH
subdue COW; QUELL; TAME
subdued LOW; QUIET
subject MATTER; THEME; TOPIC
subject to LIABLE; ST; UNDER
subjective CASE
sublime LOFTY
submariner NEMO
submit CEDE; DEFER; TABLE; YIELD
submit to ENDURE
subordinate BELOW; LOWER; UNDER; can indicate that one element should follow another
subscribe SIGN
subsequent AFTER; LATER; NEXT; SECOND; can indicate one element should follow another
subsequently AFTER; LATER; NEXT; THEN; can indicate one element should follow another
subservient UNDER
subsidiary route BROAD (ie. B-road)
subsidise AID; BACK; HELP
substance MATTER
substantial BIG; HIGH; REAL
substitute LOCUM
subterfuge DECEPTION
subtle NICE
subtly anagram indicator
suburb KEW

succeed ENSUE; FOLLOW; PASS; WIN
succeeded S; WON
succeeded in DID
success COUP; GO; HIT; WIN
success in snooker POT
success, period of BOOM; UP
successful MADE
successful record HIT
successfully WELL
succession LINE
successor HEIR
such SO; THUS
sucker DUPE; GULL; SHOOT; *see* FOOL
sudden SNAP
sudden move LUNGE
suddenly put down PLONK
suede KID
suffer ACHE; AIL; BEAR; STAND
suffer on stage DIE
suffered anagram indicator
sufferer JOB
suffering NEEDY; PAIN; anagram indicator
sufficient AMPLE; PAT
sufficient, barely SCANT
sugar BEAT; CANE
sugar-coated ICED
sugary SWEET
suggest HINT; IMPLY; POSE; RAISE
suggestion CLUE; HINT; IDEA; THOUGHT; TIP
suggestion of initial letter indicator
suggestive RACY
suit ACTION; BEFIT; CASE; DO; ETONS; FIT; KIT; MATCH; can also refer to a card
suit CLUB, DIAMOND, HEART, SPADE (singular or plural)
suitable APT; DUE; FIT; ON
suitable place NICHE
suitably WELL
suited FOR
suitor RIVAL
sulk PET; POUT

sullen DOUR
sullied anagram indicator
sulphur S
sultanate OMAN
sultry HOT
sum ADD; BID; COUNT; TOTAL
summarise PRECIS
summary PRECIS; RESUME
summate ADD
summer ADDER; SEASON; TIME; can indicate something to do with accountancy, calculation, etc
summertime JUL; JUN; AUG
summit CAP; PEAK; TOP
summon CALL; CITE; GONG
summon loudly GONG
Sumo BASHO
sun BASK; RA; S; SOL; STAR
Sun PAPER
sun-burn TAN
sun god RA
sun-set anagram of SUN
sunbathe BASK; TAN
sunblind AWNING
Sunday School SS
sunder CLEAVE
sunny BRIGHT
sunrise DAWN; NUS; RA
sunshine, little RAY
sup DRINK
super ACE; MEGA
supercilious SNIFFY
superficial SHALLOW
superfluous EXTRA
superior A; ABOVE; ARCH; BEST; BETTER; ELDER; HIGH; OVER; PRIOR; TOP; U; UPPER; can indicate that one component should precede another; with capital letter can refer to the lake of the same name; reversal indicator
Superman HERO
supervising OVER
supper EATER
supple LITHE

supplication PLEA; PRAYER
supplied FED; GAVE
supplier CO; SOURCE
supplier, nautical CHANDLER
supply CATER; ENDUE; EQUIP; FEED; FILL; RATION; STOCK
supply of drink WELL
supply, in short LOW
supply with capital BACK; FUND
support AID; ARCH; BACK; BEAM; BEAR; BRA; BRACE; EASEL; ENDORSE: FAVOUR; FOOT; GUY; HAND; LEG; PIER; PIN; PROP; RACK; RAIL; REST; ROCK; ROOST; RUNG; SECOND; SIDE; SHORE; SLEEPER; SLING; SPINE; SPONSOR; STAGE; STAY; STEM; STRUT; TEE; TRESTLE; TRUSS; can indicate one element is to follow another; can indicate that an element is to be placed at the end
support, show ROOT
support structure ARCH
supporter ALLY; BRA; BRACKET; BUFF; FAN; FRIEND; LEG; RAFTER; STAY
supporters, royal COURT
supporting, supportive FOR; ON; PRO; can indicate that one component comes behind another
supports can mean the preceding component comes second to the one that follows in the clue
suppose GUESS; OPINE
supreme BEST; TOP
suppress CHOKE
sure BOUND; FIXED; YES
sure-fire CERT
sure thing CERT
surfeit CLOY
surge PRESS
surgeon BS; LISTER; VET
surgery OP
surgical instrument PROBE
surgical procedure OP
surly GRUFF
surpass CAP; TOP
surplus OVER
surprise START; STARTLE
surprise, by ABACK

surprise, cry, expression of BOY; COR; GEE; GOD; MY
surprisingly anagram indicator
surrealist DALI
surrender CEDE; FALL; YIELD
surround RING
surrounded AMID
surroundings nesting indicator
Surrey SY
survey CENSUS; EYE; POLL; SEE; WATCH
surveyor EYE; can refer to a particular mountain
survive LAST; LIVE
suspect FISHY; IFFY; anagram indicator
suspend DANGLE; HANG
suspended DANGLED; HUNG; STRUNG
suspense, in ONICE (ie. on ice)
suspension STAY
suspicion IDEA; INKLING; TOUCH; TRACE
Sussex rem: can refer to a breed of cow
Sussex town RYE
sustained BORE
swab MOP
swag LOOT
swagger BLUSTER
swallow DOWN; EAT; GULP; nesting indicator
swallowed ATE; nesting indicator
swallowing DOWNING; EATING; nesting indicator
swamp BOG; DROWN; ENGULF; MARSH
swan COB; PEN
swanning about anagram indicator
swap DEAL; CHANGE; TRADE; can indicate letters or components are to be changed over
swapped can indicate letters or components are to be changed over
sward GRASS; TURF
swarm HORDE
swarming anagram indicator
swat KILL
sway REIGN; TOTTER
swear CURSE; CUSS; VOW
swearword CUSS
sweat LATHER; SPOT; STEW

sweep BRUSH; RANGE
sweep away anagram indicator
sweeper BROOM; BRUSH
sweet AFTERS; CANDY; COMFIT; CUTE; FUDGE; HONEY; KISS; LOLLY; MINT; PUDDING; TART; *see* DESSERT
sweet, cold ICE
sweet, not BITTER; DRY; TART
sweet sauce TOPPING
sweet, sentimentally TWEE
sweet stick ROCK
sweetheart E; FLAME; LOVE; LOVER
sweetness HONEY
swell FOP; NOB; ROLLER; TOFF
swelling BOIL; BUNION
swerve YAW
swift BIRD; FAST; FLEET; NIPPY; QUICK
swig SHOT; SLUG
swim BATHE; DIP
swimmer can indicate a fish or other aquatic animal eg. OTTER; *see* FISH
swimmer, young ELVER
swimmers, lots of SCHOOL(S)
swimming anagram indicator
swimming-stroke BREAST; CRAWL
swindle CON; DO; NOBBLE; RAMP; ROB; ROOK; SCAM; SKIN; STING
swindled BITTEN; STUNG
swindler CROOK; FRAUD; ROOK; SHARP
swine CAD; HEEL; HOG; PIG; RAT
swing HANG; LURCH; SLEW
swinging HIP
swipe LIFT; NICK
swipes BEER
swirling anagram indicator
swish CHIC; SMART; anagram indicator
Swiss mountain RIGI
Swiss subdivision CANTON
Swiss toboggan LUGE
switch BEAT; CANE; HAIR; LASH; ROD; SHOOT; STICK; TRESS; TURN; TWIG; anagram indicator; reversal indicator
switch on anagram to include ON

switched, switching anagram indicator; reversal indicator
Switzerland CH
swivel SWING
swivelling, swivels reverse indicator
sword EPEE; FOIL; SABRE
sword-fighter FENCER
swot CRAM
symbol BADGE; CROWN; FLAG; LETTER; LION; LOGO; MACE; STAR; TOKEN; TOTEM
symbol of innocence LAMB
symbol of rank STAR
sympathetic word THERE
sympathy, expression of THERE
symphony FIFTH
syncopated music RAG
synthetic, synthesized anagram indicator

Tt

T-shirt TOP
tab FLAP
table BOARD; CHART; DESK; LIST; ROTA
tablet PILL; SLAB
tabloid MIRROR; SUN
tack NAIL; SEW; SHEER; VEER; can indicate something to do with saddlery
tackle FACE; GEAR; HANDLE; HARNESS; KIT; TRY
tactless remark GAFFE
tag AGLET; LABEL; IAMB
tail BRUSH; DOG; END; SCUT; end of word indicator
tailor FIT; STYLE
tainted anagram indicator
take BAG; FILCH; HACK; HAVE; HOOK; NET; NICK; SEIZE;

STEAL; TRAP; *see* OPINION
take action SUE
take away MINUS; REMOVE
take exam SIT
take home EARN
take in EAT; INHALE
take it easy REST
take food EAT
take off APE; COPY; DOCK; DROP; SHED; SKIT; STRIP [IMITATE]
take on FACE; HIRE; PLAY
take out DATE; DELETE; KILL; SLAY
take part ENTER
take steps DANCE
take to task RATE
taken GOT
taking CUTE
taking half a day off omission of SUN, MON etc
taking place ON
tale FABLE; LIE; MYTH; SAGA; STORY; YARN
talent ART; FLAIR; KNACK; SKILL
tales, told SANG
talisman CHARM
talk BABBLE; BANTER; CHAT; GAB; GAS; JAW; LINGO; ORATE; PRATE; RABBIT; RAP; RATTLE; SPEAK; YABBER; homophone indicator; *see* BELOW
talk boringly DRONE
talk, empty WIND
talk foolishly PRATE
talk, glib PATTER
talk, idle CHATTER; GAS
talk idly CHATTER; GAS; PRATE; NATTER; PRATTLE; *see* TALK
talk, sales PITCH
talking homophone indicator
tall BIG
tall structure TOWER
tamper with FIX; RIG
tampered with anagram indicator
tan BAKE; BROWN
tang SMACK

tangible REAL
tangle KNOT; MESS; RAVEL; anagram indicator
tank VAT
tanker OILER; OILSS (ie. oil SS)
tanned BROWN; RUDDY
tap BUG; C; COLD; H; HOT; PAT
tar PITCH
tardy LATE; SLOW
target AIM; BULL; END; GOAL; HOME; INNER; OUTER; TEE
target, part of BULL; INNER; OUTER
Tarka OTTER
tarry LINGER; STALL; STAY; WAIT
tart ACID; FLAN; HARLOT; PIE; SHARP; SWEET; SOUR
tartan PLAID
task CHORE
taste DROP; FLAVOUR; LICK; SAMPLE; SIP; SMACK; TANG
taste, with CHIC
tatty anagram indicator
taunt MOCK; SCOFF; TWIT
taut TENSE
tautological, tautology can indicate that a word is repeated (or sometimes its synonym) to give solutions such as THAT'S THAT, HOT-SHOT
tax CESS; CUSTOM; DRAIN; DUTY; RATE; RATES; SCOT; STRAIN; STRESS; TITHE; TOLL; VAT
taxation RATES
taxi CAB
tea CHA; CHAR
tea-maker POT; URN
teach TRAIN
teacher BEAK; DON; HEAD; MASTER; MISS; RABBI; TUTOR
teacher, female MISS
teacher, leading HEAD
teacher, old USHER
teachers NUT; STAFF; *see* TEACHER
teaching CLASS; LESSON
teaching union NUT
team COLOUR; CREW; GANG; GROUP; SIDE; SQUAD; STAFF; XI; *see* TEAM, FOOTBALL
team, football FOREST; ORIENT; VILLA
tear REND; RENT; RIP

tear-jerker MACE
tease BAIT; KID; RAG; RIB; TWIT
teasing ARCH; RIBBING
technique ART; MODE; STYLE; TOUCH; TRICK; WAY
technology IT
teddy bear TOY
tedious DRAGGING; DRY; DULL; LONG
tedious, be DRAG
tedious, become PALL
tedious type BORE
tee T
teenage rebel TED
teenager MOD; ROCKER; TED; YOUTH
teeter YAW
teetering anagram indicator
teeth SET
teeth, bare GRIN
telepathy ESP
telephone CALL; RING; TEL
television BOX; CABLE; SET; TELLY; TUBE; TV
television regulator ITC
television supplier BBC; CABLE; SKY
tell COUNT; INFORM; RELATE
Tell SWISS
tell-off RATE
tell the tale LIE
temper BATE; HUFF; INURE; IRISH; MOOD; PET; RAGE; SEASON; TONE
temperament BLOOD; MOOD
temperamental MOODY
temperature C; F; T
temperature, running a high HOT
tempo RATE
temporary ACTING
temporary accommodation, cover, shelter TENT
temporise STALL
tempt DRAW; eg.G; LURE
temptress SIREN
ten X
ten percent TITHE

tenant LEASER
tend CARE; LEAN; MIND; NURSE
tendency BENT; DRIFT; LEANING; TREND; VEIN
tendency, natural STRAIN
tender BID; DOUGH; OFFER; PUT; READY; SORE; SOFT; can refer to money; *see* CASH, MONEY, CURRENCY; can indicate something to do with a railway
tending PRONE
tennis champ BORG
tennis decision LET; NET; OUT
tennis facility COURT
tennis, game of DOUBLES; SET; SETS
tennis, some SET; SETS
tennis star SEED
Tennyson poem MAUD
tenor COURSE
tense BRACE; DRAWN; FUTURE; PAST; PERFECT; TAUT; TIGHT
tension, create TIGHTEN
tenth TITHE
term CALL; HILARY (university term); LENT; NAME; SESSION; SPELL; TIME; WORD
terminal END; FINAL; last letter indicator
termination last letter indicator
terminology USAGE
terrace ROW; TER; TIER
terrible, terribly anagram indicator
territory PATCH; TER; *see* REGION
terrorist group CELL
terse CURT
test CHECK; EXAM; MATCH; MOT; ORAL; ORDEAL; PROBE; RUN; SAMPLE; SOUND; TASTE; TRIAL; TRY; VET
Test RIVER
Testament NT; OT; VERSE
testy CROSS
tether CHAIN; ROPE; TIE
Texas TX
text MS; PROSE; WORDS
text, some PARA
textbook READER
textile JUTE

textile, instrument CARD; LOOM
textile worker DYER
Thailand SIAM
Thank God DG
thank you, thanks TA
that WHO; YON; YONDER
that chap, fellow HIM
that hurts OW
that in France QUE
that is IB; ID (ie. idem); IDEST; SC
that place THERE
that's IE
that woman HER
thatch HAIR; ROOF
Thatcherite DRY
thatching REED
thaw MELT
the beware that this innocent article can itself be part of an anagram or the solution
the first T
the French LA; LE; LES
the German DER; DIE
the Italian IL
the northern T
the old YE
the Spanish EL; LAS; LOS
theatre ARENA; LYRIC; ODEON; REP; SHOW; STAGE; rem: theatre can mean an operating theatre
theatre company CAST; REP
theatre, foreign NOH
theatre of war FRONT
theatre, part of APRON; CIRCLE; PIT; STAGE; STALLS
theatrical CAMP
theologian DD
theory IDEA; ISM; NOTION
these days AD; LATELY; NOW; PRESENT
therapy ECT
there, over YONDER
therefore ERGO; SO; THUS
thermal rating TOG

thesis PAPER; TRACT
thespian ACTOR
they say homophone indicator
thick DENSE; DIM; DUMB; FAT
thicket BRAKE; COPSE; GROVE
thieve NICK; ROB; STEAL; WHIP
thigh HAM
thin BONY; FINE; LAME; LEAN; RARE; SHEER; SPARE; WEAK
thing ARTICLE; IT; OBJECT; can indicate an obsession, enthusiasm or mania as "A thing for lighting fires?" clues PYROMANIA
thing, delightful GAS
thing, funny HOOT
things worn WEAR
think DEEM; FEEL; MULL; MUSE; PONDER; WONDER
thinker MUSER
thinking PENSIVE
third of third letter of succeeding word
third-rate C
thirst ITCH
thirsty DRY
thirty days can indicate a month of thirty days (usually abbreviated form) namely APR, JUNE, SEPT, NOV
thirty-one days can indicate a month of thirty-one days (usually abbreviated form) namely JAN, MAR, MAY, JUL. AUG, OCT, DEC
thirty seconds MIN
this country GB; UK
this French CE
this month INST
this place HERE
this state UK
this writer I; ME
thong TAW; TAWS
thoroughfare LANE; RD; ROAD; ST
those, those people EM (ie. 'em); THEM; THEY
though IF; THO
thought BELIEF; IDEA; MUSED; NOTION
thoughtful KIND
thousand GRAND; K; M; THOU
thousand, two MM
thousandth THOU

thrash BEAT; LAM; TAN; WHIP
thread CORD; FLOSS; LACE; STRAND; YARN
threat PERIL
threat to king CHECK
threatening BLACK
three TRIO
three couples, pairs VI
thresh BEAT
threshing anagram indicator
threw CAST; FLUNG
thrice TER (L.)
thrifty CANNY
thrill KICK
thrive BLOOM
throat CRAW
throaty sound COUGH
throb BEAT; PULSE
throne SEAT
through BY; PER; VIA
throughout DURING
throw CAST; FLING; HURL; LOB; PITCH; SHY; SLING; SPIT; TOSS
throwing anagram indicator
thrown CAST; FLUNG; anagram indicator
thrown about anagram indicator
thrown out of omission indicator
thrown up reversal indicator
thrust DRIVE; LUNGE; TILT
thug GOON; HEAVY; ROUGH; TOUGH
thump BANG; BEAT
thunder CLAP
Thunderer THOR; TIMES
thundering, thunderous LOUD
thurible CENSER
thus ERGO; SIC; SO; with particular wording can indicate AS eg. "thus primed" gives ASSET (ie. as set); anagram indicator
thus, Latin HOC
thwart FOIL; SEAT
Tibet, native of YAK
tick BEAT; MO; SEC

ticket FINE; PASS; TOKEN
ticket, meal LV
ticket seller, supplier TOUT
tidal flood *see* TIDAL WAVE
tidal flow RIP
tidal wave BORE; EAGRE
tide SEA; can indicate something to do with DRIFT
tidy CLEAN; COVER; HOE; NEAT; TRIM; anagram indicator
tie BAND; BIND; BOND; DRAW; EQUAL; FIX; LACE; LINK; TETHER
tie up BIND; FIX; MOOR; STAKE
tied BOUND; DREW
tier BAND; BANK; RANK; ROW
tiff BRUSH; PET; ROW; SPAT
tight CLOSE; SNUG; anagram indicator
tight-fisted MEAN; NEAR; STINGY; can indicate something to do with being tense
tight spot FIX; HOLE; SCRAPE; *see* DIFFICULTY
tile BOWLER
tiler ROOFER
tilt LEAN; LIST
timber ASH; BOARD; BEAM; FIR; LOG; PINE; PLANK; TREE; WOOD; can refer to specific wood or tree
time on earth LIFE
time AGE; AM; BIRD; DATE; DAY; ENEMY; EON; ERA; HOUR; MIN; MO; PERIOD; PM; SEASON; SEC; SHIFT; SPAN; SPELL; T; TEMPO; TERM; TICK; YEAR; can indicate something to do with prison term
time after that SINCE
time, astronomical EPACT
time, at that THEN
time, before EARLY
time being NONCE
time, good BALL; FUN
time, little MO; SEC; T; TICK
time, of past OLDEN
time on earth LIFE
time, our AD
time, passing of indicates that T is to be omitted from associated word
time-serve TRIM

timeless indicator for the omission of T, AGE, ERA, etc.; *see* TIME
timepiece CLOCK; HUNTER; WATCH
times X
times, behind the DATED; RUSTY
times gone by AGO
times, old BC
times, the AGE
timid person MOUSE
tin CAN; PRESERVE; SN
tin-plated component to be nested within SN as "Tin-plated uranium" gives SUN
tine POINT; PRONG; SPIKE
tinge DASH; TRACE
tinker FIDDLE; SLY (ie. Shakespearian character)
tint DYE
tiny BABY; INFANT; SMALL; WEE
tiny amount DOT; DROP; MIL; SPLASH
tiny distance MIL
tip CUE; CLUE; HEAD; HINT; LEAN; LIST; PEAK; POINT; TOE; initial letter indicator
tip-off initial letter to be omitted
tipple DRAM; RUM; SHOT; TOT
tipster TOUT
tipsy HIGH; TIGHT; anagram indicator
tiptop SPIRE
tirade RANT
tire FLAG
tiresome work CHORE; FAG
tired DRAWN; STALE; WEARY
tiredness FLAG
tissue FLESH; PAPER; SINEW
title CLAIM; COUNT; EARL; HANDLE; LORD; MISTER; MR; NAME; PASHA; SIR; RIGHT
title holder CHAMP
titled lady DAME
TNT, use BLAST
to be (with some indication of French) ETRE
to the French A; ALA; AU; AUX
to wit VIZ
toast BREAD; CHEER; CHEERS

toast, half of CHIN (ie. from chin-chin)
toboggan, Swiss LUGE
today AD; NOW; OURAGE (ie. our age); when the crossword is in a daily newspaper, can indicate the day of publication, either full or abbreviated
toddle AMBLE; STROLL
toe TIP
toff GENT
toffee SWEET
toilet GENTS; HEAD; HEADS; JOHN; LOO; WC
token COUNTER; DISC; EARNEST; HOLLOW (as in a token gesture); TICKET
token of love RING
told homophone indicator
told, be HEAR
told off CHID
told tales SANG
Toledo SWORD
tolerance GIVE
tolerate BEAR; HACK; STAND; WEAR
toleration LATITUDE
toll COST; CHARGE; DUTY; FEE; RING; STROKE; TAX
Tom CAT; MOGGY; PUSS; PUSSY; THOS; THUMB
tomb GRAVE
tome BOOK
Tommies *see* SOLDIERS
Tommy *see* SOLDIERS
tone SOUND
tone down TEMPER
tongue LINGO; SPIT; can indicate a specific language, FRENCH, etc.
too ABOVE; DITTO; can indicate a verb beginning with OVER
too far OVER
too many can indicate a word beginning with OVER
too much EXCESS; OTT; OVER
too soon EARLY
took action DID; SUED
took a lift RODE
took chair SAT
took cover HID
took exam SAT

took in ATE
took off SHED
took refuge HID
tool AWL; AXE; BRACE; BIT; CLAMP; FILE; FORK; HAMMER; HATCHET; HOE; JIG; LATHE; PICK; PLANE; RASP; SAW; *see* SEE IMPLEMENT, INSTRUMENT
tooth MOLAR; TUSK
top ARCH; BEST; CAP; COVER; HEAD; LID; ROOF; [UP]; initial letter indicator; can indicate something to do with head; *see* HEAD, TOP OF
top award GOLD
top car GT
top class AI; SUPERB; U
top commander CINC (ie. C-in-C)
top drawer U
top honour ACE
top light RED
top man CHIEF; BOSS; HEAD; KING; LEADER
top mark A
top marks can indicate high-ranking grade consisting of letters A,B,C
top of initial letter indicator
top, over the OTT
top (performance etc) RECORD
top person QUEEN; ROYAL; *see* TOP MAN
top player ACE; SEED; STAR
top quality AI; *see* TOP
top room ATTIC
toper SOT
topic THEME
topping BRILL; ICING
topless omission indicator for first letter
torch LIGHT
torment HELL; NAG
torn RENT; SPLIT
torn apart RIVEN
torn up anagram indicator
torrid anagram indicator
torso TRUNK
torture RACK
Tory BLUE; CON; RIGHT
toss FLING; ROLL; SPIN; THROW

tossed FLUNG; SPUR; anagram indicator
tossing anagram indicator
tot ADD; DRAM; KID; NIP; NIPPER; SHOT; SUM; TIPPLE
tot up ADD
total ADD; ALL; LOT; SUM; WHOLE
totally different anagram indicator
total, one finding SUMMER
totter QUIVER; ROCK; REEL; SHAKE
touch CADGE; CONTACT; KISS; MOVE; PAT; TINGE; TRACE
touch-down LAND
touch, in can indicate something to do with field game eg. linesman
touch lightly BRUSH; KISS
touch of initial letter indicator
touch regularly SPONGE
touched MAD; MET
touchy TESTY
tough FIRM; HOOD (ie. gangster); HARD; STERN; STRICT; STRINGY
tough Cockney ARD
tough exterior SHELL
tour TRIP; anagram indicator
tour of duty STINT
tourist attraction DOME
tourist, visit as a DO
tourney, take part in JOUST
tout BARKER; HAWK; PEDDLE
tow DRAG; HAUL; PULL
towards AT
towel CLOTH
tower BROCH; KEEP; LOOM; PEEL; PILE; SPIRE; STACK; rem: the less common pronunciation which can indicate TUGBOAT etc
town BARROW; BATH; BURY; CITY; CREWE; DEAL; DISS; IVER; LEEK; SLOUGH; STREET
town, big CITY
town centre OW
town, Irish *see* IRISH TOWN
town, to UP
townee CIT
toy DALLY; DOLL; PLAY; RATTLE; TRIFLE
toy explosive CAP

toying anagram indicator
trace DRAW; FIND; HINT; SIGN; SNIFF; TINGE
traces of first letter indicator
track DOG; FOLLOW; LANE; LINE; PATH; ROW; RUT; SCENT; SPOOR; STALK; TAIL; TRAIL; WAY
tract PLOT; SPREAD
trade ART; BARTER; CRAFT; DEAL; LINE; MARKET; SELL; SWOP; TRAFFIC
trade association EFTA
trade-centre MALL; MART
trade-mark BRAND; LOGO
trade-name BRAND
trade route CANAL
trade union TU
tradesman BAKER; MONGER; PLUMBER
trading place MALL; MART
trading station FORT
traditional OLD; TRAD
traffic CARS; DEAL; TRADE; TRUCK; *see* TRADE
traffic controller LIGHT
traffic marker CONE
tragically anagram indicator
trail DOG; DRAG; FOLLOW; PATH; RETINUE; ROUTE; SCENT; SIGN; SPOOR; STALK; TRACK; WAY
train AIM; COACH; POINT; RY; SCHOOL; TEACH [TRACK]
trained TAME; TAUGHT; anagram indicator
trainee CADET; INTERN
trainer COACH; SHOE
training COURSE; DRILL; PE; PT; anagram indicator
trains RY
traipse TRAIL
traitor CAD; RAT; WEASEL
traitorous type *see* TRAITOR
tramp DOSSER; HOBO; PLOD; TREAD
tranquiliser DOWNER
tranquility CALM; PEACE
transaction DEAL
transfer DECAL; PASS
transfiguration, transfigured anagram indicator
transformed, transforming anagram indicator

transgress SIN
transgression OFFENCE; SIN
translate RENDER; anagram indicator
translated anagram indicator
translation CRIB; anagram indicator
translation, illicit CRIB
translator TR
transmit PIPE; SEND
transmitted SENT
transmitter SENDER
transport BEAR; BUS; CAR; CARRY; CART; DELIGHT; ENTRANCE; RY; SEND; SHIP; TRAIN; TUBE; *see* VEHICLE
transport, free LIFT
transport, public BUS; TRAIN; TRAM; RY
transport, sea *see* BOAT
transport system, old BR
transported CARTED
transporter *see* VEHICLE
transposed anagram indicator
trap CATCH; FLY; GIN; NET; WEB
trash DRECK
trashed anagram indicator
trauma SHOCK
travail WORK
travel GO; RIDE; TOUR
travel document VISA
travel fast RUSH; SPEED
travel guide NAP
travelled RODE
traveled on the Underground TUBED
traveller FARER; HOBO; POLO; REP; TRAMP; TRIPPER
travelling anagram indicator
Travels the capital initial can indicate the reference is to “Gulliver’s Travels”, its author (SWIFT) or its characters (eg. YAHOO)
travesty FARCE
treacherous daughter REGAN
treacherous person, type RAT; RATTER; WEASEL
treachery TREASON
tread STEP; TRAMP
treadle LEVER

treasure VALUE
treasurer TR
treat DRESS; STAND; USE [ENTERTAIN]
treated anagram indicator
treatment CURE; DEAL; ECT; anagram indicator
treaty PACT; PEACE
trek leader MOSES; T
tree ACER; ASH; ALDER; BAY; BEECH; BIRCH; BOX; ELDER; ELM; FIR; GUM; HOLLY; LARCH; LIME; OAK; PALM; PEAR; PINE; PLANE; POPLAR; SORB; TEAK; WILLOW; can indicate something to do with ancestors, lineage; can indicate something to do with shoe
tree trunk BOLE
trees CLUMP; COPSE; FOREST; GROVE; STAND; WOOD
tremble QUAVER; SHAKE; SHIVER
tremulous anagram indicator
trench DITCH; PIT
trenchant CUTTING
trend TIDE; VOGUE
trendy HEP; HIP; IN
trespass SIN
tress LOCK
trial GO; HEARING; ORDEAL; TEST; TRY
trial, appearing for UP
trial, on UP
tribe CLAN; GAD; LEVI; RACE; SEPT
tribe, ancient GAD
tribesman ANGLE; GOTHI; LEVI
tribunal ROTA
tribute TOAST
trick CHEAT; CON; DO; DIDO (U.S.); FEAT; FLANKER; FOX; HOAX; JAPE; JOKE; KID; PLANT; PRANK; RIG; RUSE; SCAM; anagram indicator
tricked, tricky anagram indicator
trifle DALLY; TOY
trifling LIGHT; PETTY
trilby HAT
trill QUAVER; SING; TRA; WARBLE
trim CUT; LOP; NEAT; PARE; PRUNE
trimmed omission indicator, either first or last letter or both
trio THREE

trip CATCH; CRUISE; DANCE; DRIVE; FALL; FLIGHT; ROW; SPIN; STUMBLE; TOUR; anagram indicator
trip, French TOUR
trip, on a HIGH
tripe ROT
trite BANAL
trite jokes CORN
trite quotation TAG
triumph WIN
triumph, expression of AHA; HA
trivial LIGHT; LITTLE
Trojan PARIS
troll ELF
trollop DOXY; SLUT
troop, member of GUIDE
troops RA; RE; SAS
troops, crack SAS
trophy CUP; POT; SCALP; URN
tropical HOT
trot PACE
troth PLEDGE
Trotsky LEON
trouble ADO; AIL; BANE; BOTHER; BUG; CARE; FUSS; ILL; IRK; JAM; PAIN; PEST; SCRAPE; STINK; TRIAL; reversal indicator; anagram indicator; can indicate a specific illness
trouble, in anagram indicator
troubled anagram indicator
troublemaker IMP
troubles ILL
troublesome anagram indicator
trough CHUTE
trousers BAGS; PANTS; TREWS
trowel SCOOP
truck LORRY; TRADE
truculent anagram indicator
true LOYAL; REAL; RIGHT; SO
true, not BENT
truism MAXIM
truly, yours I; ME
trump BEAT; RUFF

trumpet BUGLE; LUR
trunk BOLE; TORSO
trustee TR
truth FACT
truth, old SOOTH
try DO; GO; HEAR; SAMPLE; SHOT; TACKLE; TASTE; TAX; TEST
try hard STRAIN
try to find out PRY; SPOON
try to win COURT; WOO
trying to get AFTER
tsar IVAN; PETER
tub BATH
tube ARTERY; DUCT; PIPE; VEIN
tuber SPUD; YAM
tuck DART; PLEAT
Tuck FRIAR
tuck in EAT
Tucker's companion BIB
tucked in ATE
tucking in nesting indicator
tuft BOBBLE
tug BOAT; LUG; PULL; TOW; YANK
tumble FALL
tumbler GLASS
tumbling anagram indicator
tummy pain GRIPE
tumulus MOUND
tun CASK
tundra PLAIN
tune AIR; ARIA; MARCH; NUMBER; PORT (Gael.); SONG
tungsten W
tunnel BORE; HOLE; BURROW
tup RAM
turbulent anagram indicator
turf GRASS; LAW; SWARD
turkey FLOP
Turkey TR
Turkish chief, commander, leader AGA; AGHA
Turkish governor BEY

turmoil, in anagram indicator
turn ACT; BEND; CRACK; FIT; GO; HINGE; LUFF; PIVOT; ROLL; ROUND; SCREW; SHOW; SOUR; SPIN; TED; TWIST; U; WHEEL; WIND; anagram indicator
turn inside out EVERT
turn out COME; DRESS; anagram indicator
turn over PTO; TO; reversal indicator
turn tail FLEE; RUN; the last two letters of a word to be interchanged
turn, take a STROLL
turn up APPEAR; COCK; COME; FOLD; OG (ie. reverse of GO); SHOW
turn-up anagram indicator
turncoat RAT
turned OFF; SPUN; anagram indicator; reversal indicator
turned out anagram indicator
turner SPIT
turned over reversal indicator; anagram indicator
turning BEND; CORNER; SOURING; reversal indicator; anagram indicator
turnover reversal indicator
turns anagram indicator
turns up PU (ie. reverse of UP); reversal indicator
tutor COACH; DON; TEACH; TRAIN; TRAINER
TV TELLY; *see* TELEVISION
TV doctor WHO
TV programme usually SOAP OPERA
TV relay OB
twelve NOON
twenties DECADE
twenty-eight/nine days FEB
twenty-five pounds PONY
twenty-four hours DAY
twig BRANCH; GET; SEE; SHOOT; STICK
twilight DUSK
twin REMUS
twinkling TRICE
twirl SPIN
twirling anagram indicator
twist COIL; SNAKE; SPIN; TURN; WRITHE
twisted WRY; anagram indicator
twisted back reversal indicator

twisting TORTUOUS
twit DUNCE; PUDDING
twitch JERK; TIC; anagram indicator
twitched anagram indicator
twitching TIC; anagram indicator
two BI; BOTH; BRACE; COUPLE; DUET; DUO; II; PAIR; TWAIN
two couples IV
252d GUINEA
two pints QUART
two, the BOTH
two thousand MM
two-sided LR; RL
two-under score EAGLE
two-way can indicate a palindrome
Tyneside NE
type CLASS; ELITE; FACE; FOUNT; ILK; MAKE; SORT; KIND; PICA; PRINT; ROMAN (ie. printing);STYLE; can refer to printer's type; can refer to a particular type of person as "possessive type" clues OWNER
type, mixed up PI; PIE
type of wood *see* WOOD, TREE
typically can indicate that a group term is required as "panthers typically" requires CATS; can indicate something to do with printing type as "Typically leaning to the right" clues ITALIC
typist TEMP
typo ERROR
tyrant NERO
tyre RADIAL

Uu

U-boat SUB
U-turn reversal indicator
ugly anagram indicator

UK citizen BRIT
Ulster NI; rem: can also refer to a coat
ultimate ALL; LAST
ultimately LAST; last letter indicator
Umberto ECO
umbrella COVER
umpire REP
UN body WHO
unable to, am CANT
unable to, is CANT
unacceptable NOTON (ie. not on); OFF; OUT
unaccompanied ALONE; LONE
unaccompanied (flight) SOLO
unaccountably anagram indicator
unadorned BALD; PLAIN
unadulterated NEAT; SHEER
unassertive type MOUSE
unattracted OFF
unavailable OFF; OUT; omission indicator
unbelievable TALL
unbiased FAIR; JUST
unblock FREE
unbound FREE
unbusy DEAD
unceremoniously anagram indicator
uncertain IFFY
uncertainly anagram indicator
uncertainty DOUBT; IF
uncivil RUDE
uncivilised RUDE ; WILD
uncle SAM
unclear FOGGY
unclosed last letter of associated word to be omitted
unclothed BARE; NAKED; NUDE
unclouded CLEAR
uncomfortable place HOLE
uncomfortably anagram indicator
uncommon NOTABLE; RARE; ROYAL
uncommonly anagram indicator
uncomplicated PLAIN; SIMPLE; anagram indicator

unconcealed OPEN; OUT; OVERT
unconscious OUT
unconscious, knock STUN
uncontrollable anagram indicator
uncontrollably anagram indicator
unconventional anagram indicator
unconvincing LAME
uncouth anagram indicator
uncouth person BEAR; LOUT; OAF
uncovered BARE; NUDE
uncultivated RUDE
uncultivated area MOOR
undecided, be HOVER
undemanding CUSHY; EASY; LIGHT
under SUB; BELOW; NEATH; can indicate something to do with anaesthetics
under attack IN CHECK
under-eighteen MINOR
undercut SAP
undergarment *see* UNDERWEAR
undergo SUFFER
Underground TUBE
underground church CRYPT
underground river LETHE
underground takeaway service SEWER
underground worker MINER
undermine SAP
underneath BELOW
underside SOLE
understand DIG; FOLLOW; GATHER; GET; GRASP; KEN; KNOW; READ; SEE; TWIG
understanding DEAL; GRASP; INSIGHT; LIGHTS (ie. according to one's); SENSE
understood GOT; READ; ROGER; SAW
undertaking MISSION; VOW
underwear BASQUE; BRA; BRAS; SHOE; SLIP; SLIPPER; SLIPS; VEST
underweight LIGHT
underworld DIS; HELL
undesirable person LOUT; OAF
undiluted NEAT

undisciplined anagram indicator
undisguised BALD
undo RUIN
undone anagram indicator
undress STRIP
undressed first and last letter to be omitted as "swimmer feels undressed" clues EEL
unduly TOO
unelected OUT
unemotional COOL; STOLID
unemployment benefit DOLE; UB
unenlightened DARK
unenthusiastic LAME
unexpected SNAP; SUDDEN; anagram indicator
unexpectedly anagram indicator
uneven BUMPY; ODD
uneven, make RUFFLE
unfairly anagram indicator
unfamiliar NEW; anagram indicator
unfashionable OUT
unfavourable ADVERSE
unfeeling COLD; NUMB
unfilled VOID
unfinished omission indicator, usually of last letter
unfit ILL
unfit for service US (ie. colloquialism for 'useless)
unforthcoming SHY
unfortunately ALACK; ALAS; anagram indicator
unfriendly COLD
unfurled anagram indicator
unfurnished BARE
ungenerous MEAN
unhappily anagram indicator
unhappy GLUM; SAD; SOMBRE; anagram indicator
unhealthy PASTY
uniform EQUAL; EVEN; LEVEL; SUIT
unidentified SOME
unimportant SMALL
uninhibited FREE
uninspired STALE

union CONCERT; TU; can signal something to do with marriage or wedding
union, teaching NUT
Unionist politician UMP
unique ALONE; LONE; ONE; ONLY; SINGLE; SOLE
uniquely ONCE
unit I; ONE; PART; SQUAD; WATT; *see* MEASURE
unit, Morse DASH; DOT
unit, sound BEL
unit of speed KNOT
unit of weight K; KILO; L; LB; OZ; ST; TON
unite ALLY; BOND; JOIN; KNIT; LINK; MARRY; TIE; WELD
united ONE; U; UTD; WED
United player RED
universal U
universe ALL; COSMOS
university ASTON; BATH; KEELE; LSE; MIT; OU; OXFORD; READING; U; UNI
university, at UP
university crew ISIS
university period TERM
university position CHAIR
university sportsman BLUE
unjustified anagram indicator
unkind ILL
unknown ANON; X; Y; Z
unknown amount X; Y; Z
unknown author ANON
unknown quantity X; Y; Z
unlicensed driver L
unlike opposite indicator
unlikely anagram indicator
unlit DARK
unlucky EVIL
unmarried FREE; SINGLE; M to be omitted from associated word as "Unmarried girl said to be accomplished" clues ABLE (ie. M from MABLE)
unoccupied FREE
unofficially anagram indicator
unopened indicator that initial letter should be omitted
unoriginal OLD; STALE

unorthodox anagram indicator
unplanned anagram indicator
unpleasant AWFUL; FOUL; ICKY; NASTY; ROUGH
unpleasant person CRUD
unpleasant smell BO
unpleasant woman TROUT; WITCH
unpopular name MUD
unpractised RUSTY
unpredictably anagram indicator
unprepared RASH
unproductive LEAN
unqualified LAY; SHEER; UTTER
unravelling anagram indicator
unreasonably anagram indicator
unrecorded LIVE
unrefined RAW
unreliable IFFY; GAMMY; anagram indicator
unreliably anagram indicator
unresolved LOOSE
unrest anagram indicator
unrestrained FREE; LOOSE
unruffled EVEN
unruly anagram indicator
unruly crowd MOB
unruly youngster, youth TED
unsatisfactory BAD
unseasoned RAW
unseated U
unserviceable US (ie. colloquialism for 'useless)
unskilful player HAM
unskilled GREEN; RAW
unsociable type LONER
unspeaking MUTE
unspecified amount SOME
unstable anagram indicator
unsteady gait ROLL
unstuck anagram indicator
unsuitable INAPT
unsullied CHASTE
unsympathetic HARD

untamed WILD
untidiness MESS
untidy SLOPPY; anagram indicator
until TILL
untrue FALSE
untruth, tell LIE
unusual EXTRA; NOVEL; ODD; OUTRE; RARE; RUM; STRANGE; anagram indicator
unusually anagram indicator
unused GREEN; NEW; RAW; UN (ie. "un" to be used)
unwavering CONSTANT
unwelcoming FIRM; FROSTY; ICY
unwell AILING; ILL; SICK
unwell, become AIL
unwilling SHY
unwisely anagram indicator
unwritten ORAL
up FAR; HIGH; OVER; RAISED; RIDING; RISEN; STANDING; UP; anagram indicator; reversal indicator; can indicate something to do with flying, pilot, trapeze artiste
up-market TRAM (think about it)
up to TILL
up-to-date HIP; MODERN; NEW; RECENT
upbeat MAL (ie. LAM reversed)
upfront AHEAD; OPEN; OVERT
upheaval anagram indicator
upland area *see* UPLANDS
uplands MOOR
uplifted reversal indicator
upon NO
upper-class POSH; U
upper class chap, type TOFF
upper leg THIGH
uppers, on BROKE; SKINT
upright ERECT; POST; STRAIGHT; WORTHY
uprising REVOLT; reversal indicator
uproar CRY; RACKET
upset RATTLE; RILE; SPILL; TES (ie. 'up' a reversal indicator for 'set'); reversal indicator; anagram indicator
upset, be CRY; WEEP
upsetting anagram indicator; reverse indicator

upside-down anagram indicator; reversal indicator
upstanding ERECT
upturned PU
upward/s reversal indicator
uranium U
urchin ARAB
urge DRIVE; eg.G; GOAD; ITCH; PRESS; PROD; YEN
urgent message SOS
Uruguay U
US agent FED
US car DODGE
US city LA; EC; NY; RENO; WACO
US college MIT
US explorers NASA
US friend BUD
US intelligence CIA
US industrialist FORD
US investigator GMAN
US investigators CIA; GMEN
US lawyer DA
US mag LIFE; TIME
US mail ARMOR
US novelist COOPER
US quarters CASH
US president ABE; BUSH; CARTER; FORD
US sports stadium BOWL
US student COED; MAJOR
US volume LITER
us, of OUR
usual NORMAL; PAR
use APPLY; AVAIL; DO; EMPLOY; FUNCTION; WEAR; anagram indicator
use force PRESS
use of drugs TRIP
use, to be of AVAIL
use wrong words LIE
used anagram indicator
used by run indicator
used to be WAS; WERE
used up anagram indicator; reversal indicator

useful BOOT; HANDY
useful quality ASSET
useless DUFF; IDLE; OFF; US; VAIN
useless article LEMON
using ON; PER
usual PAR
usurping replacement indicator
Utah UT
utensil FORK; SPOON
utter ISSUE; SAY; SPEAK; STATE; VOICE

vacant BARE; BLANK; FREE; HOLLOW; VAIN
vacation REST; VAC
vacillating anagram indicator
vacuous middle letters of associated word to be omitted
vacuum VOID
vagrant HOBO; TRAMP; anagram indicator
vague HAZY; anagram indicator
vaguely IDLY; anagram indicator
vain IDLE
vain display POMP
vale CHEERIO
valid RIGHT
valid, no longer UP
valley COMBE; DALE; DENE; DELL; DINGLE; DIP; GLADE; GLEN; GULLY
valuable ASSET
valuable card TRUMP
value PRICE; RATE; RESPECT; WORTH
van FRONT; LEAD
van, in the LEADS; can indicate component to be placed at the

beginning
vandalised anagram indicator
vanish END; GO
vanished GONE
vapid DULL
vaporizer MISTER
vapour FOG; MIST; STEAM
variation anagram indicator
varied anagram indicator
variegated anagram indicator
variety KIND; MAKE; SORT; TYPE; anagram indicator
various DIVERSE; anagram indicator
varnish GLOSS; can indicate something to do with finger-nail
vary CHANGE; WAVER
vase POT; URN
vast SEA
vault CLEAR; CRYPT; LEAP; anagram indicator
vegetable BEAN; BEET; CHARD; PEA; LEEK; ONION; SWEDE
vegetarian food PULSE
vehicle AGENT; BIKE; BRAKE; BUS; CAB; CAR; CART; COACH; FLOAT; GIG; LIMO; MINI; ROLLS; SLED; SLEDGE; SLEIGH; TANK; TRAIN; TRAM; TRAP; TRIKE; TRUCK; VAN
vehicle, electric FLOAT
vehicle, old CRATE
vehicle, slow-moving HEARSE
veil COVER; SCREEN
vein LODE; MOOD
vendor SELLER
venerable churchman BEDE
Venetian BLIND
Venetian merchant POLO
Venetian lawman DOGE
venison, source of DEER
venom SPITE
venomous indicative of a snake, scorpion etc.
vent FLUE
ventilate AIR
ventilated AIRED; AIRY
venture BET; CHANCE; DARE; GAMBLE; PRESUME; RISK; STAKE; TRY

venture, commercial SPEC
venue FAIR; PLACE; SITE
veracity TRUTH
verbal, verbally can signal a colloquialism; homophone indicator
verdant GREEN; LUSH
Verdi opera AIDA
verge BRIM; EDGE; HEM; LIP; SIDE; TEND
verisimilitude REALISM; TRUTH
vermin RAT
verminous RATTY
vermouth IT; ITALIAN
vernacular CANT; SLANG
Veronica can indicate something to do with speedwell
versatile anagram indicator
verse CANTO; DITTY; LINES; ODE; POEM; STAVE; V
versed, well UP
version EDITION; KIND; SORT; TYPE; anagram indicator
vertiginous STEEP
very SO; TOO; V
very bad CHRONIC; DIRE
very big OS
very cold ICY
very fast PRESTO
very fat OS
very fit AI
very French TRES
very good ACE; AI; BOFFO (U.S.); CLASS; CLASSI (ie. class 1); OK; PI; RIGHT; SO; STAR
very good, not omission of PI
very keen MAD
very large OS
very little WHIT
very loud FF
very much FAR
very musical ASSAI; MOLTO
very precise NICE
very quiet PP
very same SPIT
very small MINI; WEE; TEENY
vessel ARK; BARQUE; BATH; BIN; BOAT; BOTTLE; BOWL;

BRIG; CAN; CHURN; CRAFT; CROCK; CRUSE; CUP; EWER; FONT; FLUTE; GLASS; JAR; KETCH; KETTLE; LAUNCH; LINER; PAIL; PAN; POT; SHE; SHIP; SS; STEAMER; SUB; TIN; TUN; URN, VASE; VAT; VEIN; WOK; YAWL; *see* BOAT, CONTAINER, SHIP

vessel, American US; USS

vessel, Chinese WOK

vestibule HALL

vestment ALB

vet CHECK; SCREEN; SURGEON

veteran OLD

veto BAN; BAR; BLACK

vex GALL; IRK; NAG; RILE; SORE

via BY; THROUGH; WAY

vicar CURATE; REV

vicar's home BRAY; MANSE

vice GRIPPER; PORN; SIN

Vichy water EAU

vicinity CLOSE; NEAR; NIGH

vicious anagram indicator

victim ABEL; PREY

victim of disease LEPER

victor WINNER

Victoria V; VR; also can indicate something to do with the railway station

victory MATE; VE (ie. VE Day); WIN

victory, easy ROMP

victory, gain a WIN

victory, gained a WON

view ANGLE; EYE; FACET; GAZE; PEER; PEEK; SCENE; SEE; SIGHT; STANCE; TAKE; VISTA

viewer EYE; OPTIC

viewpoint ANGLE

vigilant AWAKE; AWARE

vigorous WELL

vigorous activity GO

vigorously anagram indicator

vigour GO; GUSTO; DRIVE; FIRE; PEP

vile BASE

villain CAD; CHEAT; CROOK; HEAVY; ROGUE

villainy EVIL

vindicate CLEAR
vineyard CRU
vintage AGE; CROP; YEAR
violated anagram indicator
violent RABID
violently anagram indicator
Violet VI
violin part NECK
violinist STERN
VIP CELEB; NIB; SWELL
virgin NEW
Virginia VA; can indicate something to do with tobacco
Virgo SIGN
virtue HOPE
virtue of being, by QUA
virtuous PI; MORAL
virtuoso ACE; EXPERT; PRO
virtuous person ST
virus BUG; FLU
viscosity, measure of STOKE
visible OUT
visible in run indicator
vision DREAM; SIGHT
visit CALL; HAUNT; SEE; STAY
visiting nesting indicator as "Judge visiting fine islands" clues FIJI
vista VIEW
vital KEY; LIVE; can refer to some vital function or part of the body, organ etc.
vital part ORGAN
vitality GO; VIM; ZEST
vitiate FLAW
vivacity BRIO; GO
vivid BRIGHT; GRAPHIC
Vivien LEIGH
vocal LOUD
vocal expression TONE; homophone indicator
vocalise SING
vocalised homophone indicator
vocalist SINGER
vocally homophone indicator

vociferous homophone indicator

vogue FAD; TREND

voice AIR; ALTO; BASS; EMIT; PART; PASSIVE; SAY; SINGER; TENOR; TONE; UTTER

voice, given homophone indicator

voiced homophone indicator

voiced disapproval TUT

void EMPTY; NULL; SPACE

void of omission indicator

volley BURST

volume BOOK; BULK; CC; CL; GAL; MASS; QUART; SIZE; SPACE; TOMB; V; VOL

volume, American LITER

volume, negligible CC

volunteer OFFER

volunteer force TA

volunteers TA

vomit SPEW

vote AYE; CROSS; NAY; NO; POLL; X; YES

vote against NAY; NO

vote, consenting (for, in favour) AY; AYE; YES

voucher TOKEN

vow OATH; WORD

voyage CRUISE; SAIL; TRIP

voyager see sailor

vulgar CHEAP; CRASS; FLASHY; GROSS; LOUD; LOW; RUDE; TACKY; colloquialism indicator; can indicate the omission of an initial H

vulgar, not PURE

vulgar people, those EM (ie. 'em)

vulnerable anagram indicator

Ww

wad BUN; ROLL
wag CARD; WIT
wage PAY; SCREW
wage deduction NI
wager BET; PUNT
wages HIRE; *see* WAGE
wagging anagram indicator
wagon CART; DRAY; VAN; WAIN
wail HOWL; KEEN; YAMMER
wain CART
waistcoat, American VEST
wait LINGER; STAY; TARRY
wake ROUSE; WASH
waking UP
walk AMBLE; GAIT; MALL; MARCH; PACE; PLOD; PROM; RAMBLE; REEL; STEP; STRIDE; STROLL; TRAMP; TURN
walk affectedly MINCE
walk clumsily LUMBER
walk lamely HOBBLE; LIMP
walk-out STRIKE
walk out on LEAVE; STRAND
walk quietly SNEAK
walker LEG
wall DYKE
wall, part of, under roof GABLE
wallop ALE; BEAT; BEER; HIT; THUMP
Walter SCOTT
wander ERR; GAD; ROAM; ROVE; STRAY
wander aimlessly MOON
wandering ASTRAY; ERRANT; MAD; anagram indicator
wandering around anagram indicator
want DEARTH; DESIRE; LACK; LONG; NEED; WISH
want, badly LONG
wanted, exactly what's IT

wanting omission indicator
wantonly anagram indicator
war SCRAP
War Department MOD
war hero ACE; BADER
War Ministry MOD
war, prepare for ARM
war-time hero, pilot see war hero
warble QUAVER; TRILL
ward off FEND; PARRY
warder GUARD; SCREW
wardrobe GARB
warehouse DEPOT
warfare ACTION
warm AIR; COSY; FAIR; HEAT; HEARTY; HOT; NEAR (ie. clue in guessing game)
warm covering FUR
warm up HEAT
warmonger HAWK
warmth HEAT; SUN
warmth, source of COAL; FIRE; SUN
warn BEEP
warning ALARM; CAVE; FORE; HOOTER; HORN; OMEN; SIREN
warning, give BEEP; HOOT; TOOT
warning light AMBER
warning, player's FORE
warped, warps anagram indicator
warplane FIGHTER; ZERO
warrant-officer SM
warren MAZE
warring anagram indicator
warrior BRAVE; KNIGHT
warriors IMPI
warship RAM; SUB
Warwick EARL
was first LED
was informed HEARD; TOLD
was MP SAT
was obliged HAD
was quick RAN; SPED

wash BATHE; CLEAN; FLUSH; LAVE; RINSE; WAKE
wash gently LAP
washed out PALE; WAN
Washington WA
Washington area DC
waste BLUE (spend extravagantly); GASH; KILL; LOSE; REFUSE; SLAG
waste away ATROPHY
wasted anagram indicator; omission indicator eg. "with nothing wasted" instructs that O be omitted
wasting anagram indicator
watch EYE; HUNTER; SCAN; SHIFT; TIMER; TICKER; WAKE; VIGIL
watch out CAVE (Latin); MIND
watchword MOTTO
water AQUA; BROOK; BURN; CHANNEL; MAIN; MED; OUSE; POND; POOL; RAIN; REACH; SEA; SOUND; SPRING; STREAM; TARN; TIDE; URE; URINE; *see* RIVER, SEA
water bird SWAN
water channel GUTTER
water control TAP
water, out of, short of ARID; DRY
water, salt SOLENT; *see* SEA
water, shallow FORD
water, source of WELL
water supply SPA; SPRING; WELL
water, take to SWIM
watered, being can indicate a component is to be nested within a form of water eg. rain
Waterloo ROUT; can indicate something to do with the battle or the railway station
waterproof MAC
waters SEAS; SWELL
waterside BANK; BEACH; SHORE
waterway CANAL; RIVER
Waugh novel SCOOP
wave BILLOW; BREAKER; EAGRE; FLAG; RIPPLE; ROLLER; SIGN; WASH; *see* WAVES
waver ROCK; VARY
wavering sound TRILL
waves can indicate something to do with hair or hairdressing; also *see*

WAVE

wax IRE

way AISLE; AVE; DOOR; HOW; LANE; MALL; NODE; PASS; PATH; RD; ROAD; ROUTE; ST; TRAIL; VIA

way back can indicate the reversal of a 'way', so we get DR, ROOD, TS and so on

way, by the can indicate something to do with street furniture

way, long FAR

way of doing things HOW

way of looking ANGLE

way of working MO

way things are, the ASIS (ie. as is)

way, this SO

way though mountains COL; PASS

wayward anagram indicator

we had WED

we hear homophone indicator

we objectively US

weak FAINT; FEEBLE; FRAIL; LAME; LAX; LIGHT; PUNY; SLIGHT; THIN

weak person SOP

weaken SAP

weakling RUNT

weakness LAPSE; VICE; can indicate something to do with Achilles' heel

wealth MEANS; MONEY

wealthy RICH; ROLLING

weapon ARM; ARROW; AXE; BILL; BOMB; BOW; DART; GUN; LANCE; LUGER; MAUSER; PIKE; RIFLE; SPEAR; SWORD

weapon in US AX

weapons, position of PORT

wear LAST; SPORT; STAND; STICK; USE

wear away, down ERODE

wearing IN; ON; nesting indicator

weary FLAG; TIRE; TIRED

weary, get FLAG; TIRE

weaselly type STOAT

weather, bad RAIN; STORM

weather forecasters MET

weather, indication of COCK, GLASS, VANE

weaver BOTTOM

web TRAP
wedding UNION
wedding, before the NEE
wedding response IDO
wedge CHOCK; SCOTCH
weed DOCK; GRASS; HOE
week WK
weekend K
weekly COMIC
weft WOOF
weight CT; GRAMME; KG; LB; MASS; OUNCE; OZ; PLUMB; ST; STONE; TON, TONNE
weir DAM
weird CREEPY; EERIE; ODD; RUM; anagram indicator
welcome AVE; GREET; HELLO; HI; SALUTE
weld BOND; FUSE
well BORE; FIT; HALE; PIT; SO (as in 'So?'); SPA; SPRING
well-being HEALTH
well-cooked DONE
well-dressed anagram indicator
well-earned DUE
well-endowed FLUSH; RICH; ROLLING
well-groomed NEAT; SLEEK
well in France BIEN
well-informed ABREAST; UPIN (ie. up in)
well-kept TRIM
well-organised TOGETHER
well-turned anagram indicator
well versed UP
Wellington BOOT; can refer to the general, or something to do specifically with New Zealand eg. KIWI
Welsh W
Welsh county GLAM
Welsh port BARRY
Welshman DAI; EVAN
went LEFT; WENDED
went ahead, first LED
went fast RAN
went off anagram indicator
went to court SUED

we're told homophone indicator
west W; reversal indicator
West MAE
West Country area DORSET
West End T
west, heading W; reversal indicator
West Indian, Indies WI
West Indian music REGGAE
wet DAMP; RET; SODDEN; TACKY; WIMP
whacked anagram indicator
whales POD
what EH; SOME (as used in the exclamation "What cheek!")
what French QUOI
what should not be said DIE
what Spanish QUE
wheat CROP
wheedle CADGE
wheel CASTER; ROLL; TURN; reverse indicator as "cart-wheel" denotes that CART is to be reversed
wheeling reverse indicator
wheeze IDEA
whelp PUP
when AS
whenever ONCE
where French OU
where in France OU
whet HONE
which THAT
whichever way you look at it palindrome indicator
while AS; TIME
while away PASS
whim CRAZE; FAD
whine SNIVEL
whip CAT; LASH; KNOUT; LEATHER; STEAL; TROUNCE
whirl EDDY; SPIN
whirl, in a anagram indicator; reversal indicator
whirlpool EDDY
whisk STIR
whisker HAIR
whisky BLEND; GRAIN; HOOCH; MALT; RYE; SCOTCH

whistle BLOW
whistler REF
white GLAIR; LILY; PURE
white, go PALE
White House trainee INTERN
white, South African BLANK
whitish PALE
Who can refer to the TV doctor, DALEK etc
who in France QUI
whole ALL; LOT; SUM; TOTAL
wholly ALL
why REASON
why I hear Y
WI can indicate something to do with West Indies or Women's Institute eg. jam.
wicked BAD; EVIL; SINFUL
wicked deed CRIME ; SIN
wickedness EVIL; SIN; VICE
wicket DOOR; GATE; STUMP
wicket, at the BAT; BATTING; IN
wicket, part of BAIL; STUMP
wide BROAD, EXTRA; V
wide-eyed NAIVE
widespread RIFE
widow RELICT
wielded anagram indicator
wife BRIDE; DUTCH; KATE; RIB; W
wife-batterer PUNCH
wife, new BRIDE
wife, old EX
wig RUG
wild CROSS; FERAL; MAD; STORMY; anagram indicator
wild animals GAME
wild birds GAME
wild card JOKER
wild youth BLOOD
wildebeest GNU
wildlife DEER
wildly anagram indicator
will LEAVE; SHALL

Will can refer to Shakespeare; or William I and so indicate something to do with the Norman Conquest
will, he HELL
will, I ILL
will, in short LL
will possibly MAY
willing ABLE; KEEN; ON; READY
willingly LIEF
willing participant SPORT
William BILL; TELL; WILL; can indicate something to do with the Norman Conquest, or orange ie. William of Orange
willow BAT
willy-nilly anagram indicator
wilt DROOP; FLAG
Wimbledon game TENNIS
wimp DRIP; WEED; WET
wimpish WEEDY; WET
win BEAT; GAIN; MATE; TAKE
win, try to WOO
winch CRANK
Winchester RIFLE; SCHOOL
wind AIR; COIL; GALE; GUST; LOOP; PUFF; RACK; REEL; ROLL; TURN; TWINE; can refer to the wind instruments of the orchestra
wind, indicator of COCK; VANE
wind up END; ROLL
winding device REEL
windlass WINCH
window BAY; GLASS; LANCET; LIGHT; ORIEL; PANE; SASH
window cleaner WIPER
window frame SASH
Windsor CHAIR; KNOT; SOUP; can indicate something to do with the Royal family, or something to do with a neck-tie
Windsor, women in WIVES
wine ASTI; CRU; HOCK; MEDOC; MUST; PLONK; PORT; RED; ROSE; SACK; SAKE; SOAVE; TENT; VIN; WHITE
wine collection CELLAR
wine, German HOCK; WEIN
wine, new MUST
wing FLY; LIMB; SIDE
winged ALIATE

winger can refer to a bird
wings LR; RL; indicator of first and last letters
wings off first and last letters to be omitted
winner BEST; CHAMP; GOLD; NAP; TOP
winning SWEET; UP
Winter festival NOEL
wipe RUB
wisdom DEPTH; LORE; SENSE
wise SAGE; SOUND
wise man MAGE; SAGE
wise men MAGI
wise old man NESTOR
wise words SAW
wisecrack BARB
wised-up SAGE
wit CARD; ESPRIT; JOKER; PUN; WAG
wit, to VIZ
witch HAG
witch's place ENDOR
with AND; BY; CON; W; run indicator
with German MIT
with it COOL; HIP
with Italian CON
with no points NOSE (ie. no SE) to be added to a word or component
with no sides first and last letters of a word to be omitted
withdraw BACK; RECANT; SCRATCH
withdrawing reversal indicator; omission indicator
withdrawn COY; OFF; SHY; omission indicator
wither DIE
withered DEAD; SEAR
withhold omission indicator
within nesting indicator; run indicator
within confines of can signify use of first and last letters only
without EX; LESS; OUT OF; nesting indicator; NO to be followed by another component as "without identification" clues NOID (ie. no ID) for instance in building up PARANOID
without borders, verges first and last letters to be omitted
without charge (cost, rental) FREE
without drink TT
without liquid DRY

without limit ALL
without prejudice OPEN
witness SEE; SEER
witty DROLL; FUNNY
witty remark SALLY
wizard-place OZ
wizards MAGI
wobble TEETER
wobbly anagram indicator
woe DOLE; can indicate something to do with Wednesday (eg. WED) as in "Wednesday's child"
wolf GORGE; ROMEO; SCOFF
wolves PACK
woman ADA; AMY; ANGIE; ANNA; ANNE; ANNIE; AVA; CATH; CORA; DI; DOLL; DORA; EMMA; ENA; ENID; EVA; EVE; HEN; HER; HESTER; INA; JO; KAY; LADY; LASS; MAE; MEG; MO; MOLLY; NELL; NINA; PAM; RITA; RUTH; SHE; UNA; W; WENCH; *see* GIRL
woman, beautiful BELLE; VENUS
woman, disreputable TRULL
woman, dowdy FRUMP
woman, enchanting CIRCE
woman, evil WITCH
woman had SHED (ie. she'd)
woman, horrible old (ugly, unpleasant) HAG; TROUT
woman, of HERS
woman, old HAG; TROUT
woman, OT RIB
woman's HER
woman, spiteful CAT
woman, that HER
woman, that Cockney ER
woman, ugly HAG; TROUT
woman, young CHICK; MAID; MISS
women HENS; WENCHES
women, excluding STAG
women only NOMEN (ie. no men)
women's organisation WI
women's quarters HAREM
wonder AWE; MARVEL
wonder, expression of COR; LOR

wonderful SUPER; WIZARD
woo COURT; SPOON
wood ARDEN; BEECH; BOX; BRANCH; ASH; COPSE; DEAL; EBONY; ELM; FIR; GROVE; LOG; LUMBER; LATH; PINE; SHAW (thicket); SLAT; TEAK; TIMBER; TINDER; *see* TREE
wood, a lot of FOREST
wood, piece of STICK
wooded area WEALD
woof WEFT
wooden STOLID; TREEN
woolly VAGUE
woolly jumper EWE; LAMB; RAM; SHEEP; TUP
Worcester can refer to race course, sauce, cathedral, apple (pearmain), porcelain
word MOT; NAME; NOUN; OATH; PLEDGE; TERM; VERB
word, last AMEN
words PROSE; VERSE
words, few NOTE
words, in other SC
words, play with PUN
words. use wrong LIE
wordy TALKING
work ACT; ART; BOOK; CHORE; DO; ERG; FUNCTION; GO; GRAFT; GRIND; HARNESS; JOB; KNEAD; LINE; OEUVRE; OP; OPUS; PLAY; PLY; SERVE; SLAVE; STRIVE; STUDY; TASK; TILL; TOIL; TRACT; anagram indicator
work, body of CORPUS
work diligently PLY
work for SERVE
work for a time TEMP
work, hard FAG; GRAFT; GRIND; SLAVE
work in America LABOR
work in restaurant WAIT
work, not IDLE; LAZE; REST
work, not at OFF
work of art BUST; MURAL; OIL; PAINTING; STATUE
work out SOLVE
work-related talk SHOP
work, religious AV; BIBLE; NT; OT; TRACT
work, some ERG
work steadily PEG; PLY; PLOD

work, tiresome CHORE; DRAG; *see* WORK, HARD
work unit ERG
work, very little STROKE
work, without IDLE
worked DID; PLIED; anagram indicator
worked out CRACKED; SOLVED; anagram indicator
worker ANT; BEE; HAND; POTTER; RIGGER; TEMP
worker, hard BEE
worker, paid PRO
workers CREW; GUILD; MEN; STAFF; TU; UNION
workers, group of GANG; *see* WORKERS
working ACTIVE; ON; USING; anagram indicator
working, not DOWN; OFF; OUT
working on AT
working time SHIFT; STINT
workplace FORGE; STUDIO; PLANT
workroom DEN; LAB; OFFICE; STUDIO; STUDY
workshop *see* WORKROOM
works FACTORY; OPS; PLANT; anagram indicator
world EARTH
worn OLD; ON; anagram indicator
worn-out DONE; OVER; STALE; STOCK
worn track RUT
worried anagram indicator
worried look FROWN
worry AIL; BROOD; CARE; EAT; FRET; FUSS; NAG; QUAIL; STEW; WORRY
worse VILER
worse luck ALAS
worship ADORE; LOVE; PRAISE; DEIFY
worshipper FAN; VOTARY
worst BEST
worst situation PITS
worsted SERGE
worthless IDLE; POXY; TRASHY
worthy UPRIGHT
would, I ID
wound CUT; LESION; MAIM; SCAR; STAB
wounded BLED; CUT; HURT
woven anagram indicator

wow AMAZE
wow! BOY; COR
wrap SCARF; SHAWL
wrapped (around) nesting indicator
wrath ANGER; IRE; RAGE
wreath LEI
wreathe WIND
wreck RUIN; UNDO; anagram indicator
wrecked SORRY; anagram indicator
wrench RICK
wrestling SUMO; anagram indicator
wrestling event BASHO
wretch CUR; DOG
wretched ABJECT; anagram indicator
wretched fellow CUR; RAT
wriggling anagram indicator
wring EXTORT
wrinkle CREASE; KNIT; LINE; RUT
wrinkled LINED
writ anagram indicator
write PEN; POST; SPELL
write in ENTER
writer AUTHOR; BARRIE; BIRO; DAHL; FLEMING; GIBBON; GREENE; MAILER; ME; NIB; PEN; POE; QUILL; SAKI; SCRIBE; STEIN; WELLS; *see* AUTHOR, NOVELIST, POET
writer, controversial MARX
writer, French GIDE
writer, poor HACK
writer, this I; ME
writer's MINE; MY
writer's complaint BLOCK; CRAMP
writer's material INK
writer, uninspired HACK
writhe TURN; TWIST
writing COPY; HAND; MS; PROSE; SCRIPT; TEXT
written after letter PS
written work MS; TRACT
wrong ASTRAY; ILL; OUT; SIN; TORT; X (ie. teacher's mark); anagram indicator
wrong-doing SIN

wrong way anagram indicator
wrong, do SIN
wrong, go ERR
wrong, went ERRED
wrong words, use LIE
wrongdoer SINNER
wrongdoer briefly CRIM
wrongdoing CRIME; EVIL; SIN
wrongly anagram indicator
wry DROLL

Xx Yy Zz

X TEN
XX SCORE
yahoo BOOR; LOUT
Yale can indicate something to do with key, lock
yank TUG
Yank GI; TUG
Yankee BET
yap BARK
yard PATIO; QUAD; SPAR; YD
yarn LISLE; TALE; THREAD
yawn GAPE
year ANNO; ANNUM; DATE; Y; rem: when age is expressed as "in the xth year", it signifies the previous year. Example: "in the fifth year" signifies the number FOUR
yearbook can indicate something to do with Orwell's "1984"
yearn ITCH; LONG; WAIT
years DECADE; TIME
yell SCREAM; SHOUT
yellow AMBER; CHICKEN; CRAVEN; GOLD; GOLDEN; OR; SALLOW

yellowish SALLOW
yellowish-brown AMBER; TAN
yen ITCH; NEED; URGE; WAIT; Y
yes AY; AYE; OK; RIGHT; YEA; YUP
yesteryear PAST
yet EVEN; STILL
yet to be paid OWING
yield BEAR; CEDE; CROP; GIVE; GRANT; RENDER; RETURN; anagram indicator
yielding SUPPLE; anagram indicator
Yippee! BOY
yob TED; LOUT; OIK
York HOUSE
Yorkshire can indicate RIDING
Yorkshireman TIKE; TYKE
you SOLVER; THOU; Y; YE
you and I US; WE
you and me US
you, belonging to THY; YOURS
you declared U
you old, once THEE; THOU; YE
young BROOD; FRY; ISSUE; LITTER; SPAWN
young animal CHICK; COLT; CUB; KID; KIT; LAMB; PUP
young cricketer, footballer, etc COLT
young fellow BOY; LAD; PUP; SPRIG
young lady GAL; LASS; MISS
young man BEAU; LAD; MASTER
young man, aristocratic BUCK
young, no longer AGED; OLD
young, produce BREED; SPAWN
young reporter CUB
young woman GAL; LASS; MAID; MISS
younger member SCION; SPRIG
youngster COLT; CUB; KID; LAD; MINOR; NIPPER; PUP; SHAVER; *see* YOUNG ANIMAL
youngster, Scottish WEAN
youngster, impudent BRAT; IMP
your THY; YR
your old THY
yours truly ME; SETTER

yours truly, owned by MINE
youth BOY; LAD; SPEAR; SPRIG; *see* YOUNG MAN
youth, wild BLOOD
yuk UGH
zeal ARDOUR
zealous EAGER; KEEN
zero O; NIL; NOUGHT
zest GUSTO
Zeus's wife HERA
zigzag TACK
zinc ZN
zing GO; OOMPH
zip RUSH
Zola can indicate something to do with "J'accuse"
Zola's coquette NANA
zone AREA; SECTOR
zoological group GENUS
zoom SOAR

Bradford's Crossword Key Dictionary

The *Key* makes it easy to find words to fit a space or to finish a partly-solved solution. It provides a comprehensive, unique listing of over 350,000 entries organised into chapters according to the number of letters in each word.

Within each chapter, the words are then listed alphabetically in separate sections according to each letter position within the word. For example, if you are looking for a six-letter word with 'b' as the second letter, you would look in the chapter on six-letter words, then for the section listing the words alphabetically by their second letter.

paperback, 1180pages, ISBN 1-901659-40-2

Bradford's Crossword Solver's Dictionary

The *Solver* provides a comprehensive guide to help you solve cryptic crossword puzzles. This dictionary is the result of over 35 years' work compiling answers to over 300,000 crossword clues and then cross-referencing the results. The book contains over 200,000 entries arranged under 18,000 headwords: look up one of the words featured in your crossword clue and the dictionary lists possible solutions.

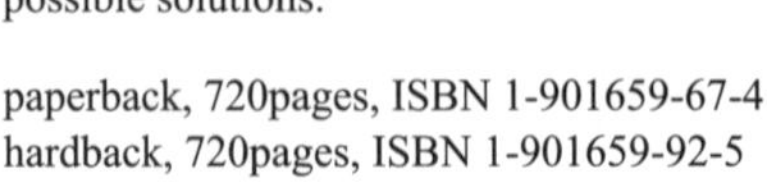

paperback, 720pages, ISBN 1-901659-67-4
hardback, 720pages, ISBN 1-901659-92-5

For full details of all our titles, visit our website: **www petercollin com**
All our titles are available from good bookshops or direct from the publisher:
Peter Collin Publishing
UK: 32-34 Great Peter Street, London, SW1P 2DB
USA: PO Box 1321, Oak Park, IL 60304-0321